THE UNITED STATES AND

EUROPEAN RECONSTRUCTION,

1945–1960

BAAS Paperbacks

General Editor: Philip John Davies, Reader in American Studies at De Montfort University

Associate Editor: George McKay, Senior Lecturer in Cultural Studies at the University of Central Lancashire

Published in association with the British Association for American Studies, this exciting series is destined to become an indispensable collection in American Studies. Each volume tackles an important area and is written by an accepted academic expert within the discipline. Books selected for the series are clearly written introductions designed to offer students definitive short surveys of key topics in the field.

Titles in the series include:

The American Landscape
Stephen F. Mills

Gender and Sexuality in Contemporary American Film
Jude Davies and Carol Smith

Political Scandals in the USA
Robert Williams

The United States and European Reconstruction, 1945–1960

JOHN KILLICK

KEELEUNIVERSITY**PRESS**

© John Killick, 1997

Keele University Press
22 George Square, Edinburgh

Typeset in Monotype Fournier by
Carnegie Publishing, Lancaster and
printed and bound in Great Britain

A CIP record for this book is available
from the British Library

ISBN 1 85331 178 2

Contents

List of Figures

List of Tables

Abbreviations

CEEC	Committee of European Economic Cooperation
CIO	Congress of Industrial Organizations
DRs	Drawing Rights
ECA	Economic Cooperation Administration
EEC	European Economic Community
EFTA	European Free Trade Association
EPU	European Payments Union
ERP	European Recovery Program
ECSC	European Coal and Steel Community
FME	Fond de Modernisation et d'Équipement
GARIOA	Government and Relief in Occupied Areas
GATT	General Agreement on Tariffs and Trade
GFCF	Gross Fixed Capital Formation
GNP	Gross National Product
IBRD	International Bank for Reconstruction and Development
ICU	International Clearing Union
IMF	International Monetary Fund
ITO	International Trade Organization
MSA	Mutual Security Administration
NATO	North Atlantic Treaty Organization
OECD	Organization for Economic Cooperation and Development
OEEC	Organization for European Economic Cooperation
OMGUS	Office of Military Government, USA
PPS	Policy Planning Staff
RTAA	Reciprocal Trade Agreements Act
SF	Stabilization Fund
SWNCC	State–War–Navy Coordinating Committee
TUC	Trades Union Congress
UN	United Nations
UNRRA	United Nations Relief and Rehabilitation Administration
WFTU	World Federation of Trade Unions

I

Introduction

Europe recovered and developed much more rapidly after World War II
than after World War I. Clearly, American influence was an important
part of this process, but its exact impact is still not clear. The Marshall
Plan has traditionally been seen as a decisive turning-point, but many
contemporary scholars argue that Europe revived spontaneously during
1945–6, and that American 'dollars did not save the world' in 1947–8.
Similarly, the early postwar recovery apparently led into the long
European boom of 1948–73, but it is still uncertain whether this boom
was simply a natural rebound from interwar stagnation, *or* was caused
by purposeful changes in European government policies, *or* was part of
an international process in which American influence and example were
predominant. Finally, since 1950 there has been obvious convergence
around the North Atlantic basin, – not only in productivity and incomes,
but also in social mores and political norms. The latter include the
general adoption of competitive and meritocratic systems, the relative
decline of class and national distinctions, the drift from socialism, and
the weakening of the nation-state. To what extent were these due
to immediate postwar American predominance, *or* to later American
influences, *or* to purely European or general development processes that
were bound to happen anyway?[1]

Scholarship on the Marshall Plan has moved through several stages.
During the late 1940s and early 1950s there was a spate of analysis
about US economic relations with Europe, generally emphasising the
American contribution. However, most academic interest from the
middle 1950s to the early 1980s focused on political problems, and
especially on the origins of the Cold War. As part of this political
analysis, it became received wisdom that, immediately after the war,
the USA attempted global approaches to world economic problems.
She helped to create the United Nations (UN), the International Monetary Fund (IMF) and the other international organisations. She hoped
that the wartime alliances with Britain, France and Russia would last,
and that loans to individual countries would help to restore prosperity.

She only became particularly concerned with Europe in early 1947, when the Potsdam settlement of 1945 began to fail, communist threats developed in Greece, Italy and France, and the postwar recovery faltered.[2]

This traditional version describes how the danger of Russian dominance over a bankrupt Europe forced the USA to act. Hence, on 12 March 1947 President Truman – referring to the communist insurrection in Greece – declared: 'I believe that it must be the policy of the United States to support free peoples who are resisting attempted subjugation by armed minorities or by outside pressure.' This became the Truman Doctrine. Then, on 5 June, General Marshall recognised in his famous Harvard Commencement address that:

> Europe's requirements ... are so much greater than her present ability to pay that she must have substantial additional help, or face economic, social and political deterioration of a very grave character ... Our policy is directed not against any country or doctrine but against hunger, poverty, desperation, and chaos.

This became the Marshall Plan.[3]

Political historians then went on to describe how the North Atlantic Alliance and the Marshall Plan secured and revived western Europe. By 1950, therefore, European output was well above 1938 levels. European integration began with the European Payments Union and the Schuman Plan of 1950, which helped to free European trade and integrate European heavy industry. By the mid-1950s Europe was becoming prosperous and in 1957 the Treaty of Rome created the European Common Market. The European economic miracle then continued until the crises of the early 1970s, by which time the United States, rather than the stronger European countries, was revealing economic weaknesses. Thus, the postwar American recovery programmes and the Marshall Plan were usually treated as successful or – for the conspiracy-minded – devious subsidiaries of the Cold War. For many years most economic historians gave them a parallel customary obeisance or ignored them almost completely.[4]

In the 1980s, however, as the Cold War faded, economic historians became more seriously concerned about the effects of American economic policy in Europe. Alan Milward in particular questioned the macroeconomic and socio-political importance of the Marshall Plan. He argued that Europe recovered very rapidly, using her own resources, in 1945–6; that the crisis of 1947 was marginal; and that European reconstruction and unity were achieved almost despite the Marshall Plan, not because of it. On the other hand, many writers like Michael Hogan emphasised the importance of American ideas and influences on Europe. These led to a widespread Americanisation and a new European neo-capitalism, but within limits. 'But ... these impressive gains not-withstanding ...', he wrote:

> participating countries were not clay in the hands of American potters ... They resisted the social-democratic elements in the New Deal synthesis, adapted other elements to their own needs and traditions, and thus retained much of their original form. In the beginning, the Marshall Plan had aimed to remake Europe in the American mode. In the end, [this] America was made the European way.[5]

More recently, historians have attempted to find compromises between these different views. Generally, economic historians accept Milward's findings on the relative smallness, compared to GNP, of the Marshall Plan resource inputs. On the other hand, political historians have continued to emphasise the many favourable effects of American policy. They argue that it is difficult to understand how European recovery could have happened at the speed that it did without American assistance in opening trade channels and assuring investment. Some interesting research suggests that the American input was critical in sealing a very effective social contract post-1945. The aid may have been small compared to GNP, but it was sufficient to clinch productive deals between many old enemies, economic, social and national. In the 1920s this widespread social consensus never really happened. Post-1945, with better-planned American aid, it did – and everyone gained. This book surveys the debate between these points of view.[6]

American dominance was the unifying factor underlying the whole period 1945–60. Figure 1.1 shows that America was producing about 40% of world manufacturing at this time, a proportion never equalled before and unlikely ever to be achieved again. In the late 1940s American industry appeared so technically advanced that it seemed as if Europe would never be able to catch up. This predominance was partly a function of long-term trends dating from the mid-nineteenth century, partly the temporary results of the war. But, however caused, it gave the USA an extraordinary temporary leverage in Europe. If ever there was a time when the USA should have been able to influence international affairs, it was then. After about 1960 Europe (and East Asia) began to catch up and American dominance waned.[7]

Figure 1.1. *American Share of World Manufacturing (% distribution), 1820–1961*

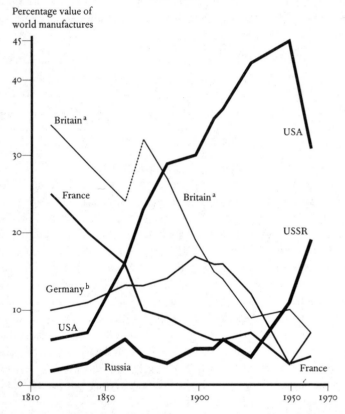

Percentage value of world manufactures

[a] Discontinuity in British figures between 1860 and 1870 is caused by a shift in sources.
[b] 1961: German Federal Republic only.
Sources: For 1820–60: Michael G. Mulhall, *Dictionary of Statistics* (London, 1909), p. 365; for 1870–1929: League of Nations, *Industrialisation and Foreign Trade* (Geneva, 1945), p. 13; for 1948–61: United Nations, *The Growth of World Industry, 1938–1961* (New York, 1965), pp. 230–76.

A major symptom of American power in international economic relations in the early twentieth century was the 'dollar gap'. Figure 1.2 shows the American–European trade deficit over the very long term. Exports and imports from Europe are shown as a % of total US exports and imports. The measure therefore conceals both the huge growth in trade volume across the Atlantic and the absolute size of the gap, but it does show the relative size of transatlantic, as against total American, trade and the relative size of the European trade gap. Until 1860, American trade with Europe was a very high proportion of total US trade and was more or less balanced. From 1865 onwards, however, US imports of European goods declined relatively as the USA industrialised and began to buy raw materials and luxuries from Canada, Latin America and Asia. High American tariffs insulated the US market even further.[8]

On the other hand, American exports of cotton, wheat, oil and the 'high tech' goods of the time, such as cars, cameras, and machine tools, grew very rapidly. Britain in particular needed the food and raw materials and had low tariffs. The USA found that she could 'free ride on British free trade' without fear of retaliation. The other European nations were less exposed, but generally had trade deficits with the USA. Towards 1900 the deficit declined – as relatively less American wheat was shipped – but it then expanded enormously in World War I as the allied war effort drew in American supplies. Before 1914 the deficit was covered by emigrant remittances, receipts from such European services as shipping and insurance, and the earnings of those European empires and Third World countries which had deficits with Europe, but surpluses with the USA. India, for instance, had a deficit with Britain, but a surplus with China and Japan, which in turn had surpluses with the USA. During World War I the gap was covered by such extraordinary measures as the sale of British-owned American railroad securities and American loans.[9]

In the 1920s high American productivity and tariffs still excluded most European goods, and the consequent deficits continued to be covered in roundabout ways – usually through Third World, empire or service earnings. Britain's colony Malaya, for instance, sold rubber and tin for use in American cars. The Dutch East Indies sold oil to the USA. The British and Norwegians provided freight. Italy and France earned dollars from wealthy American tourists and expatriates; Italy also received large immigrant remittances. In the late 1920s the balance was covered by American loans. When these dried up in 1929, the European nations, pressed by depression, resorted to a great variety of national and imperial trade and exchange controls. All the European countries, for instance, reduced their US cotton and grain imports and attempted to find alternative sources.[10]

Figure 1.2. *American Trade with Europe (as % of total US trade),*
1821–1970

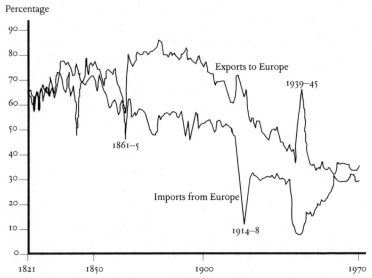

Source: United States, Bureau of the Census, *Historical Statistics of the United States:*
Colonial Times to 1970 (United States Government Printing Office: Washington, DC,
1975), pp. 903–7.

Transatlantic trade collapsed in the 1930s, but recovered dramatically
during and after World War II. The share of transatlantic trade in total
US trade continued to decline until about 1950 and then stabilised. There
was a last great expansion of the gap, 1939–50, before it finally closed.
Lend-Lease – the free pooling of all allied supplies during the war –
covered the British trade deficit until 1945, but the postwar years were
especially difficult for Europe. The leading countries had lost, or
were about to lose, their empires and Third World surpluses which had
hitherto funded the gap. They had also lost most of their investment,
shipping and other invisible earnings. Yet they desperately needed
American supplies and machinery to re-equip.

It was therefore the main function of the Marshall Plan to help the
European nations through this difficult transition. They were encouraged to copy American production methods, to expand exports to
America and to increase intra-European trade. Even Britain was eventually pulled into the European orbit. However, Figure 1.2 suggests that,

to a certain extent, the Marshall Planners were swimming with the tide. Underlying technical developments – the spread of American technology, the displacement of certain raw materials (like cotton), the growth of European agriculture – all tended to reduce European dependence on America. Europe had good chances of success, whatever the external assistance. (The dollar gap is discussed in Chapter 2, and its decline in Chapter 15.)

In the immediate aftermath of the war, the degree of imbalance with the USA seemed overwhelming. The Europeans knew that they would need huge quantities of North American food, raw materials and machinery to rebuild their economies. Many of the alternative supplies had been destroyed or had dried up. Tight import controls and deflation at home might limit demand, but the 1930s depression had convinced leading economists such as Keynes that planned autarchy was self-defeating. The Bretton Woods debates about postwar financial and commercial organisation – held in New Hampshire in 1944 – therefore revolved around the likely USA–European trade deficits and how to accommodate them with reasonably free trade. All liberal economists wanted to avoid the excessive controls of the 1930s, with their dangerous economic and political consequences, but most recognised that these could only be avoided by generous US grants or severe European retrenchment. At Bretton Woods, Keynes and the leading American economist, Harry Dexter White, suggested an intellectual framework for the solution of the consequent transatlantic imbalances, but there was no political commitment in the USA or Europe for the critical decisions that would make it work. (The Bretton Woods debates are considered in Chapter 3.)

The first test of the Bretton Woods ideas came much sooner than anticipated, with the American loan to Britain in 1946. Keynes had hoped that Britain would be able to recover her old markets in what was expected to be the fairly long period between the predicted victory in Europe in, say, late 1944 or early 1945, and the expected fall of Japan in, say, early 1946. In practice, however, this period – 'Phase 2' to the Americans, 'Stage 2' to the British – was foreshortened to a few months in mid-1945 by the determined German resistance during the winter of 1944/5 on the one hand, and by the atom bomb on the other. As soon as Japan surrendered in August 1945, Lend-Lease was terminated and Britain was forced to send Keynes to Washington to beg for aid.

The whole of Europe was short of dollars to buy essential American goods. The USA was faced with the strong possibility that Britain and the larger European countries would re-create the trade barriers and imperial preference systems of the 1930s. In response to Keynes's mission, therefore, the USA offered Britain a very large loan – the 'American loan' – as a way of pre-empting this autarchic trend and opening up transatlantic and international trade. It was supplemented by smaller loans to France and generous grants to the United Nations Relief and Rehabilitation Administration (UNRRA) to encourage multilateral recovery and expansion. Canada also extended substantial loans to Britain and Europe. (The American loan to Britain, and American and international aid for Europe are discussed in Chapters 4 and 5.)

This aid was crucial in assisting the first stage of European recovery. The traditional view suggests that the recovery was painfully slow – hence the need for Marshall Aid in 1947. In practice, popular expectations forced European governments to revive their economies as fast as possible and to ignore the growing dollar gap. For some countries, these pre-Marshall Plan loans were probably of a greater magnitude, as a % of GNP, than the grants under the Marshall Plan. Hence, by late 1946 most countries except Italy and Germany were making a remarkably rapid, not a painfully slow, recovery. It was not, however, a balanced recovery, and by late 1946 it was becoming clear that full employment and production were not compatible with a lasting international balance, either with or without autarchic controls. The terms of trade had swung so far against Europe since the 1930s that only very large increases in regional productivity or continued loans would enable the area to import the food and raw materials required for full production. (The 1945–7 recovery is discussed in Chapter 6.)

By early 1947 this crisis, foreseen at Bretton Woods, had arrived. Most European countries had developed serious payments deficits with the USA and were running short of credit. Milward and others have suggested that the commercial and financial crisis concealed the extent of the underlying recovery. However, contemporary authors and most analyses of specific countries confirm a really painful pressure on resources which would have wrecked the recovery and led to widespread social collapse. Simultaneously, political crises between the West and Russia and in France, Germany, Greece and Italy exacerbated the situation and forced the USA to introduce the Truman Doctrine and the Marshall Plan. President Truman's advisers feared that European economic collapse might lead either to a revived 1930s autarchy and nationalism or to a communist takeover supported by Russia. They were also reasonably confident that America had the methods and resources to help. (The crisis of 1947 is discussed in Chapter 7.)

General Marshall announced his 'plan' on 5 June 1947, but a great deal of detailed work had to be done before the European Recovery Program (ERP) became law on 3 April 1948. It was transformed from a short open invitation to the Europeans to volunteer proposals to a well-organised programme with as much emphasis on encouraging reform as on providing resources. The legislation laid down targets for improved output, inflation, and trade over a four-year period. In practice, these targets were mostly achieved by 1951. The trade and inflation figures relapsed with the Korean War emergency, 1950–3, but the recovery continued through the 1950s and developed into the long European boom which finally ended in 1973.

The interesting question is to determine to what extent the aid provided by America during 1948–51 was responsible for stimulating European recovery. As a proportion of GNP, the aid varied considerably between countries; overall, it was probably too small to have a dramatic effect, but it did have critical effects in particular situations and countries. In addition, the American influence was much wider than the aid alone. In West Germany, for instance, Marshall Aid arrived little and late, yet it is difficult to believe that the wider effects of American policy on security and trade were not crucial for German recovery. (The debate over the aims and macroeconomic effects of the Marshall Plan both in general and in individual countries is discussed in Chapters 8–11.)

Many of the central concepts of European unity were first discussed in the Marshall Plan. The administrators of the plan, the Economic Cooperation Administration (ECA), hoped that increased intra-European trade would reduce the European call on American resources and improve European productivity. The US administration also hoped that European integration would bring France and Germany together. Initially, the Americans anticipated that the Organization for European Economic Cooperation (OEEC) – created in 1948 to represent the Europeans in the Marshall Plan process – would perform this task. Then, when the Europeans rejected this form of supranational control, the Americans helped to establish the European Payments Union (EPU) to encourage intra-European trade. The US administration continued to support European integration – for instance, the Schuman Plan in

1950 and the Treaty of Rome in 1957. Many commentators see these as solely European endeavours, but strong US influence was apparent in both cases. However, the Americans failed to persuade Britain to go any further towards integration than joining the EPU. (The Marshall Plan and European unity are discussed in Chapters 12 and 13.)

The Marshall Plan administrators hoped that the Europeans would adopt what they regarded as the best features of the US economy – a continental-size market, correspondingly large modern firms and trade unions, tough but fair competition, modern technology, modern welfare and labour management systems, and a limited federal system of government. Many ECA administrators were relatively liberal academics or politicians who had absorbed New Deal attitudes and Keynesian ideas; even the businessmen in the ECA were generally forward-looking. The ECA hoped to use Marshall money to modernise not only European productivity, but also political and social attitudes. However, the contemporary European leadership, left and right, wanted US dollars, but without the strings attached. Hence many of the American ideas were rejected initially, but were then – after generational change – adopted later.

Charles Maier and Michael Hogan have argued that the ECA was successful in giving Europe an initial push towards the 'politics of productivity' and a moderate neo-capitalism. Maier's argument is that rapidly rising productivity took the harsh edge off disputes between capital and labour – which had inhibited growth between the wars – and led to two decades of productive growth and social stability. Anthony Carew shows how the mere promise of the Marshall Plan split the left in several countries, leading to 1950s centralism. The EPU and other American policies initiated the rapid growth of intra-European trade – which in turn led to the Treaty of Rome and widespread industrial change. Similarly, the continent-wide market gradually produced European-wide multinational firms and institutions. Simultaneously, American scholarship captured the high ground in many disciplines, – in industrial relations, for example – and gradually converted European public policy on such matters as business competition (or anti-trust). More subtle changes in attitudes to government and business only matured with generational change. (The debate about the Marshall Plan and European productivity and industrial structure is discussed in Chapter 14.[11])

By the mid-1950s European output had risen far above 1938 levels and the dollar gap was becoming far less of a problem. The most striking development was the improvement in the current account. Despite European hopes, the improvement was halting, with frequent relapses during 1951–4, 1956–7 and in the early 1960s, but the trend towards a more reasonable balance was clear. The westward flow was only 17% of the eastward flow in 1947, but had reached 60% by 1958 and 83% in the unusually good year of 1959. By the mid-1950s it was possible to calculate that the long-run US trade surplus over Europe would probably end by the mid-1970s.[12]

Marshall Plan policy initially supported this change by encouraging Europe to discriminate against American goods. The aim was to keep Europe in the (open) international market and on the US side in the Cold War. It was not until the early 1960s that the USA really began to complain about European Economic Community (EEC) discrimination. The US capital account also changed dramatically. By the early 1960s the huge outflow of government money had been replaced by a massive flow of private investment to Europe. Europe had been rescued and was in the process of being transformed. The first major postwar thrust of US influence was over. (The end of the dollar gap and the development of transatlantic trade relations in the 1950s and 1960s are discussed in Chapter 15.)

The European economy grew extremely rapidly in the next twenty years; far from achieving mere viability, much of the productivity gap with the United States had been closed by 1990. There was also a great deal of convergence between Europe and the United States in methods and styles of personal consumption, commercial organisation, and even government administration. On the other hand, the gap between western European prosperity and eastern European austerity grew throughout the postwar period. There were many reasons for the collapse of the Russian empire in eastern Europe in the late 1980s, of course, but this gnawing differential was a major factor.

There were many forces working for this convergence across the Atlantic (and across the Pacific). In particular, the huge advantage that America had enjoyed over Europe from, say, 1920 to 1950 – a productivity gap of about 3:1 in terms of manufacturing output per head – was obviously the product of very exceptional circumstances and was bound to diminish as Europe recovered, technology developed and diffused, and international contacts increased. Nevertheless, the recovery programmes can claim to have had a catalytic effect on this process, pushing just at the right time and at the right points to have major effects on the outcome. (The long-run effects of the Marshall Plan are discussed in Chapter 16.)

Notes

1. Derek Aldcroft, Michael Collins, Helen Mercer, Michael Oliver, Martin Thornton, Rhiannon Vickers, and Malcolm Walles have provided helpful comments. I am also very grateful for Nicola Pike's hard work and cheerful support. The phrase 'dollars did not save the world' comes from the book by Henry Hazlitt, *Will Dollars save the World?* (Appleton-Century: New York, 1947).

2. Some contemporary analyses are listed in the section on *'Further Reading'*, below, pp. 189–98.

3. *Public Papers of the Presidents of the United States: Harry S. Truman, 1947* (United States Government Printing Office: Washington, DC, 1963), pp. 178–9; United States, Department of State, *Foreign Relations of the United States: 1947* (United States Government Printing Office: Washington, DC, 1972), vol. 3, pp. 237–9 (henceforth *FRUS*).

4. See Peter G. Boyle, *American–Soviet Relations: From the Russian Revolution to the Fall of Communism* (Routledge: London, 1993), pp. 54–70, for the Marshall Plan as diplomatic history.

5. Alan S. Milward, *The Reconstruction of Western Europe, 1945–51* (Methuen: London, 1984), pp. 1–55; Michael Hogan, *The Marshall Plan: America, Britain, and the Reconstruction of Western Europe, 1947–1952* (Cambridge University Press: Cambridge, 1987), pp. 427–51 (p. 445).

6. Barry Eichengreen and Marc Uzan, 'The Marshall Plan: economic effects and implications for Eastern Europe and the former USSR', *Economic Policy* 14 (1992), pp. 14–75.

7. Richard R. Nelson and Gavin Wright, 'The rise and fall of American technological leadership: the postwar era in historical perspective', *Journal of Economic Literature* 30 (1992), pp. 1931–64, surveys the ground.

8. S. B. Saul, *Studies in British Overseas Trade, 1870–1914* (Liverpool University Press: Liverpool, 1960), *passim*; Matthew Simon and David E. Novack, 'Some dimensions of the American commercial invasion of Europe, 1871–1914: an introductory essay', *Journal of Economic History* 24 (1964), pp. 591–605.

9. David A. Lake, *Power Protection and Free Trade: International Sources of US Commercial Strategy, 1887–1939* (Cornell University Press: Ithaca, New York, 1988), pp. 91–147; Kathleen Burk, *Britain, America and the Sinews of War, 1914–1918* (George, Allen and Unwin: Boston, 1985).

10. M. C. Falkus, 'United States economic policy and the 'Dollar Gap' of the 1920s', *Economic History Review*, 2nd ser., 24 (1971), pp. 599–623; Hal B. Lary *et al.*, *The United States in the World Economy: The International Transactions of the United States in the Interwar Period* (United States Government Printing Office: Washington, DC, 1944), *passim*.

11. Anthony Carew, *Labour under the Marshall Plan: The Politics of Productivity and the Marketing of Management Science* (Manchester University Press: Manchester, 1987); Hogan, *The Marshall Plan*; Charles S. Maier, 'The politics of productivity: the foundations of American economic policy after World War 2', in *idem* (ed.),

In Search of Stability: Explorations in Historical Political Economy (Cambridge University Press: Cambridge, 1987), pp. 121–52.

12. Eastward and westward trade flows are calculated from United States, Bureau of the Census, *Historical Statistics of the United States: Colonial Times to 1970* (United States Government Printing Office, Washington, DC, 1975), pp. 902–5; United Nations, *Economic Survey of Europe in 1957* (Economic Commission for Europe: Geneva, 1958), Chapter 5, 'Prospective trade structures'.

2

Overview: Atlantic Trade and Payments, 1945–1960

International recovery was faster after World War II than after World War I, although the variation depends a great deal on the dates and indices used. Table 2.1 compares the two postwar recoveries with 1913 and 1937 respectively. The first bloc of statistics compares index numbers of post-World War I performance with 1913 (1913 = 100). The second bloc compares index numbers of post-World War II performance with 1937 (1937 = 100). The starting points for the two recoveries are rather different. In 1913 there was a mild recession, but 1937 was the best year in a bad decade. Secondly, World War II damaged Europe more than World War I, but also enforced more new investment. Comparisons of the two postwar eras are complex, therefore, but it is possible to make some brief general observations. After World War I most countries enjoyed a quick postwar boom, but then relapsed into depression in 1920–1. The long-run mid-1920s boom started in America in 1922 and in Germany in 1924, but had begun the descent into depression in most countries by 1930. After World War II, by contrast, the expansion of production was almost continuous and led into the economic miracle of the 1950s and 1960s.[1]

The third bloc of figures compares the difference between the two recoveries in the major countries. There is an assumption that 1920 and 1946 are fair equivalent starting-points from which to make comparisons. America gained most from both wars, but even more from World War II. This was because of her relatively low starting-point in 1937, her greater expansion in the war itself, and her better immediate postwar performance. In the late 1940s she did no better than in the mid-1920s, but the difference was much greater by 1930/1956. Britain came out of both wars with very full output, but grew much more quickly post-World War II. France did slightly better post-World War II, especially by the mid-1950s. Germany, after a slow start – the result of the bombing

Table 2.1. *Industrial Growth and Postwar Recovery, USA and Europe, 1920–1930[a] and 1946–1956[b]*

	1920	*1922*	*1924*	*1926*	*1928*	*1930*
USA	123	126	134	157	163	148
Britain	98	92	108	106	119	120
France	70	88	118	131	135	141
Germany	59	82	82	91	118	102
Italy	95	108	141	163	175	184

	1946	*1948*	*1950*	*1952*	*1954*	*1956*
USA	152	178	196	222	226	265
Britain	100	114	128	130	144	152
France	76	103	117	133	148	180
Germany	—	63	112	145	174	219
Italy	71	99	124	147	173	203

Difference	*1946/ 1920*	*1948/ 1922*	*1950/ 1924*	*1952/ 1926*	*1954/ 1928*	*1956/ 1930*
USA	30[c]	52	62	65	63	117
Britain	2	22	20	23[c]	25	32
France	6	15	−1	2	13	39
Germany	—	−19	31[c]	54	55[c]	117
Italy	−24	−9	−17	−16	−2	19

Notes: In this, and in all subsequent tables, '—' = n/a; 'o' = zero or less than 0.5 (after rounding).
[a] 1913 = 100.
[b] 1937 = 100.
[c] Statistics have been rounded.
Sources: B. R. Mitchell, *European Historical Statistics, 1750–1975* (Macmillan: London, 1980), pp. 376–9; United States, Bureau of the Census, *Historical Statistics of the United States: Colonial Times to 1970* (United States Government Printing Office: Washington, DC, 1975), p. 667; Ingvar Svennilson, *Growth and Stagnation in the European Economy* (United Nations, Economic Commission for Europe: Geneva, 1954), pp. 304–5.

and invasion – did very much better. Italy did worse after World War II, but gradually caught up.

The table only measures industrial output. GNP and per capita incomes did not do as well as industry after World War II. Agriculture recovered very slowly, pulling down GNP. High investment also reduced consumption, as countries attempted to make up for the shortfall during the depression and to take advantage of new technology, taking resources from consumption. Adverse swings in the terms of trade meant that imports also absorbed more resources. Nevertheless, after World War II there was greater social harmony and less industrial strife in Europe than during 1919–29. The starting-point of the two recoveries is critical. The idea that there was more technological ground to be made up after 1945 than after 1918, because of the lost years of the 1930s, is discussed in Chapter 16.[2]

As the leading world power in 1945, America had a very important role in this recovery. The USA was the leading – or certainly a very large – supplier of most European countries in 1948 and in 1956: see Table 2.2, col. 1. The Europeans found it far more difficult to export to the USA, especially in 1948 (col. 3). Hence the USA provided a substantial percentage of the imports of most European countries, but received a much smaller share of their exports in return. These values are expressed as percentages in cols. 2 and 4 and as ratios in col. 5. In 1948, for instance, Britain received nearly three times as much from America as she sent to America, and Germany fifteen times as much. There were substantial differences in the values of American exports to Europe in 1948 as reported by the recipients and by the USA. Cols 1–5 are based on European statistics of imports from, and exports to, the USA, converted into dollars at the prevailing rate. Col. 6 gives the corresponding ratio to col. 5, but uses American trade figures. Austria and Germany are the extreme cases. US export figures include US civilian relief, UNRRA, and ECA commodities, whereas the corresponding European figures exclude or undervalue non-commercial relief. Including all items, therefore, Germany rather than Britain was the largest receiver of US goods in 1948.

In 1948 Britain was still the leading European importer from America (according to European statistics). Britain had by far the largest viable economy in western Europe in 1948, with a massive demand for imports of raw materials and food. However, she used import controls to divert much of her demand to the sterling area to save dollars – and hence a relatively small share of her imports came from the USA (col. 2). Most of the other European countries, especially France, Germany and Italy, had to import very large quantities of American food, raw materials and machines not available elsewhere in order to recover. As they had few exports to offer in return, these supplies were only maintained by large American credits and loans. By 1956, however, the transatlantic

Table 2.2. *US Trade with Europe, 1948 and 1956*

	Imports from USA		Exports to USA		Ratio of imports:exports	
	$m (1)	% (2)	$m (3)	% (4)	(5)	(6)
1948						
Austria	17	4	10	5	1.7	16.3
Belgium	357	18	102	6	3.5	3.0
Britain	737	9	266	4	2.8	2.2
Denmark	103	14	31	5	3.4	9.1
France	593	18	79	4	7.5	8.1
Germany	473	50	31	6	15.4	28.0
Greece(1)	236	47	19	14	13.0	12.1
Italy	572	38	92	9	6.2	4.4
Norway	100	13	32	8	3.1	2.5
1956						
Austria	125	13	44	5	2.8	1.6
Belgium	409	12	302	10	1.4	1.4
Britain	1142	11	680	8	1.7	1.3
Denmark	130	10	81	7	1.6	1.4
France	682	12	224	5	3.0	2.4
Germany	945	14	494	7	1.9	1.6
Greece	78	17	23	12	3.5	3.6
Italy	521	16	201	9	2.6	2.4
Norway	93	8	58	8	1.6	1.3

Sources: Cols 1–5: Mitchell, *European Historical Statistics*; exchange rates are from International Monetary Fund, *Balance of Payments Yearbooks* (International Monetary Fund: Washington, DC, various years), henceforth IMF, *Payments Yearbooks*; col. 6: United States, Bureau of the Census, *Statistical Abstract of the United States* (United States Government Printing Office: Washington, DC, 1949 and 1958), henceforth US, *Statistical Abstract*. (1) Cols 1, 3 and 6 are from US, *Statistical Abstract*; cols 3, 4 and 5 are from Mitchell, *European Historical Statistics*.

relationship had normalised considerably. Trade had grown in both directions, but European exports to America had developed much faster than US exports to Europe (cols 5 and 6). The problem of the 'dollar gap' had mostly been solved. Simultaneously, the growth of Europe's interior trade was diverting volume from the Atlantic and preparing the ground for the Common Market.[3]

The European balance of payments with America improved immen-

Table 2.3. *US Balance of Payments with Europe, 1946–1950 ($bn.)*

	1946	*1947*	*1948*	*1949*	*1950*
Exports to Europe (1)	4.4	5.2	4.5	4.3	3.4
Imports from Europe (2)	−0.8	−0.8	−1.2	−1.0	−1.3
Trade net (3)	3.6	4.4	3.3	3.2	2.2
Services net (4)	0.6	1.0	0.3	−0.1	−0.3
Private capital net (5)	−0.5	−0.7	−0.6	−0.2	−0.2
Government misc. (6)	0.3	0.2	0.2	0.0	−0.6
Residual/multilateral (7)	0.5	2.8	1.2	0.9	0.3
Total normal balance (8)	4.5	7.7	4.4	3.8	1.4
Compensatory finance					
US government grants (9)	−0.5	−0.9	−2.4	−3.0	−2.8
US government loans (10)	−2.7	−3.6	−1.2	−0.6	−0.1
International institutions (11)	−0.5	−0.9	−0.3	0.0	0.0
Foreign gold + dollars (12)	−0.8	−2.3	−0.5	−0.2	1.5
Total aid	−3.7	−5.4	−3.9	−3.6	−2.9
Compensatory balance	−4.5	−7.7	−4.4	−3.8	−1.4
Ratios (× 100)					
Imports : exports	17	16	27	24	38
Aid : US exports	90	103	89	85	86
Aid : G & S deficit[a]	89	101	108	126	153

[a] G & S = goods and services.
Sources: IMF, *Payments Yearbook*, vol. 1, pp. 368–9; IMF, *Payments Yearbook*, vol. 3, pp. 416–20.

sely, 1946–60. The main reason for this was the very rapid recovery of exports from Europe to the USA compared with the relative stagnation of American exports to Europe. This came as a surprise to contemporaries. As late as 1953, well-informed economists doubted if Europe would ever solve the 'dollar gap' and thought that the relatively favourable trade returns in 1950 – see Table 2.3 – were an illusion based on temporarily high US rearmament needs. By the mid-1950s, however, the European 'economic miracle' had obviously begun; twenty-year forecasts based on the relative potential of typical American and European exports were estimating that, in the long run, the European deficit would be eliminated. It was possible to see, for instance, that whereas Europe could displace considerable quantities of American wheat, cotton and mass-produced manufactured goods with home, Third World or synthetic production, the American demand for cheap European mass-produced products, such as Volkswagens, was likely to be buoyant.[4]

Before 1950, however, the picture seemed very grim. Table 2.3, shown from the American point of view, shows (rows 1 and 2) US goods flooding in to Europe to help reconstruction, but very little going back in return. The net trade balance (row 3), therefore, was strongly against Europe in 1946–9, but improved substantially in 1950. In addition, the Europeans had deficits (row 4) from service income in 1946–8. Services had been a traditional dollar earner before 1939, but nearly all the main components of the service account had problems in 1946. Europe had sold or lost many of her dollar-earning investments during the war, leaving a deficit on investment earnings. Similarly, she had lost most of her ships in the war. The British and Norwegians rebuilt their fleets rapidly, but the USA had already built a large fleet, 1942–5, and had secured congressional preferences (for instance) in carrying Marshall Aid supplies. American tourists were not initially attracted by the bomb-shattered cities of postwar Europe, but explored Canada and Latin America instead. Nor were the traditional City of London services, like insurance, large net earners pre-1950. Hence, European services as a whole only regained a surplus (i.e. a '—' sign, from the American point of view) in 1949.[5]

Flows of American private capital to Europe had helped to balance Atlantic payments in the 1920s. In 1945 – row 5 – the major components of this flow had also slackened. American private institutions – charities, churches, etc. – continued to give substantial sums for European good causes, but immigrant remittances were far less than in the 1920s – presumably because of the long fallow period in European immigration to Europe, and the disruption of family relationships during the war. Private American investment capital was also not attracted to Europe until the mid-1950s because of high profits in America and the obvious risks in Europe. Instead, there was a small net outflow of funds as Europeans sold securities in the USA to raise resources, especially during 1946–8. In addition to private finance, all governments spent quite large sums overseas on 'normal' miscellaneous governmental business – row 6 – which was in favour of the USA, 1946–8. These sums included interest and repayment of existing loans, military and civilian expenditure overseas, and regular contributions to organisations like the UN, the IMF and the World Bank.

Before 1939 Europe's Third World triangular trades had been large dollar-earners. However, after 1945 these earnings – included in row 7 – earned far fewer dollars. European – especially British – exports to the Third World expanded enormously in 1946–56. This enabled Britain to buy a great deal of her food and raw material requirements in the sterling area and to avoid dollar purchases. However, the terms of trade had swung so much in favour of food and raw materials since the 1930s that Europe could not generate large surpluses with the Third World. Instead, American products were so attractive to the Third World countries that, whenever they could extract dollars from Europe in place of sterling or francs, they attempted to spend the surpluses that they had earned with Europe in the USA. Hence, the residual and multilateral entries that contain these balances were adverse to Europe immediately after the war and only swung into surplus when primary prices began to fall after the Korean War.

The net balance of normal transactions – row 8 – therefore had to be covered by various forms of 'compensatory' government aid and finance – rows 9–12. The use of the term 'compensatory' is unusual and significant. Immediately after the war the IMF differentiated between two main types of intergovernmental transactions: 'government miscellaneous', described above and included in the normal balance; and 'compensatory official finance'. The latter included all the residual government items required to balance the international payments, such as US government grants and loans, US contributions to the grants and loans of international organisations, and US and foreign government sales of gold and dollars. The major items in 1946–50 were the American loan to Britain and the Marshall Plan grants. After 1950, as Europe recovered, 'compensatory finance' became less important, but US resources continued to be transferred to Europe via military grants and spending. From 1946–8 the Europeans also kept themselves afloat by transferring gold and dollars to the USA and selling securities, but this flow slackened in 1949, and in 1950 they began to rebuild their reserves.[6]

The exact importance of the aid element in compensatory finance has been debated endlessly. There is no doubt that US aid was vital in maintaining the flow of US goods and services to Europe. The ratios in Table 2.3 compare the aid with trade. It can be seen that, throughout the period, European exports to the USA were only a small percentage of imports. Instead, US aid paid for a large proportion of her exports and covered, or more than covered, the whole European trade deficit. In addition, the USA provided critical supplies – machinery, coal, cotton – that Europe could not easily have acquired in other ways. On the other hand, aid was always a small proportion of total western European investment and income. There are no global European figures for GNP and investment, so it is impossible to present global ratios. However, on average, the Marshall Plan grants, in 1948–51 represented less than 3% of total European income, and less than 20% of gross investment in recipient countries.

Most commentators have therefore argued that, in global terms, the amounts received may have been sufficient to oil the wheels, but they were certainly not enough to fuel the recovery. However, it is possible to argue that the effects may have been more critical at particular times and in specific situations – and that a failure in any one may have been crucial for the whole. Firstly (see Table 2.3), deficits and aid generally – apart from 1947 – either remained at similar levels or fell from 1946 onwards, while national incomes rose from 1946 onwards; this means that aid, as a proportion of GNP, must have fallen quickly. The largest amounts were allocated before the Marshall Plan started, suggesting that what was novel about the ERP was not the volume of aid, but the effectiveness with which the programme was organised, presented and applied. Both the earlier aid and the Marshall Aid also varied a great deal between countries and end-uses. In 1948–9, for instance, aid varied from being 2.4% and 2.9% of national income in the case of Britain and Germany, to 10.8% and 14% in the case of The Netherlands and Austria. End-uses of the aid also varied a great deal, making it essential to examine the geographical and functional impact of the aid and the way in which the conditions attached to it attempted to link the whole European system together.

Notes

1. The faster post-World War II recovery was already evident in 1947. See United Nations, Department of Economic Affairs, *A Survey of the Economic Situation and Prospects of Europe* (Economic Commission for Europe: Geneva, 1948), pp. 14–21; J. Bradford de Long and Barry Eichengreen, 'The Marshall Plan: history's most successful structural adjustment program', in Rudiger Dornbusch, Wilhelm Nolling and Richard Layard (eds), *Post War Economic Reconstruction and Lessons for the East Today* (MIT Press: Cambridge, Mass., 1993), pp. 189–230, which has clear charts comparing global European output after each war.

2. Charles Maier, 'The two postwar eras and the conditions for stability in twentieth-century western Europe', in *idem, In Search of Stability* (Cambridge University Press: Cambridge, 1987), pp. 153–84.

3. Charles P. Kindleberger, *Europe and the Dollar* (MIT Press: Cambridge, Mass., 1966), surveys the dollar gap in the twentieth century.

4. United Nations, *Economic Survey of Europe in 1957* (Economic Commission for Europe: Geneva, 1958), Chapter 4, 'The changing pattern of Western Europe's trade'.

5. UN, *Survey of the Economic Situation and Prospects of Europe*, pp. 31–74, and Alan S. Milward, *The Reconstruction of Western Europe, 1945–51* (Methuen: London, 1984), pp. 19–55, survey Europe's trade and balance of payments with the USA in 1946–7.

6. *Payments Yearbook*, vol. 1, pp. 4–38, discusses 'compensatory finance'.

3

Anglo-American Plans
for Postwar Reconstruction

The belligerents drew their plans for postwar reconstruction from their ideology and war aims, their experience in the 1930s, and their perception of how the war had begun. The German aims were based on a 'New Order for Europe'. In some ways, these harked back to the old *Mitteleuropa* ideas of World War I – envisaging a self-sufficient, land-based European economy, with Germany at its heart. Nazi ideas were strengthened by the decline of international trade in the 1930s, which they thought was a long-run phenomenon based on the rise of new industries and synthetics. Research seemed to show that Europe, Russia and North Africa, taken together, could be almost self-sufficient in most foods and raw materials. Hitler's first rapid conquests suggested that such a European empire could be quite easily assembled. Hence, in 1941 he commented:

> Once the Asiatics have been driven out, Europe will no longer be dependent on any outside power; America, too can 'get lost' as far as we are concerned. Europe will itself provide all the raw materials it needs and have its own markets in the Russian area, so that we will no longer have any need of other world trade ...[1]

After the war the armaments minister, Albert Speer, recalled that, at the height of German success, he had envisaged some sort of European free-trade area, organised in the German interest to gain economies of scale: 'The tariff [would have been] lifted from this large economic area and through this a mutual production ... really achieved ... it is clear that the tariffs which we have in western Europe are unbearable. So the possibility of producing on a large scale only exists through this scheme.' In practice, the Nazis were soon forced to replace these fleeting dreams of 1941–2 by a feverish attempt to reorganise Europe for defence and to wring resources from the conquered territories. Even so, Milward comments that 'After the German occupation of France, the pattern of west European trade as it now exists began to emerge.'[2]

The British and Americans rejected this continental view, which diminished their role and cut them off from Europe; instead they offered a vision of the world that linked Europe with the Atlantic economy, the British empire and the Third World. The British recognised that they would have to do more than just discredit German propaganda to win the ideological contest. Leading economists such as Keynes argued that Britain could not just offer a return to private capitalism, the gold standard and narrow bilateralism. These values were too linked with the inequity and unemployment of the 1920s and 1930s. Britain would have to present a more humane and optimistic view of the future to win the necessary moral and political support to defeat the Axis powers. The domestic element of this vision was later embodied in the Beveridge Report and the social programmes of the postwar Labour government.[3]

In addition, Keynes and other economists argued in favour of a liberal international programme linking Britain, the Commonwealth and the rest of the world in a free and equitable trading system. Similarly, more enlightened American politicians recognised that they would have permanently to reject traditional American isolationism and high tariffs, and project the domestic dynamism of the New Deal overseas. Britain and America together would have to persuade all the major trading nations to abandon the restrictive 'beggar my neighbour' and deflationary policies of the 1930s and to secure full employment at home and expanding trade overseas. This was the task outlined at Bretton Woods and achieved by the Marshall Plan and other international agreements in the late 1940s and 1950s. Whether it also included the abandonment of regional or imperial preference schemes was a moot point.[4]

Although the US Reciprocal Trade Agreements Act (RTAA) of 1934, pushed through by Roosevelt's liberal Secretary of State Cordell Hull, exhibited early signs of the internationalism that flowered after the war, American policy in the 1930s was still very isolationist. The USA remained very self-sufficient, and foreign trade was only a small percentage of GNP. The strong constitutional position of domestic interests and lobbies made an outgoing foreign policy difficult. However, many Americans blamed the Senate's rejection of the Treaty of Versailles and the breakdown of the Atlantic economy after the Wall Street Crash for the rise of Hitler and, like Hull, concluded that 'If trade does not cross frontiers, soldiers will'. American trade recovered far more slowly than domestic and foreign GNP in the 1930s, because the USA lacked its own empire and was excluded from so many foreign trade blocs. Hence, although the war temporarily created full employment, many American economists calculated that the USA would have to prise open these blocs in order to maintain full employment after the war.[5]

British economists and politicians were far more concerned about the immediate problems of winning the war and surviving the peace. They knew that, while the fighting continued, Britain could secure essential supplies from Lend-Lease and from empire and Third World countries. But they also knew that this situation would end with victory. Lend-Lease would stop, the Americans would claim some sort of 'consideration' for their help, and the Third World allies would clamour for repayment. The economy would take time to convert to peacetime production. There would inevitably be an international restocking boom and relatively easy sales before Germany and Japan recovered, but most economists doubted that this would be enough to carry Britain through the difficult postwar period. They therefore predicted the continuation of tight planning and rationing at home and state trading and bilateral controls overseas. These would mock both the domestic promises and the multilateral dream for which the war had been fought. Since Britain had the largest trading empire, the other European nations were likely to follow her example, frustrating all the American hopes.[6]

However, many forecasters also saw some powerful positive factors that would enable active and intelligent governments to avoid renewed depression. The most important of these was the huge increase in capital, output and technology in the USA. America now had sufficient knowledge, output and capital to fund a considerable domestic and external recovery. There was a backlog of technology awaiting exploitation, great consumer hunger for new products, and large reserves of consumer savings ready to spend. These would be useless, however, if American unemployment returned or if renewed isolationism denied these resources to the Atlantic economy. By 1960 the recognised antidote to deep unemployment was Keynesian monetary and fiscal policies. These ideas had been developed in America in the mid-1930s, after the cartel planning experiments of the early New Deal had been discredited. Keynesian methods were only part of a package of New Deal measures, including anti-trust, social, farm and labour policies, that provided the liberal consensus for the next forty years.[7]

In 1939, however, despite fairly widespread knowledge of Keynesian methods in Britain and the USA, there had been no confidence that they would work in practice. In the USA, there was no political consensus for the establishment of the experiment on a sufficiently large scale to give it a chance of success; even if Congress had voted the funds, business might well have reduced investment expenditure to offset the government increase. In Britain, similarly, fears about the effects of an expansionary fiscal policy on investment and the overseas balance inhibited experiment. In both countries, war expenditure provided the crucial breakthrough into high employment. In the USA, business became far less critical of government expansion, and a generation of economists were convinced that their ideas were right. In Britain, too, wartime full employment had convinced economists and politicians that active and intelligent government planning could produce better results. This was expressed in Britain in the 1944 White Paper on *Employment Policy*, and in the USA in the Employment Act of 1946.[8]

Bretton Woods, which led to the creation of the International Monetary Fund (IMF), was one of the first victories for these economists, notably for the leading negotiators, Keynes and White. Parallel negotiations on tariff and preference differences between the USA and Britain were less successful, but they did lay the intellectual groundwork for the GATT agreement (General Agreement on Tariffs and Trade). Keynes had become interested in the problems of reconstruction when he visited Washington in May 1941. At this time the idea was developing in the USA that payment for Lend-Lease would be waived in return for some form of 'consideration' after the war. This would be a better solution than the war debts–reparations tangle of 1918. It was Hull's *idée fixe* that this 'consideration' should end, *inter alia*, British bilateral trade controls, especially imperial preference. Article 7 of the Mutual Aid Agreement of February 1942 incorporated a vague British promise – over Churchill's protests – to meet this obligation after the war.[9]

Of course, Keynes, like every British official, recognised that it was just these protective bilateral trade arrangements and their parallel domestic controls that might allow Britain to survive after the war; he described the plan as the 'lunatic proposals of Mr Hull'. Yet, at heart, Keynes, like Hull, was a liberal internationalist and he recognised the ultimate superiority of a multilateral trade regime, both in principle and for a trading nation like Britain. He was challenged to find some way of making the old verities – free trade and the gold standard – work in a modern context. In principle, stable exchange parities, which all sides agreed were essential, would only be accepted if those countries facing severe trade deficits and runs on their currency were offered sufficiently generous loans to carry them through, without excessive controls, while they reorganised their finance and industry. Such loans in the early 1930s might have pre-empted the disastrous deflation and unemployment in Germany, or prevented Britain's abandonment of the gold standard. In Keynes's opinion, they were the minimum price for accepting Article 7.

Keynes's suggestion was the formation of the International Clearing Union – the ICU – which would act as an international central bank, making very large loans available to countries in trouble. If the guarantees were convincing enough, many disasters might never begin and the domestic authorities would have time to put their house in order. In fact, a country in Britain's potential postwar position would be able to continue reconstruction despite temporary balance of payments deficits that would otherwise be crippling and necessitate all the standard bilateral, unemployment and rationing devices. In America, almost simultaneously, White was fashioning a similar plan, the Stabilization Fund (SF), which would make short-term loans to debtors to avoid exchange crises and prevent currency devaluations. There were, however, considerable differences in the size and generosity of the two schemes.[10]

This was partly because, in the first drafts of the White plan, a short-term fund was complemented by a much larger plan for an international bank which, as well as making long-term loans, would undertake many of the functions covered by Keynes's ICU. It was derived from a combination of Hoover and Roosevelt programmes such as the Reconstruction Finance Corporation for supporting industry, and the Tennessee Valley Authority for encouraging regional economic development, and meant that the SF idea was correspondingly limited. However, this plan seemed too ambitious to US departmental officials, especially when they realised that the USA would have to provide most of the funds for the bank. Many conservative Republicans who were sceptical of New Deal methods were returned to Congress in the elections in November 1942, and there were corresponding changes in the administration. Consequently, Lend-Lease and the more generous postwar plans were whittled down, leaving the SF as the major US proposal. The British, too, were sceptical about the idea of a world bank. They did not expect to receive financial aid from it; nor did they want to commit themselves to provide substantial resources to it. Hence, it emerged in 1945 not as a powerful reconstruction agency, but as a conservative bank, making cautious commercial loans.

The Keynes and White plans were exchanged in late 1942. Both sides agreed on the main aim of the proposals and on large parts of the detail – for instance, the plan to introduce stable exchange rates and prevent competitive depreciation. However, there were also major differences. Keynes was concerned that the reserves of the SF were just not large enough – $5bn. compared to $25bn. in the ICU – to have the planned effects, and that the burden of adjustment in the scheme was placed on the Europeans. The major problem in the 1920s had been the huge US surpluses, combined with her restrictive tariffs, which made it very difficult for the Europeans to export to her.[11]

In December 1942 White recognised this problem by introducing a 'scarce currency' clause in the SF, which authorised debtor countries to discriminate against the exports of over-successful creditors. Even though it was whittled down at Bretton Woods, Keynes felt that this was a most important change. The Americans, on the other hand, felt that the ICU would be too generous to European debtors and potentially very expensive for them. What would prevent the Europeans from continually drawing on the fund and never mending their ways? The USA insisted that the SF should have the power to enforce changes in debtor policy in return for loans, and that voting power in the SF would not reflect trading size, which would have helped Britain, but be in proportion to GNP and gold subscriptions.[12]

The final form of the agreements that were presented to the international conference at Bretton Woods in July 1944 was mostly hammered out between British and American delegations in Washington in September 1943. The ICU plan was dropped, but Keynes managed to introduce some of its ideas into the SF. White argued that Congress would never accept the ICU, but Keynes countered that the scheme had to be reasonably attractive to potential debtors to have the effects intended. The size of the SF was increased to $8.8bn., therefore, debtors were given greater freedom to devalue their currencies if they were in 'fundamental disequilibrium' and to manage their internal affairs without SF controls. Both sides agreed that there would be a difficult 'transition' period for several years after the war, when the Bretton Woods disciplines would not apply. During this period countries could use restrictive policies to control their trade, but there would be no IMF help. The immediate problems of relief and rehabilitation would be dealt with by separate agencies such as UNRRA and the Export–Import Bank (of Washington), which were given additional funds, principally by the USA.[13]

The parallel commercial discussions proceeded more slowly than the financial debate. The background was the American conviction in 1943 that 'A great expansion in the volume of international trade after the war will be essential to the attainment of full and effective employment in the United States and elsewhere ...' They feared that postwar European tariffs, quantitative restrictions, exchange controls and state trading would freeze out private American traders, prevent the USA from ending its own internal controls, and exacerbate international tensions. The Americans therefore offered to reduce their tariffs substantially, through the mechanism of the RTAA, if the British and other Europeans would end their preference systems. They hoped to create an International Trade Organization (ITO) similar to the IMF to monitor and control commercial restrictions.[14]

As with the IMF negotiations, there were frequent meetings in London and Washington, but the central issues did not change much. The main American negotiator, the Houston cotton merchant Will Clayton, argued so strongly for free trade that the British dubbed him 'Ideological Willie'. However, they doubted that he could carry his ideas through Congress. The British position in 1945 was that, if the Americans would transform the world trading situation by removing trade barriers and restrictions all over the world, including their own tariffs, then they would end imperial preference. But they knew that this was not likely. Instead, they did promise to discuss mutual concessions at a conference to be held in Geneva in 1947.[15]

The Bretton Woods agreements aroused considerable debate in Britain and America. In Britain, opposition came from both left and right. It was difficult for left-wing socialists who believed in a controlled economy to accept an American plan based on free-trade multilateralism and fixed exchange rates reminiscent of the gold standard. Many on the right also believed in some form of planning in the context of the empire, the sterling area and the Ottawa agreements. Many industrialists and most farmers knew that they depended on protected markets, either at home or abroad, to survive, and these seemed threatened by Bretton Woods. The agreement therefore relied on somewhat lukewarm support from traditional liberal and moderate Conservative and Labour supporters, energised by Churchill and Keynes, who emphasised – from the British viewpoint – the most attractive features of the scheme. In America there was opposition from old isolationists in the Mid-West, who questioned the need for overseas commitments, and eastern bankers, who opposed New Deal experiments. Members of the east coast intellectual establishment, who believed in the Atlantic commitments, pushed it through Congress, however, similarly emphasising the pro-creditor, pro-American features in the end of war euphoria.[16]

Similarly, when the preparatory committee to charter the International Trade Organization (ITO) met in London in late 1946, both sides clouded their agreement to proceed with extensive qualifications. The British, for instance, insisted on the right to impose controls to preserve full employment in case of a US depression, – which, remembering the sharp post-World War I depression of 1921, many expected soon. Consequently, when hard bargaining began in Geneva and Havana in 1947–8, there was only limited success. The USA did reduce her tariffs considerably at Geneva, and Britain and the dominions made substantial cuts in their preference systems. They also agreed to repeat the GATT meetings regularly, creating a periodic mechanism for further reductions. However, the planned ITO parallel to the IMF was stillborn. A charter was agreed at Havana in March 1948, but the American negotiators soon realised that they had made so many concessions that it would not pass Congress and it was quietly dropped in late 1950. It would also probably have failed in Britain.[17]

All the difficulties with these institutions and with international relations in 1946–7 were not yet apparent in 1945. During the latter stages of the war, therefore, the western allies were able to present a better view of a peaceful world than the sterile conservatism of the 1930s. This gave added moral justification to the allied invasion of Europe. They had also created a network of institutions, – the UN, UNRRA, the IMF, the International Bank for Reconstruction and Development (IBRD), etc. – to complement and control the national interests and vision of each country, to provide mutual assistance and to improve the international system. In principle, Europe would be linked to America and to the outside world. However, there were still no hard agreements on exactly how the resources required to make the system work were to be raised and distributed. The old problem of the huge trading imbalance between Europe and North America was still unsolved and was likely to be worse after World War II than it had been in the 1920s. In this sense, the new agreements and institutions merely concealed the old differences. Only time would show if the hard political and financial decisions could be made to allow an Atlantic system to work.

Notes

1. Alan S. Milward, *The New Order and the French Economy* (Oxford University Press: London, 1970), p. 25. Tenses have been changed to clarify this quotation.
2. *Ibid.*, pp. 147, 283.
3. Roy F. Harrod, *The Life of John Maynard Keynes* (Macmillan: London, 1951), pp. 503–14.
4. Richard N. Gardner, *Sterling–Dollar Diplomacy in Current Perspective: The Origins and Prospects of Our International Order* (Columbia University Press: New York, 1980), pp. 24–39.
5. *Ibid.*, pp. 1–23; Hal B. Lary *et al.*, *The United States in the World Economy* (United States Government Printing Office: Washington, DC, 1944), pp. 54–71.
6. Sir Alec Cairncross, *Years of Recovery: British Economic Policy, 1945–51* (Methuen: London, 1985), pp. 1–16; Sir Richard Clarke, *Anglo-American Collaboration in War and Peace, 1942–49* (Oxford University Press: Oxford, 1982), pp. 46–65, 94–125.
7. Michael Hogan, *The Marshall Plan* (Cambridge University Press: Cambridge, 1987), pp. 1–25; Charles Maier, 'The politics of productivity: foundations of American international economic policy after World War 2', in *idem* (ed.), *In Search of Stability: Explorations in Historical Political Economy* (Cambridge University Press: Cambridge, 1987), pp. 121–52.
8. Herbert Stein, *The Fiscal Revolution in America* (University of Chicago Press: Chicago, 1969), pp. 169–96; Alan Booth, 'The "Keynesian Revolution" in economic policy-making', *Economic History Review* 36 (1983), pp. 103–23.
9. Alan P. Dobson, *The Politics of the Anglo-American Economic Special Relationship* (Wheatsheaf: Sussex, 1988), pp. 20–34; Gardner, *Sterling–Dollar Diplomacy*, pp. 40–68; Harrod, *Keynes*, pp. 505–17.
10. Gardner, *Sterling–Dollar Diplomacy*, pp. 71–80; Harrod, *Keynes*, pp. 525–34, 537–43, provide background for this and the following paragraph.
11. Gardner, *Sterling–Dollar Diplomacy*, pp. 80–100; Harrod, *Keynes*, pp. 548–55, summarise the differences between the two plans.
12. Harrod, *Keynes*, pp. 543–8, describes the invention of the 'scarce currency' clause.
13. *Ibid.*, pp. 555–66; Gardner, *Sterling–Dollar Diplomacy*, pp. 110–21, describe the compromises reached in 1943–4.
14. Gardner, *Sterling–Dollar Diplomacy*, pp. 101–9.
15. Gregory A. Fossedal, *Our Finest Hour: Will Clayton, the Marshall Plan and the Triumph of Democracy* (Hoover Institution Press: Stanford, California, 1993), pp. 110–36; Gardner, *Sterling–Dollar Diplomacy*, pp. 145–60.
16. Fossedal, *Clayton*, pp. 137–49; Gardner, *Sterling–Dollar Diplomacy*, pp. 110–44.
17. Fossedal, *Clayton*, pp. 235–54; Gardner, *Sterling–Dollar Diplomacy*, pp. 348–80.

4

The North American Loans

The first large North American credits to Europe were the American loan of $3.75 billion and the Canadian loan of $1.25 billion to Britain in mid-1946. The background to these loans was that, as victory had come nearer in 1945, knowledgeable British economists and ministers had realised that the war austerity would continue, and possibly even become worse in 1946. The key variables were the resources used and the debts incurred during the war, and Britain's ability to adapt to the postwar situation. Table 4.1 shows the essential statistics. Britain had developed a massive trade deficit during the war as imports for war use soared and exports collapsed (rows 1–3). The fall in exports is obscured in the table by the rise in 'other credits' (row 2). During the war, imports had been financed by Lend-Lease, by sales of British assets overseas, and by borrowing from the empire and sterling area (rows 4–8). For instance, essential supplies for the forces overseas had usually been purchased with sterling, which often could not be spent locally. Hence, Argentina, Egypt and India built up large sterling claims in London – the sterling debts in Table 4.1 (row 10). However, the government could see that, as soon as the war ended, Lend-Lease would cease, Britain's creditors would claim their assets, and Britain would have few other reserves with which to buy essential food and raw materials.[1]

Fortunately, Britain's debts to the USA, unlike 1919, were small – row 9 – because Lend-Lease had been provided free. However, debts to the sterling area and other countries were very large (row 10). Britain's gold and dollar reserves – the security that she needed as a banker to defend her credibility and finance her trade – had been increased slightly during the war by careful management, by hard bargaining and by GI spending in Britain in 1944 (row 13). The USA, however, monitored the reserves and, towards the end of the war, began to ration Lend-Lease to limit their rise. The USA also hoped that Britain would be able to persuade the sterling area countries to write off at least part of their very large claims. British ministers questioned the parallel with Lend-Lease. The USA had needed British military and strategic support

Table 4.1. *British Financial Position, 1939–1945*
(£bn., current value)

	1940	1941	1942	1943	1944	1945
Imports + all debits (1)	1.5	1.9	2.6	3.6	4.2	2.8
Exports + all credits (2)	0.7	0.8	0.9	1.5	1.7	1.2
Total deficits (3)	0.8	1.1	1.7	2.1	2.5	1.6
Financed by						
Net US + Canadian grants (4)	—	0.3	1.1	1.4	1.8	0.8
Sales of assets (5)	0.2	0.3	0.2	0.2	0.1	0.1
Overseas borrowing (6)	0.2	0.6	0.5	0.7	0.7	0.7
Fall in reserves (7)	0.4	−0.1	−0.1	−0.2	−0.1	0.0
Total financing (8)	0.8	1.1	1.7	2.1	2.5	1.6
Reserves/debts						
Dollar debts (9)	—	0.2	0.0	0.0	0.1	0.0
Sterling debts (10)	0.5	0.7	1.0	1.4	1.9	2.5
Other debts (11)	0.1	0.4	0.6	0.9	1.0	1.2
Total debts (12)	0.7[a]	1.3	1.6	2.3	3.0	3.7
Gold + dollar reserves (13)	0.1	0.1	0.3	0.5	0.6	0.6

[a] Statistics have been rounded.

Source: R. S. Sayers, *Financial Policy, 1939–45: History of the Second World War, UK Civil Series* (HMSO: London, 1956), pp. 496–9.

during the war and had provided Lend-Lease free. The sterling area claims on Britain by relatively poor countries like Egypt and India were obviously different, both commercially and morally.[2]

Britain therefore faced very difficult problems in securing vital supplies in 1945. Reconversion and her future export capacity would depend on access to credit, which was threatened by the debt overhang and the weak reserves. Keynes had originally suggested that his proposed International Clearing Union (ICU) would provide 'an agreed plan for starting off every country after the war with a stock of reserves appropriate to its importance in world commerce, so that without undue anxiety it can set its house in order during the transitional period to full peace time conditions'. At Bretton Woods, however, the IMF was given a much more limited role, which was only to start *after* the transition period. Immediate demands for relief, recovery and reconstruction were left to United Nations organisations such as UNRRA. This was created to help the poorer countries, and Britain was expected to be a contributor, not a recipient.[3]

Looking ahead in 1943 and 1944, therefore, British planners foresaw an ominous gap from the end of Lend-Lease until full trade recovery. Britain would initially gain in the postwar restocking boom, because most of her factories would be intact, while Germany and Japan would be crippled. However, many of Britain's own factories were old and run-down and her import bill was bound to be large. Her economy was also very dependent on foreign trade and, therefore, very vulnerable to autarchic measures by other countries intent on domestic recovery. The government wanted to start winning back overseas markets before the end of the war, but the Americans initially would not allow Lend-Lease material to be used for reconstruction or export. They only reluctantly allowed her to begin exports with purchased raw materials in January 1945.[4]

Keynes's comment on the figures outlined above and on Britain's likely prospects were set out in a paper written in March 1945, 'Overseas Policy in Stage III'. His conclusion was that Britain had done well so far, but that she still faced great dangers. She had built up some reserves, and her liabilities were in sterling, under her control, not in gold or dollars. At current exchange rates, her wages and prices were sufficiently low to offset any industrial inefficiency. However, he added acidly:

> If by some sad geographical slip, the American Air Force (it seems too late now to hope for much from the enemy) were to destroy every factory on the North-east coast and in Lancashire (at an hour in the day when the directors were sitting there and no one else) we should have nothing to fear.

Nevertheless, he estimated that Britain's likely postwar external expenditures – for troops overseas, for German relief and domestic restocking – were so large that she would need help from the USA for three or four more years just to get by.[5]

Keynes saw three choices. The first was 'Austerity', i.e., complete financial independence from the USA – a tightly planned autarchic economy, with direction of foreign trade 'somewhat on the Russian model' and withdrawal from nearly all military commitments and colonial development. The second was 'Temptation' – i.e., taking large easy loans from the USA at commercial rates, with too many strings. The third was 'Justice' – i.e., an appeal to the USA and the sterling area countries for reasonable aid in return for Britain's special war effort. Keynes naturally wanted an immediate formal request for 'Justice' to be made before the wartime alliance faded from the American mind, but in practice he thought that the choice was between combinations of these alternatives.[6]

Some British economists, more sanguine than Keynes, thought that Britain might just wriggle through the transition period without too much explicit help or controls. They argued that all would depend on just how quickly the US and world economies grew, how world trade responded, how well British industry reacted, and what trade policies were followed by other countries. If there was a general rush for controls, then Britain would have to follow suit. Hence, instead of the grand negotiation that Keynes planned, some economists – for instance, Sir Richard Clarke – thought that there were good arguments for waiting for the situation to clarify.[7]

In the event, however, the end of the European war (Stage 1) was delayed until May 1945 by the Ardennes offensive, but the Japanese war (Stage 2) was cut short by the atom bombs (6 and 9 August). After the Quebec conference in September 1944, Churchill had expected that Britain would be able to use Lend-Lease to re-equip and re-establish exports during Stage 2, but this hope was dashed. In fact, Lend-Lease was stopped, including goods in the pipeline, on 19 August. The decision was taken by Leo Crowley, the conservative foreign-aid administrator. It was endorsed by Truman, who had become President in April 1945, when Roosevelt died. Truman was relatively inexperienced in foreign economic policy, but was also constrained by the Lend-Lease legislation. State department officials who were more friendly to Britain, like Dean Acheson or Will Clayton, were out of Washington at the time.[8]

Keynes, who had just introduced his plans to a meeting of British and American officials in London, immediately persuaded the new British Labour Cabinet that he could win a degree of 'Justice'. He was given a relatively free hand to negotiate, and sailed to Washington to argue the case for a large loan, recalculating his estimates en route. When he arrived, however, he found that the atmosphere in Washington had changed completely. In American eyes, the war was over; Britain still seemed a powerful and wealthy country; the UN had been created to regulate international relations; and the Potsdam Conference (of July–August 1945) had settled the German question. Real destitution in Europe would be dealt with by UNRRA. Many far poorer nations than

Britain were clamouring for assistance; the Russians were still friendly allies.[9]

Keynes found, therefore, that he could appeal neither to 'Justice' nor to fear of Russia, but was driven back to explaining the implications of British poverty for world trade. Fortunately, although ordinary congressmen wanted to concentrate on domestic issues, the leading American officials, such as Will Clayton and Dean Acheson, did understand the British problem and wanted to establish genuine multilateralism. Keynes persuaded them that, if Britain did not receive a loan, she would be forced back on bilateralism, the world economy would crystallise into rival trading blocs and the Bretton Woods dream would be delayed for years. It was agreed to give Britain a substantial loan of $3.75bn., plus a further $650m. to write off her debt for Lend-Lease supplies in the pipeline, but delivered after VJ Day.[10]

This amount was based on shrewd assessments by Clayton and other US officials of Britain's likely balance of payments deficits over 1946–8, plus some 'back of an envelope' bargaining. Table 4.2 gives one estimate, made in early 1946, which proved far too pessimistic for 1946, but was reasonably near Britain's actual accumulated payments deficits for 1947–8. In addition, the Lend-Lease debt of $20bn. was wiped out and US war-surplus supplies in Britain were sold for a knock-down price. Goods in the pipeline were sold for the full price, but the loan, the war surplus and the pipeline debts were all payable on the same very easy terms of 2% p. a. over fifty years, with liberal waivers if Britain experienced payment difficulties. In financial terms, the whole package was very generous, as long as the 'Justice' mentioned in Keynes's paper of March 1945, quoted above, was ignored. This was the unquantifiably much greater length and depth of the British war effort. However, it was insufficient to prevent the massive run on the pound that developed in mid-1947. This crisis – discussed in Chapter 7 – could only have been prevented by a very much larger ICU-type guarantee.[11]

In return for the loan, the Americans demanded the multilateral 'considerations' – the end of British transition period controls – much sooner than had been agreed at Bretton Woods. Keynes warded off attempts to abolish imperial preference, but Britain had to agree not to discriminate against US goods after 31 December 1946. Other elements of the Bretton Woods conference were introduced more quickly and, after a great battle, Keynes agreed that sterling would be made fully convertible one year after the ratification of the loan by Congress. Britain

Table 4.2. *Early 1946 Estimates of British Balance of Payments,*
1946–1948 (£bn.)

	1946	*1947*	*1948*	*1946–8*
Imports FOB (excl. oil)	−1.1	−1.2	−1.4	−3.7
Overseas government expenditure	−0.5	−0.4	−0.2	−1.0
Exports	0.6	1.0	1.2	2.8
Net invisibles	0.2	0.2	0.2	0.5
1946 estimate of deficit	−0.8	−0.4	−0.2	−1.4
Actual G & S deficit	−0.2	−0.4	0.06	−0.6

Sources: Estimated deficit from Sir Richard Clarke, *Anglo-American Collaboration in War and Peace* (Oxford University Press: Oxford, 1982), p. 153; actual deficit from IMF, *Payments Yearbook*, vol. 5.

as well as America had obvious interests in multilateralism, and there were good arguments for introducing convertibility before any alternative system had had a chance to crystallise. The British government, after some hesitation, was forced to accept the terms because of the Bretton Woods timetable, which required all members of the IMF to accede before 1 January 1946. The debate in the Commons was sour; there was an overwhelming sense that these were 'dollars with strings' which they had to accept. However, the government pushed the agreement through the Commons, and Keynes won approval from the liberal middle ground in the Lords with a persuasive speech emphasising Britain's long-run interests in multilateralism.[12]

Congress delayed ratification until July 1946 because of lack of US public interest and support. In Britain, the delay in Congress and the possibility that the loan might fail forced economists and politicians to consider alternative possibilities. Calculations showed that, if Britain re-enforced the sterling area system energetically and borrowed smaller sums from the USA and elsewhere, then she might just achieve viability in 1948. This could not be done without great costs, however, which would threaten the balance of world trade and security. Britain could not cut her imports of machinery and raw materials and still hope to recover; neither could she reduce her food imports below 1946 levels. Manufactures might be diverted a little more from home consumption to exports; dollar imports might be cut drastically by switching to sources in the empire for food, cotton and oil. Government advisers reckoned that the empire countries would then have to spend their earnings on British exports. Some countries like Canada might be pressed further because they needed British markets. There were limits, however, to how far Britain could discriminate against the USA, squeeze her sterling area trading partners, and prejudice her own recovery in this way.[13]

The Americans were finally persuaded to help by the growing recognition of the value of British troops in many areas around the world. Overseas British government expenditure, which included heavy expenditure in Germany and in many parts of the empire, is listed in Table 4.2 and approximated to the value of the loan. Keynes argued in February 1946 that:

> The American Loan is primarily required to meet the political and military expenditure overseas. If it were not for that we could scrape through without excessive interruption of our domestic programme ... The main consequence of the failure of the loan must, therefore, be a large-scale withdrawal on our part from international responsibilities. (Perhaps there would be no harm, in private conversation, in letting the State Department appreciate [this] a little more vividly than I think they do at present.)

In late 1945, in the euphoria of victory, the USA saw the UN as the answer to all problems and was not averse to the crumbling of empires, including Britain's. However, by early 1946 Russia's ambitions in central Europe were obvious and the value of British help to the USA had increased. Hence, by mid-1946 even the most conservative congressman supported the loan. The effects of the loan for British recovery and the collapse of convertibility in 1947 are discussed below.[14]

Britain also received a loan of $1.25bn. from Canada in early 1946. In addition, Canada made smaller loans to France ($199m.), other European countries like Belgium, Holland and Norway, and several British Commonwealth countries ($112m.). In total, she extended $1.85bn. in loans to other countries between the end of the war and early 1947. This was a major effort for a country with a population about one tenth the size of the USA and a GNP in 1946 of about $13bn. These loans ceased almost completely after the British financial crisis of late 1947, but in the late 1940s and early 1950s Canada continued to sell large volumes of wheat overseas, especially to Britain, either at cheap rates on fixed government contracts or through the Marshall Plan. Canadian support for Britain throughout and after the war can be explained by her traditional 'national policy', which emphasised internal self-development and her North Atlantic links, and as mutual

Commonwealth aid. She also followed the American lead and, like the USA, was committed to multilateralism. The loans, however, involved some uniquely Canadian economic characteristics and deserve separate analysis.[15]

Table 4.3. *Canadian Balance of Payments with Major Partners, 1947–1951 ($Canadian m.)*

	1946	1947	1948	1949	1950	1951
With sterling area						
Net G & S	664	875	615	581	1	199
Net long-term capital	47	63	59	6	48	56
Government loans	−540	−423	−52	−120	−50	—
Short-term capital	2	3	0	27	15	−79
Gold and exchange	−173	−518	−622	−494	−14	−176
With other countries						
Net G & S	306	308	229	197	65	235
Loans	−210	−142	−90	—	—	—
Misc.	7	−55	17	−20	54	25
Gold and exchange	−103	−111	−156	−177	−119	−260
With USA						
Net trade	−430	−890	−289	−378	−47	−516
Gold	96	99	119	139	163	150
Services, donations	−273	−343	−223	−362	−516	−585
Net LT capital	−217	−228	−22	66	193	510
Monetary movements	548	733	−363	−136	74	5
Gold and exchange	276	629	778	671	133	436

Source: IMF, *Payments Yearbook*, vol. 5. Each block of figures sums to zero. The gold and foreign exchange movements also sum to zero.

The essential features of the Canadian balance of payments are summarised in Table 4.3 and help to explain Canadian diplomacy. The table is presented in three separate sections, each of which sums to zero. These analyse Canadian relations with the sterling area – primarily Britain, with other overseas countries – principally in Europe and with the USA. The balance between the three areas was completed by gold and foreign exchange payments, which also sum to zero. The rationale for the triangular North Atlantic relationship was that, since 1900 or so, Canada had normally earned large surpluses with Britain and Europe for her food and raw materials, but had had large deficits with the USA, mostly for modern consumer and producer goods and services. The goods and services entries in Table 4.3 show the continuation of this characteristic pattern after the war. Then the payment of British dollar earnings to Canada evened the balance. Canada still relied on foreign trade far more than most countries of her geographical size. Trade was about 25% of Canadian GNP, compared to only 5% of American GNP. Canadian trade was also still unusually specialised in a limited number of staples such as wheat and timber. Hence she was often the world's third largest trader and provided a large share of international supplies of wheat and timber. Canadian national identity and sense of distinction from the USA derived from this staple producing role in the North Atlantic economy.[16]

Canadian agriculture and industry grew rapidly during the war, funded by American Lend-Lease and Canadian Mutual Aid. By 1945 the Canadian government had salted away substantial gold and dollar reserves, but felt even more threatened than the USA by potential British protectionism, which might divert demand for food to domestic or non-dollar suppliers. The statements by R. S. Hudson, British Minister of Agriculture, that Britain might in the future be able to provide far more of her own food worried the Canadian government. Canada therefore consistently supported the American case for multilateral trade after the war. By contrast, the other Commonwealth countries, such as Australia and New Zealand, preferred to stay in the sterling area and to draw manufactured imports and capital from Britain. Hence, in early 1945 Canada boldly initiated a debate about postwar British policy. This led to detailed discussions in late 1945 and early 1946 which interlocked with the American loan discussions. The British and Canadian governments were both afraid that their negotiations might affect, or be affected by, the much larger American loan in some way, and so proceeded cautiously. The discussions covered the settlement of the other outstanding war accounts, the size of the loan, the repayment period, and the rate of interest etc. The Canadian loan was finally activated when Congress approved the American loan and committed Britain to an accelerated multilateral programme.[17]

The combined effect of the American and Canadian loans was to help to maintain high levels of Canadian exports to Britain until the Marshall Plan took over in 1948. As expected, Britain had little to offer Canada in return after the war, and inevitably developed large deficits which were paid for in both sterling and dollars (see Table 4.3). Canadian consumers and industry, on the other hand, had a huge pent-up demand for American consumer and producer goods – cars, radios, refrigerators, machinery, etc. Canadians also bought many American services and paid large returns on US investments. Hence, in 1946–7 Canadian trade was just about in surplus overall, but in massive credit with Britain and other overseas areas and in massive deficit with the USA. Before the war Britain and Europe had earned sufficient dollars elsewhere to enable Canada to pay her US deficits, but it was only the existence of the loans that made this at all possible in 1945–7. In early 1947 Britain paid for half her Canadian purchases in dollars, using the loans, but in August 1947 the run on her gold and dollar reserves (see Chapter 7 below) forced her to make all her payments in sterling. The regional imbalance led to a financial crisis in Canada in late 1947; Canadian reserves, which had been $1.2bn. in January 1947, had almost vanished by the end of the year. Hence, in November 1947 Canada had to introduce hard import restrictions on many American goods.[18]

This seemed to challenge the traditional basis of Canadian policy. The American Ambassador in Ottawa reported in October 1947:

> In brief, it may be said that Canada today more than ever before appears ready to accept virtual economic union with the United States as a necessary substitute for the multilateralism of the Atlantic triangle now believed to have disappeared for an indefinite time to come, if not permanently.

In practice, nothing so drastic happened in the short run. In 1948 the ECA itself purchased Canadian goods 'off shore' to increase supplies in Europe and to ease the Canadian payments problem. From 1948 onwards, the Canadian goods and services surplus with Britain and other overseas areas fell as British exports to Canada rose (see Table 4.3). Similarly, her goods and services and payments deficits with the USA fell as her general and (non-monetary) gold exports to the USA rose. By 1950–1 large inflows of US capital were also alleviating Canadian deficits. The effects of the 1949–50 devaluations and the various phases of the Korean War crisis in 1950–1 are also evident in the swings in the accounts.[19]

Notes

1. R. S. Sayers, *Financial Policy, 1939–45: History of the Second World War, UK Civil Series* (HMSO: London, 1956), *passim*.
2. L. S. Pressnell, *External Economic Policy since the War, vol. 1: The Post War Financial*

Settlement (HMSO: London, 1986), pp. 1–15; Alan P. Dobson, *The Politics of the Anglo-American Economic Special Relationship* (Wheatsheaf: Sussex, 1988), pp. 20–48.

3. Keynes, quoted in Roy F. Harrod, *The Life of John Maynard Keynes* (Macmillan: London, 1951), p. 527; Richard N. Gardner, *Sterling–Dollar Diplomacy in Current Perspective* (Columbia University Press: New York, 1980), pp. 80–6, 178–84.

4. Sir Alec Cairncross, *Years of Recovery: British Economic Policy, 1945–51* (Methuen: London, 1985), pp. 3–16; Sir Richard Clarke, *Anglo-American Economic Collaboration in War and Peace* (Oxford University Press: Oxford, 1982), pp. 47–65, 94–125.

5. Clarke, *Collaboration*, pp. 52–3.

6. *Ibid.*, pp. 53–9.

7. *Ibid.*, pp. 96–122.

8. Gardner, *Sterling–Dollar Diplomacy*, pp. 184–7; Harrod, *Keynes*, pp. 591–6; Gregory A. Fossedal, *Our Finest Hour: Will Clayton, the Marshall Plan and the Triumph of Democracy* (Hoover Institution Press: Stanford, California, 1993), pp. 182–4.

9. Gardner, *Sterling–Dollar Diplomacy*, pp. 188–99; Harrod, *Keynes*, pp. 596–9; Pressnell, *External Economic Policy*, pp. 262–74.

10. Fossedal, *Clayton*, pp. 183–99; Gardner, *Sterling–Dollar Diplomacy*, pp. 188–207; Harrod, *Keynes*, pp. 599–611; Presnell, *External Economic Policy*, pp. 262–341.

11. Clarke, *Collaboration*, pp. 61–5.

12. Gardner, *Sterling–Dollar Diplomacy*, pp. 207–23.

13. Clarke, *Collaboration*, pp. 137–55; Gardner, *Sterling–Dollar Diplomacy*, pp. 225–54.

14. Keynes is quoted in Clarke, *Collaboration*, pp. 151–2.

15. See successive Canadian entries in IMF, *Payments Yearbooks*, vols 1–5.

16. United Nations, Department of Economic Affairs, *Economic Report: Salient Features of the World Economic Situation, 1945–1947* (New York, 1948), pp. 45–50 (hereafter UN, *Economic Report, 1945–47*).

17. Presnell, *External Economic Policy, passim*, especially pp. 342–55.

18. *FRUS: 1947*, vol. 3, pp. 116–33.

19. *Ibid.*, pp. 127–8; IMF, *Payments Yearbook*, vol. 5.

5

America and
Western Europe, 1944–1947

The allied conquest of Europe, 1944–5, inevitably made the liberated countries very dependent on North America. In 1938 Germany had provided supplies and markets for all the surrounding countries: see Table 5.1. The Nazis had hoped to use their victories to create an even larger integrated area from the Urals to the Atlantic, with the Ruhr at its heart. They never had time to complete their plans during the war, and the 'New Order' soon became *ad hoc* seizure. However, wartime economics did create a great deal of intra-European trade, and by 1942 Germany was extracting substantial amounts of food and other supplies from the richer western European countries in return for industrial goods and credits. Simultaneously, she had to pour resources into Italy, the Balkans and Scandinavia to keep them in the war, even though they had much less to return. The allied advance therefore required not only the provision of relief in countless bombed cities, but also the redirection of trade into new postwar channels. The immediate problem was the shortage of all supplies in the devastated areas. There had to be a massive re-victualling before recovery could begin. Hence, in 1945–6 North American (and British) imports (see Table 5.1) replaced German markets and supplies in western Europe.[1]

American concern was increased by the determination of postwar European governments to use economic planning and Keynesian methods to recover as fast as possible. The general public on the Continent, as in Britain, had inflated postwar expectations, and the new governments felt that they had to try to offer fuller employment, higher consumption and improved services. Most governments knew that living standards would probably have to fall in the short run, but they could not explain this to their electorates. All the problems were interrelated. Heavy new investment was essential to repair war damage and together with the import of new technology, absorbed resources needed for immediate consumption and risked economic and social

Table 5.1. *German and US Share of European Trade, 1938 and 1946*
(as %, excluding free relief exports)

	Germany imports from		United States exports to		United States imports from	
	1938	1946	1938	1946	1938	1946
Austria	—	—	8	5	2	7
Belgium	12	1	11	18	7	13
Britain	5	3	13	17	5	4
Czechoslovakia	14	8	14	6	14	7
Denmark	20	3	8	9	1	3
France	6	3	11	31	6	6
Greece	—	—	7	23	17	55
Holland	15	7	11	25	3	5
Italy	19	1	12	55	8	18
Norway	—	—	11	22	8	5
Sweden	18	1	16	24	9	7

Source: UN, *Economic Report*, 1945–47, pp. 176, 178.

stability. However, the weak coalition governments in many countries calculated that they had to risk expansion and quickly embarked upon expensive long-term plans which required large imports from North America. The obvious dangers were budget and payments deficits, a contorted maze of controls, accelerating inflation, economic collapse and communist takeover.[2]

American political and business leaders had been interested in European problems since World War I. In the 1920s financiers like J. P. Morgan had attempted to impose order on European governments by rationing credits. Wall Street, however, was discredited by the Crash. During the 1930s administrators of Roosevelt's New Deal developed many new techniques of government control. The wartime boom restored the confidence of American businessmen and encouraged them to work with the government. American government officials, businessmen and the military gained a great deal of useful experience in working together (and with their British opposite numbers) to organise the war effort. All these groups believed that New World technology and enlightened administration could help to heal Europe's economic and social wounds. Initially, the USA tried to work with her allies in the new international organisations. Relief was first dealt with by the Allied Control Commissions and then by UNRRA. Table 5.2 lists the very large grants and loans that were made available to Europe in 1946 and early 1947, well before the Marshall Plan.[3]

Table 5.2. *Postwar Relief, Credits and Imports of European Countries, May 1945–Autumn 1947 ($USm.)*

	UNRRA relief (1)	Other loans and credit (2)	US loans and credit (3)	Total loans and credit (4)	Imports 1946– mid-47 (5)	Credits as % of imports (6)
Austria	163	46	72	281	200	139
Belgium	0	158	205	363	2030	18
Britain	0	2926	4400	7326	8385	87
Czechoslovakia	317	96	72	485	775	62
Denmark	0	242	20	262	885	30
Finland	3	75	105	183	300	59
France	0	1202	1920	3122	3360	93
Germany[a]	0	480	670	1150	1003	115
Greece	420	40	341	801	544	147
Holland	0	502	413	915	1535	59
Hungary	5	7	30	42	—	—
Italy	505	136	325	966	1755	55
Norway	0	113	70	183	825	22
Poland	577	114	90	781	820	95
Sweden	0	0	0	0	1500	0
Switzerland	0	0	0	0	1320	0
Yugoslavia	505	2	0	507	565	90
TOTAL	2495	6139	8733	17367	25802	67

[a] Credits to Germany are British and American grants, for the whole of 1946–7, reported in IMF, *Payments Yearbook*, vol. 1; German imports for 1946 and half of 1947 are from Kramer, *The West German Economy*, p. 110.
Sources: United Nations, *Economic Report*, 1945–47, pp. 125, 183; IMF *Payments Yearbook*, vol. 1, pp. 343, 370–1.

UNRRA was established in 1943, largely through American efforts, and distributed (col. 1) about $2.5bn. in 1946 and early 1947, mostly in south-eastern Europe. UNRRA was controlled by the UN, but the first tranche of its funds came from the USA (72%), Britain (18%), and Canada (6%). However, when the second tranche was discussed in August 1945, Canada withdrew her support, concentrating her aid on her wheat credits. Britain was willing to support the second tranche – at 18% of the total – only if UNRRA took over Britain's military responsibility for relief in Italy and Austria, which had been nearer 50%

of the total. This left the USA as by far the largest contributor, but with
little control over distribution. US support for UNRRA cooled during
1946, therefore, especially when it gave large sums to eastern European
countries like Yugoslavia, and it was wound up in December 1946.
When the Marshall Plan was discussed, Will Clayton commented that
this time 'we must avoid getting into another UNRRA. The United
States must run this show.'[4]

The major credits listed in col. 2 were the Canadian loan to Britain
($1.25bn.), British drawings on sterling area countries, and several small
British and Canadian loans. The British loans, in effect, recycled American credits to Europe. The Canadian loans were intended to encourage
Canadian wheat sales. The only substantial IMF or IBRD loan before
mid-1947 was a $250m. loan to France in May 1947. The major US
credits – col. 3 – were small 'post-UNRRA' grants in early 1947 to Austria, Greece and Italy ($100m.), Lend-Lease and surplus property grants
disposing of leftover surpluses ($1.9bn.), several US Export–Import
Bank loans to western European countries ($2.0bn.), and US Treasury
credits to Britain ($3.75bn.) and Greece ($300m.). These credits collectively funded a substantial share of European imports, 1946–7. Some
south-eastern European countries relied on these credits for nearly all
their imports and then had to cut back sharply and seek help elsewhere
when they stopped in early 1947. Belgium, Sweden and Switzerland,
which either were not devastated by the war or had large reserves of
their own, received little aid. Britain and America also had to supply
their zones in Germany. 'Feeding the Germans' was a major burden on
Britain in 1946–7.[5]

After Britain, most help went to France, Italy and Germany. Discussions about French recovery were begun by de Gaulle in Algiers in
April 1944 and in Paris after the liberation. However, the turning-point
came in July 1945, when it became clear to French observers at Potsdam
that Germany, in some form, would recover. In future, the Americans
told de Gaulle, French security would be guaranteed by her economic
strength, the UN and the bomb. To the French, the message was clear;
whatever the merits of the UN and the bomb, they had to reconstruct
their economy faster than Germany. The result was the Monnet Plan
of March 1946, which aimed to draw on American and German resources
to achieve French growth and security. Jean Monnet, who had had
considerable experience in wartime planning in Britain and America,
calculated that France should achieve 125% of her 1929 level of output

by 1951. From this, his 'Commissariat au Plan' calculated targets for six main sectors of the economy – coal, electricity, steel, cement, farm machines and railways. Monnet's secret was to avoid challenging the authority of the traditional ministries, and to lay down the outlines of a reasonable plan. Detailed discussion was delegated to 'modernisation' committees in each industry. The plan required very large imports of German coal, which the French hoped would be delivered free, and American raw materials and machines, which they hoped would be covered by loans.[6]

In practice, the costs of the Free French contribution to the war, the German collapse and the Monnet Plan quickly drove France into huge deficits with the USA. Table 5.3 outlines French trade patterns in 1938–46. In 1938 France, like Britain, had a trade deficit, mostly with America, but this was offset by an equal surplus in 'invisibles'. During the war France developed – or the occupiers developed for her – large surpluses with Germany. These were paid for with unusable German marks; hence, France helped to finance the German war effort. From 1944–6 the German surplus was rapidly replaced by large deficits with America, financed by US loans or French reserves. In return, the USA attempted to commit France, like Britain, to multilateralism. American finance started with French Lend-Lease, which funded the Free French forces during the war. Like Britain, the Free French signed a master Lend-Lease agreement which included a similar Article 7.[7]

Table 5.3. *French Trade Balances with Leading Partners, 1938–1946* (*$m.*)

	USA	Algeria	Belgium + Germany	Italy + Spain	Britain	Trade balance	Invisible balance
1938	−104	−31	−8	3	9	−145	172
1943	−2	−1	571	−3	3	538	—
1944	−17	0	223	−2	1	188	—
1945	−316	9	−4	−2	−56	−861	−255
1946	−651	−95	−4	−16	−82	−1527	−225

Note: The 1943 figures are calculated at the 1939 fr–$ rate; the 1944 figures at the 1945 rate.

Source: B. R. Mitchell, *European Historical Statistics, 1750–1975* (Macmillan: London, 1980), pp. 514, 545–6, 862.

The French Lend-Lease debt was written off in the Blum–Byrnes discussions in the USA in May 1946, but there was no equivalent to the large British loan. Britain was more central to world trade than France, and the French opposed American plans for interzonal German administrations. Léon Blum, the revered ex-Prime Minister of the 1930s who had survived Buchenwald, visited Washington just after Keynes, but was honoured not rewarded. Instead, France received smaller loans from the US Export–Import Bank, from Canada, the World Bank and the IMF. France also made a formal commitment to the Bretton Woods system, but, like Britain, insisted on a long transition period and was even more vague about details. The dilemma for France was that she needed the money for security against Germany as well as for recovery, but the USA would only give it to her if she acquiesced in German recovery. Hence, agreement was grudging and delayed on both sides, but France did receive enough US money to cover her deficits in 1945–6 and to begin a rapid reconstruction.[8]

Table 5.4. *Principal Credits and Grants to France, 1941–1947 ($m.)*

1941–5	Lend-Lease to France	3.389
1941–5	Reverse Lend-Lease to USA	−870
1945 (Mar.)	Export–Import Bank	560
(Dec.)	British loan, £150m.	600
1946 (Apr.)	Canadian loan, $C253m.	253
(May)	US government	653
(July)	Export–Import Bank	650
(Dec.)	US Maritime Commission	56
1947 (May)	World Bank	250
(July)	New Zealand	20
(Sept.)	IMF	125
(Dec.)	US government	32

Source: Gérard Bossuat, 'L'Aide américaine à la France après la Seconde Guerre Mondiale', *Vingtième Siècle* 9 (1986), pp. 33–4. Interim aid of $311m. was paid in early 1948; Marshall Aid of $366m., for the remainder of 1948, began in summer 1948.

Italy also became far more dependent on the USA immediately after the war. During the slow march northwards in 1943–5 allied military assistance had been kept to the minimal levels required 'to prevent disease and unrest'; local costs were partly financed by printing lire. Despite desperate pleas, offers to adhere to Article 7 of the Atlantic Charter, and Roosevelt's promises (during the 1944 US elections) to offer a New Deal to the Mezzogiorno, only a trickle of US funds reached

Italy in 1944–5. Britain offered even less and was initially happy to see Italy weak. The north was finally liberated in April 1945 and the first Italian government was formed in June. In July 1945 Clayton voiced American expectations that Italy would promptly reduce tariffs, discontinue bilateral treaties and sell state monopolies, but, without US funds, these were pious hopes. In some ways, however, Italy was well placed to enter the international market. Although the south had been battered and many Italian railroads destroyed, large parts of industry in the north had survived the war almost intact. Unlike Germany, control was quickly handed over by the allies and there were small reparations. Unlike France, Italy had few foreign policy dilemmas.[9]

Table 5.5 outlines Italian trade. The contrast with France is interesting. Italy was less dependent on the USA than France in 1938, she did not support Germany in 1942, but, like France, she drew heavily on American resources in 1946–7. The principal aid – a $450m. UNRRA grant – was secured by the Italian centre-right Christian Democratic government, formed in late 1945 by Alcide de Gasperi. The grant provided 70% of Italian food imports in 1946, 40% of fuel, and substantial proportions of farm, industrial and medical imports. Will Clayton, the American negotiator, also arranged for cotton and coal supplies. In return, de Gasperi reduced controls on foreign trade and devalued the lira. Two large American companies, International Telegraphs and Telephones and Trans World Airlines, were given contracts to reorganise the Italian telephones and airlines. In early 1946 it seemed as if Italy was recovering quickly and fitting relatively easily into American plans for a multilateral world.[10]

Table 5.5. *Italian Trade Balance with Leading Partners, 1938–1947 ($m.)*

	USA	Britain	France	Germany + Austria + Switzerland	Visibles	Invisibles	UNRRA grants
1938	−29	−37	4	−7	−120	91	0
1942	−1	−33	3	0	146	−136	0
1946	−302	—	—	—	−512	3	588
1947	−447	—	—	—	−667	−137	315

Sources: Mitchell, *European Historical Statistics*; IMF, *Payments Yearbook*, vol. 1, p. 236; US, *Statistical Abstract*, 1949, p. 875.

Belgium adjusted to liberation more easily than any other small

European country. Her basic specialisation was in heavy industry, like the nearby Ruhr – coal, iron and steel. Table 5.6 outlines her balances (and those of Holland, Denmark and Norway) with her main trading partners, her visible and invisible balances, and, for 1946, her 'compensatory finance'. Current account deficits were, of course, normally offset by various capital movements. 'Compensatory finance' measures the additional grants, loans and gold and dollar movements that were required in the difficult postwar situation to balance international accounts. Before the war, Belgium's small deficits with the USA had been offset by surpluses with Britain and other European countries. During the occupation she shipped large quantities of heavy industrial goods to Germany. In 1945 she was well placed to exploit the recovery. Her industry was relatively untouched by the war and she had substantial overseas assets in Africa and large gold reserves. The large trade deficits with her main partners were partly offset by surpluses with other European countries, by allied military spending in Belgium, and by repatriation of capital from abroad. She was able to discontinue almost all controls immediately and to secure a quick, demand-based recovery. With the Ruhr out of action, she had very good markets for her coal and heavy industrial goods. Imports poured in, therefore, not only from America, but also from Britain, and she required relatively little compensatory finance. In 1946 even Cadillacs and light private aircraft were reported around Brussels.[11]

Holland and Denmark (see Table 5.6) also lost their chief wartime markets when German demand for food collapsed. Unfortunately, Britain, their other traditional market, had developed her own farms and domestic production during the war and severely rationed imports like Danish bacon. However, American imports, like corn, rose in price, causing serious payments deficits. Holland suffered more because she had traditionally relied on trade and invisible earnings from the Dutch East Indies to cover her large import deficit with Europe. The Japanese seized the colonies, with their valuable oil and rubber, in 1942, and the Dutch never really re-established control, despite large military costs. Norway had traditionally relied a great deal on freight earnings. Many of her ships were overseas in 1940 and were transferred to the allies. During the war she was a strategic asset to Germany, but an economic liability. However, in 1945–7 she was able to use her wartime shipping earnings to fund a large reconstruction programme, importing heavily from the USA and Britain.[12]

Table 5.6. *Trade Balances for Belgium, Denmark, Holland and Norway, 1938–1946 ($m.)*

	Britain	France	Germany	USA	Visibles	Invisibles	Compensatory finance[a]
Belgium							
1938	39	0	3	−35	−47	—	0
1943	0	−34	123	0	75	—	0
1946	−176	−74	−30	−191	−624	—	156
Denmark							
1938	65	0	−14	−24	−20	44	0
1943	0	0	25	2	23	336	0
1946	−161	−3	−9	−43	−256	61	165
Holland							
1938	61	—	−85	−59	−128	185	0
1943	0	—	134	0	118	0	0
1946	−107	—	−2	−180	−503	7	617
Norway							
1938	0	4	−24	−14	−71	92	0
1943	0	0	−69	0	−109	—	0
1946	−61	4	−12	−84	−158	51	167

[a] For the concept of compensatory finance, see the text above.
Sources: Trade figures: Mitchell, *European Historical Statistics*; compensatory finance: UN, *Economic Survey of Europe since the War* (Economic Commission for Europe: Geneva, 1953), p. 252. Exchange rates are from Svennilson, *Growth and Stagnation*, pp. 318–19; 1939 rates are used for 1943.

Victory made the allies responsible for western Germany. The old German markets and sources of supply in the east were under Russian control. In the west, the USA occupied rural south-western Germany; Britain, the industrial north-west, including the Ruhr, Hamburg, etc.; and France, the Saar and the Rhineland. The British and American zones were merged to become the Bizone in January 1947; in May 1949 the Bizone and the Rhineland formed the German Federal Republic. The allies developed policies for the whole of Germany as well as for their own zones. At the Quebec Conference in September 1944 Roosevelt had accepted the famous Morganthau Plan to deindustrialise and pastoralise Germany in favour of Britain and France, but this extreme position was quickly dropped. Instead, the USA was gradually converted to the promotion of full (non-military) German recovery, due to a growing appreciation that western Europe needed a prosperous Germany for supplies and markets and, to a lesser extent, because of growing differences with Russia.[13]

The Potsdam negotiations of July–August 1945 demonstrated the complexity of the German situation. All parties accepted the need for retribution, de-Nazification, de-militarisation and zonal division, but beyond this there was considerable disagreement. At first, the Big Three powers hoped that unified central administrations – for instance, of transport – would keep the national economy together. However, as each power developed its policies, unified administration became increasingly difficult and partition became inevitable. American policy in Germany was divided between the army, which unwillingly accepted administration of the US zone, and the State Department, which was concerned not only with Germany, but also with wider European policy.

The US Army, headed by General Lucius Clay, a professional engineer, wanted appropriate retribution and re-education, but also hoped that the occupation would be as short, humane and creative as possible. The army had absorbed the lessons of the federal occupation of the southern USA in the 1860s and of the French occupation of the Ruhr in the 1920s. The occupying forces here had initially taken a hard line, but had soon become hostages to local obstruction and passive resistance and, ultimately, had been forced to retire. The British authorities, naturally concerned about the costs of a long occupation, agreed with Clay. In practical terms, this meant rapid basic reconstruction and opposition to excessive reparations.

The State Department, however, faced urgent demands from the other west European countries for German resources. Coal, in particular, was desperately needed all over Europe. Hence, in July 1945 President Truman ordered German coal to be shipped free of charge to those areas most in need, with payment to be made later. The Monnet Plan was organised around the compulsory delivery of large volumes of cheap German coal. The USA also recognised French claims for restitution for looted property and Russian claims to a large share of reparations. The State Department was determined that these reparations should come from Germany, though, and not via some roundabout route, as in the 1920s, from the USA itself. It therefore enunciated the 'first charge' principle: proper allocations would be made to fund relief in Germany, but the cost of these necessary imports for relief should then have the first claim, before reparations, on any German exports available. Needless to say, it would have been impossible to meet all these claims immediately and still preserve Germany as a viable economy, capable of paying them in future.

In practice, the 'first charge' principle was often ignored. In the east, the Russian interpretation of 'war booty' was extremely wide; a great deal of German war-industry equipment was dismantled and shipped east. Huge amounts of civil industry plant were shipped as reparations. Ironically, much of this was too advanced for Russian use and was either wasted or, by diverse routes, shipped back to the original owners. The Russians then turned to shipping completed goods from current production, without much concern for the future of their zone. In addition, since East Germany only contained a small share of German industry, they claimed capital goods from the western zones. The Americans and British also claimed reparations; officially, they only took quite small shares in movable capital such as ships, – for instance – but the Americans did effectively scour Germany for technical ideas of potential commercial and military value. The technical details were published in 1947, but by then the Americans had gained a good start in their use. In May 1946 the US Army (and the British) eventually announced – but, curiously, did not stop – the end of all reparations to Russia from their zones.

The amount of reparations was closely connected to the 'level of industry' that the allies thought Germany should retain. It was agreed finally that the appropriate level should be 50–55% of industrial output in 1938 – approximately the same as in 1932! The Russians wanted a low level, so that they could take more surplus plant; the Americans and British a higher level to reduce their costs. In March 1946 the allies agreed a general level, not including war industries such as chemicals and steel, sufficient to achieve an average central European living standard. In practice, however, devastation and disorganisation were so widespread in Germany that production remained far below the permitted levels. Consequently, the volume of free commercial exports to the surrounding areas collapsed, and the allies had to import massive food supplies to prevent disease and unrest (see Table 5.7). Simultaneously, the commodity composition of German trade changed completely. Food replaced raw material and manufactured imports, and coal and timber replaced the traditional high-quality manufactured exports. In some respects, but without planning, this was perhaps not too far from the outcome that Morganthau or the Russians might have chosen, but it provided no long-run solution to German or European recovery.

Table 5.7. *German Trade with Leading Partners, 1936–1947*

	Total exports ($m.)		Percentage imports		Distribution of exports	
	1936	*1947*	*1936*	*1947*	*1936*	*1947*
USA	79	2	6	66	3	1
Britain	238	35	6	12	9	18
France	132	53	2	5	5	27
Belgium + Luxembourg	132	16	4	2	5	9
Holland	212	18	4	2	8	8
Percentage composition of all exports						
Agrarian	—	—	34	92	3	1
Industrial	—	—	66	8	97	99
From Bizone						
Coal	—	—	—	—	15	60
Timber	—	—	—	—	1	20
Manufactured goods	—	—	—	—	80	18

Sources: IMF, *Payments Yearbook*, vol. 1, p. 199; Alan Kramer, *The West German Economy, 1945–1955* (Berg: New York, 1991), p. 110.

Notes

1. Alan S. Milward, *The New Order and the French Economy* (Oxford University Press: London, 1970), p. 283; UN, *Economic Report*, pp. 168–80.
2. Alan S. Milward, *The Reconstruction of Western Europe, 1945–51* (Methuen: London, 1984), pp. 51–3; UN, Department of Economic Affairs, *A Survey of the Economic Situation and Prospects of Europe* (Economic Commission for Europe: Geneva, 1948), pp. 122–86.
3. Frank Costigliola, *Awkward Dominion: American Political, Economic and Cultural Relations with Europe, 1919–1933* (Cornell University Press: Ithaca, New York, 1984), pp. 111–66; Michael Hogan, *The Marshall Plan* (Cambridge University Press: Cambridge, 1987), pp. 1–25.
4. UNRRA, Operational Analysis Paper no. 49, *UNRRA in Europe, 1945–47* (UNRRA: London, 1947); Gregory A. Fossedal, *Our Finest Hour: Will Clayton, The Marshall Plan and the Triumph of Democracy* (Hoover Institution Press: Stanford, California, 1993), pp. 176–81, 230; Charles P. Kindleberger, *Marshall Plan Days* (Allen and Unwin: Boston, 1987), pp. 96–8, 112.
5. UN, *Economic Report, 1945–47*, pp. 123–7, 180–5; UN, *Economic Situation and Prospects of Europe*, pp. 62–5; Milward, *Reconstruction*, pp. 45–8.
6. Gérard Bossuat, *La France, l'aide américaine et la construction européenne, 1944–54* 2 vols, Comité pour L'Histoire Économique et Financière de la France: Paris, 1992); Frances M. B. Lynch, 'Resolving the paradox of the Monnet Plan: national and international planning in French reconstruction', *Economic History Review* 37 (1984),

pp. 229–43; François Duchêne, *Jean Monnet: The First Statesman of Interdependence* (Norton: New York, 1994), pp. 147–67.

7. Bossuat, *La France*, pp. 24–61; Duchêne, *Monnet*, pp. 126–46; Irwin W. Wall, *The United States and the Making of Postwar France, 1945–1954* (Cambridge University Press: Cambridge, 1991) pp. 35–49.

8. Bossuat, *La France*, pp. 63–98; Duchêne, *Monnet*, pp. 147–66.

9. John L. Harper, *America and the Reconstruction of Italy, 1945–48* (Cambridge University Press: New York, 1986), pp. 1–55; Wall, *France*, pp. 49–62.

10. *Ibid.*, pp. 5–75.

11. Isabelle Cassiers, '"Belgian Miracle" to slow growth: the impact of the Marshall Plan and the European Payments Union', in Barry Eichengreen (ed.), *Europe's Postwar Recovery* (Cambridge University Press: Cambridge, 1995), pp. 271–91; Kindleberger, *Marshall Plan Days*, pp. 230–44 (see p. 234 for Belgian Cadillacs); André Mommen, *The Belgian Economy in the Twentieth Century* (Routledge: London, 1994), pp. 75–98.

12. See Chapter 11 for other small countries.

13. This and the following paragraphs are based on relevant sections in *FRUS*; John Gimbel, *The Origins of The Marshall Plan* (Stanford University Press: Stanford, California, 1976), *passim*; Kindleberger, *Marshall Plan Days, passim*; Kramer, *West German Economy*, pp. 7–70; Fossedal, *Clayton*, pp. 162–75.

6

The Immediate Postwar
Recovery, 1945–1947

Two years after the end of the war, American observers were disappointed by the speed of European recovery. General Marshall broadcast to the American people in April 1947 that 'The recovery of Europe has been far slower than had been expected ...'. Will Clayton, the Assistant Secretary of State for Economic Affairs, reported in May 1947: 'it is now obvious that we grossly under-estimated the destruction of the European Economy by the war ... without further prompt and substantial aid ... economic, social and political disintegration will overwhelm Europe'. In his Harvard address on 5 June 1947 Marshall claimed: 'In considering the requirements for the rehabilitation of Europe, the physical loss of life, visible destruction of factories, mines and railroads [were] correctly estimated, but it has become obvious that this visible destruction was less serious than the dislocation of the entire fabric of the European economy.' Similarly, contemporary United Nations reports claimed: 'By the end of 1947, two and a half years after the end of the war, normal economic conditions were far from re-established in European countries.'[1]

However, contemporary statistical reports reveal another story: see Table 6.1. In practice, national governments aimed high and demobilised troops worked hard to repair war damage. Hence, from a low base, industrial output generally rose rapidly in 1945 and early 1946, but then slowed down. Individual countries recovered at different speeds. The unoccupied neutrals, who had done well during the war, grew slowly. Britain started from a high level of output, but had to make a massive conversion to peacetime production. The occupied countries, whose industry and trade had been temporarily disrupted in the German retreat, expanded very rapidly. Italy was initially held back by the fighting and by allied disinterest, but recovered very quickly in early 1946. Germany, however, did badly throughout 1946–7. The United Nations report quoted above declared: 'In general, European countries have made remarkable progress to date in restoring to working order their industrial and transport facilities and in increasing industrial production and the movement of goods.'[2]

Table 6.1. *Industrial Output and Growth in Europe, 1945–1947*

	Indexes [a]			Rates of growth p.a.[b]			
	1945	1946	1947	1946		1947	
	Oct.–Dec.	Oct.–Dec.	Jul.–Sept.	Jan.–Jun.	Jul.–Dec.	Jan.–Jun.	Jul.–Sept.
Austria	—	49–50*	—	—	—	—	—
Belgium	50	81	82	5	2	2	−1
Britain	—	100	115‡	—	—	—	—
British zone	22	33	37	—	—	—	—
Denmark	81	104	103	3	1	−1	1
France	—	90	89	7	1	2	−6
Greece	39	71	68	—	—	—	—
Holland	57	89	91	1	0	−1	−4
Ireland	96	112	109‡	—	—	—	—
Italy	—	54	72	17	−2	8	1
Norway	81	110	106	5	2	4	−1
Sweden	104	108	108	1	0	—	−1
US zone	19	45	50	—	—	—	—

[a] 1937 = 100.
[b] By six- or three-month periods.
* Jan.–Mar. 1947.
‡ Apr.–Jun. 1947.
Sources: UN, *Economic Report, 1945–47*, pp. 131, 133; Alan Kramer, *The West German Economy, 1945–1955* (Berg: New York, 1991), p. 93.

The recovery generally was substantially faster than post-1918 (see Table 2.1, above), but there was considerable variation between industries: see Table 6.2. Compared to the average, coal output recovered badly, due to long-run depletion; given the traditional importance of Germany in the total, this was a potential problem. The rapid recovery in investment industries – a weighted average of iron and steel, engineering and building – reveals the emphasis given to reconstruction and development by most governments, at the expense of light industry such as textiles.

Table 6.2. *Industrial Output in Europe, October–December 1946*[a]

	Industrial average	Coal[b]	Textiles	Investment goods[c]	Agriculture[d]	Railroad freight
Belgium	99	77	136	108	72	103
Britain	115	84	90	107	106	128
Denmark	100	—	86	85	94	144
France	94	102	79	100	73	138
Germany	31	41	24	24	65	—
Holland	83	68	72	—	79	91
Italy	61	—	62	75	77	—
Norway	110	—	99	—	87	128
Sweden	104	—	101	100	103	198

[a] 1938 = 100.
[b] Jan.–Dec. 1946.
[c] Includes iron and steel, engineering and building.
[d] For 1946/7.
Source: UN, *Economic Situation and Prospects of Europe*, pp. 3–14, 16.

Agriculture obviously recovered slowly – due to depleted soils and herds – a potential Achilles' heel of the whole process. Railroad freight, on the other hand, grew very rapidly – possibly reflecting long-run structural change and depletion of nearby resources. The high railroad activity might also have been caused by desperate attempts, as the recovery continued, to redistribute increasingly scarce stocks.[3]

Despite the large numbers of men released from the armed services, the recovery was aided by virtually full employment. In 1945–6 there was, of course, a consumer and stock-building boom as resources were released, as is the case after all wars. In addition, however, there was the obvious physical need for reconstruction and the longer-term requirement to make up for the delayed investments caused by the depression and to take advantage of the technologies that had emerged during the war. There was a massive need to improve the infrastructure, to refurbish railroads and to build new generating sets, oil refineries, etc. Finally, governments showed that they were prepared to take a risk with inflation and balance of payments problems by keeping interest rates at very low levels and, in most cases, allowing necessary imports to flow in as required, whatever the effect on the trade balance.[4]

The American and UN loans and supplies that have been detailed above played an important role in this process, both financially and physically. The helped to remove the financial restraint on imports in

1945–6 and assisted western European restocking with basic food and raw materials and specialised machinery. The UN reported:

> During 1946, the ratio of imports to the national income in most countries of Europe ... ranged from fifteen to as high as forty per cent, reflecting the fact that the reduction of indigenous production has increased the role of imports in the creation of national income ... a significant sector of the economy of Europe is working with imported raw material, and a large part of the population of Europe is being fed by imported foodstuffs.

Without these imports, Europe would have had to provide these essentials first, and the pattern of recovery might have been quite different. At each stage of recovery, new problems and bottlenecks appeared. Initially, transport problems restrained production, but these were soon solved. Next, countries placed most emphasis on re-equipping industry with new plant and machinery and on increasing the output of consumer goods for export. The cost of this, however, was slower growth of the basic industries – agriculture, mining, and iron and steel, for instance. Hence, industrial output rose rapidly, but shortages soon appeared in basic materials – coal, timber, steel and food. American imports eased these shortages by providing both the more specialised investment goods required for increased production and the basic raw materials like coal and food.[5]

In Britain the process of conversion from war to peace went remarkably well in 1946 – much better than anyone had expected. Most observers felt that the economy was well on the way to full recovery. The North American loans greatly eased policy decisions. In early 1946 officials discussed endlessly what would happen if Congress rejected the loan. Official opinion was that, with luck, Britain could probably have 'wriggled through until 1948' and then 'collected [Marshall Aid] with the rest' (of Europe). The loan enabled Britain to expand output and exports rapidly and to cover her essential defence and peace-keeping costs until there was a degree of organised disengagement in Germany, the Middle East and India. American emergency aid to Europe in early 1946 also found its way back to Britain; each successive estimate of British industrial output and exports rose in 1946 as the continentals used American loans to restock with British goods.[6]

France also recovered remarkably quickly in early 1946, partly due to American aid. The French economy was prostrate at liberation. Coal and other raw materials were almost unobtainable, the railroads had been destroyed by allied bombing, and industrial production was only 20% of its level in 1938. The farmers were producing 70% of their normal output, but keeping much of it for themselves. The French government tackled internal bottlenecks vigorously: the SNCF patched up the railways during the winter of 1944/5; coal production rose from 60% of its 1938 output in early 1945 to 100% in early 1946; large numbers of German and Italian POWs were imported to help clear rubble and work fields and mines. Successive short-run plans encouraged recon-struction and investment and controlled output and consumption. The French did a lot for themselves; also, where possible, they seized German resources.[7]

However, US loans and supplies were an important ingredient in this recovery. During 1944–6 the French economy was reorientated to the west. Table 6.3 gives monthly averages of imports, exports and industrial output. German 'demand' (see 'Exports') collapsed in mid-1944 as the German armies retreated eastwards. Simultaneously, Jean Monnet, at de Gaulle's request, designed an import programme for 1944–5 whereby 50% of French food imports, 25% of her coal, 80% of her semi-finished and 90% of her finished manufactured imports were to come from the USA. In practice, German resistance in the ports and military demands delayed civilian imports for nine months after D-Day. However, as soon as transport was made available in the spring and summer of 1945, very large supplies came in from Britain and North America. The table shows imports pouring into the western ports, spurring on industrial recovery, while exports were rigorously controlled to preserve essential supplies. By March 1946 imports were higher than they had been in 1938, industrial production had reached 78% of those levels, but exports were only 28% of those levels. The recovery continued. The French complained continually about shortages of American supplies and fin-ance, but by the end of 1946 industrial production was approaching its 1938 output.[8]

Germany had experienced far more war damage and recovered more slowly than the liberated economies. Her commercial exports (excluding reparations) fell to near zero and she had to be provisioned at considerable cost. Even in Germany, however, substantial progress was made in repairing the infrastructure and increasing industrial output. Thus, from almost zero in May 1945, overall German production had reached about 40% of its 1936 level by early 1946. The reasons for this relatively rapid

Table 6.3. *French Trade and Industrial Output, 1944–1947* [a]

	Jan.	Feb.	Mar.	Apr.	May	Jun.	Jul.	Aug.	Sept.	Oct.	Nov.	Dec.
Imports												
1944	11	11	10	9	8	7	5	4	4	2	2	2
1945	2	3	5	7	11	15	20	32	45	60	72	85
1946	92	97	105	106	124	125	127	125	120	106	100	99
1947	105	106	121	127	130	129	128	126	118	107	—	—
Industrial output												
1946	66	75	78	85	90	90	85	73	88	95	94	92
1947	91	96	99	106	106	101	98	87	101	105	99	93
Exports												
1944	49	51	48	45	39	33	26	18	12	9	6	3
1945	2	3	4	4	6	9	11	13	14	16	17	18
1946	20	24	28	33	36	39	43	45	49	54	58	65
1947	70	76	80	83	86	86	85	85	84	82	—	—

[a] 1938 = 100.

Source: Warren C. Baum, *The French Economy and the State* (Princeton University Press: Princeton, 1958), pp. 20, 89.

early recovery were twofold. First, German industrial capacity was not as badly hurt by the war as the visually dramatic bombing of the inner cities would suggest. Hence, German industrialists reported to American observers in spring 1945 that 'in general the opinion is held that the present catastrophic situation could be rapidly and fundamentally overcome ...'. Many of the largest plants and mines were quite undamaged.[9]

Secondly, despite the punitive official directives, like the famous JCS (Joint Chiefs of Staff) 1067, which ordered the US military government to organise the economy only to the extent necessary to 'meet the needs of the occupying forces and to ensure the production and maintenance of goods and services required to prevent disease and unrest, which might endanger the occupying forces', in practice, the western allies took a practical and humanitarian view of reconstruction. The military governor of the US zone, General Lucius D. Clay, was an engineer by profession and he was incensed by the directive. On the ground, local commands simply ignored it; an American Army officer in Bavaria admitted that he had not even seen the official directives: 'Brother, I don't know ... They snow me under with all sorts of papers. How'm I going to read them when I'm doing forty-eleven different things to get this burg running again.'[10]

The relatively rapid first stages of rehabilitation and recovery in large parts of southern and eastern Europe were achieved by UNRRA. UNRRA was intended to bridge the gap between the period of military rule after the liberation and full recovery. In practice, it not only prevented the worst potential effects of postwar trauma and disorganisation, but also provided many of the essential imports needed in these countries until the first Marshall Plan supplies arrived in the west and the communists took over in the east. The finance came mostly – 72% – from the USA (see pp. 45–6 above), but Britain also provided about 18%. Britain, of course, was indirectly subsidised by the USA. By the end of June 1947 UNRRA had spent $3.5bn. worldwide, 80% of which had been allocated to Europe and, of that, 86% had gone to Albania, Austria, Czechoslovakia, Greece, Italy, Poland and Yugoslavia (see Table 6.4). Thus, annual UNRRA expenditure per capita in these countries was at least as much as the later Marshall Plan grants to western Europe. All these countries, except Czechoslovakia and parts of Italy, were predominantly agricultural, with poor economies, before the war; they had been badly devastated by the fighting and would have suffered severely without outside help during the critical winter of 1945–6.[11]

Table 6.4. *UNRRA Supplies for Europe, 1944–1947 ($m.)*

	Food	Clothes Textiles Shoes	Medical Sanitation	Agricultural Rehab.	Industrial Rehab.	Military Surplus	Total[a]
Albania	7	4	2	6	7	1	26
Austria	81	2	2	19	6	25	136
Czechoslovakia	118	27	13	32	72	0	261
Finland	0	1	0	0	0	0	2
Greece	180	33	8	43	38	44	347
Hungary	3	0	0	0	0	0	4
Italy	235	50	9	13	110	1	418
Poland	202	81	25	75	95	0	478
Russia	129	24	12	22	70	0	258
Yugoslavia	135	82	20	36	108	35	416
Others	1	0	0	0	0	2	4
Total	1091	306	92	247	507	108	2351

[a] Row totals may not sum. Statistics have been rounded.
Source: George Woodbridge, *UNRRA: The History of the United Nations Relief and Rehabilitation Administration*, 3 vols (Columbia University Press: New York, 1950), pp. 428–9.

About $1bn. worth of UNRRA supplies were spent on food, with the largest amount per head – $23 – going to Greece. The aim was to raise European per capita consumption to 2,650 calories a day, but not much more than 2,000 was ever achieved, except in Czechoslovakia, which was already relatively well organised. A further $250m. was spent on seeds, fertiliser, horses, tractors etc. for agricultural rehabilitation. UNRRA also provided emergency clothing, blankets and shoes, new supplies of raw cotton and wool, and medical and sanitary aid. Large amounts of used clothes and military surplus shoes were donated from the USA, and costed in UNRRA accounts at knock-down prices. UNRRA also spent about $500m. on industrial rehabilitation, mostly on roads, rails and telecommunications and on vital equipment and raw materials. For instance, about $75m. worth of coal and oil was delivered to Italy. War surplus supplies were used wherever possible – hence about 80,000 US, British and Canadian army trucks were provided to deliver food and materials in remote areas. Some of these supplies or services were given direct to the population, but usually the governments sold them and used the receipts for other purposes. UNRRA tried to make sure that the funds were used for essential relief or rehabilitation work, like the later Marshall Plan Counterpart Funds. UNRRA's resources were probably critical in restoring transport and services and reviving production in 1945–6. In aggregate, they covered a substantial part of the cost of imports for the major recipients during 1944–7. The effects on Italy, Austria and Greece are discussed below, in Chapters 11 and 12.[12]

Notes

1. Marshall's radio message is quoted in *FRUS: 1947*, vol. 3, p. 219, from Department of State, *Bulletin*, 11 May 1947, p. 919; Clayton's memorandum is reproduced in *FRUS: 1947*, vol. 3, pp. 230–2; Marshall's speech is reprinted in *ibid.*, pp. 237–9. See also UN, *Economic Report, 1945–47*, p. 123.
2. UN, *Economic Report, 1945–47*, p. 128.
3. UN, Department of Economic Affairs, *A Survey of the Economic Situation and Prospects of Europe* (Economic Commission for Europe: Geneva, 1948), pp. 3–30.
4. Sir Alec Cairncross, *Years of Recovery: British Economic Policy, 1945–51* (Methuen: London, 1985), pp. 36–9; UN, *Economic Situation and Prospects of Europe*, pp. 27–30, 122–4.
5. UN, *Economic Situation and Prospects of Europe*, pp. 62–5, 109–21; UN, *Economic Report, 1945–47*, pp. 123–7 (passage quoted is on p. 124).
6. Cairncross, *Recovery*, pp. 20–2, 88–120; Sir Richard Clarke, *Anglo-American Collaboration in War and Peace* (Oxford University Press: Oxford, 1982), pp. 47–85.
7. Baum, *The French Economy*, pp. 16–19.

8. *Ibid.*, pp. 80–90; Gérard Bossuat, *La France, l'aide américaine et la construction européenne, 1944–54* (2 vols, Comité pour L'Histoire Économique et Financière de la France: Paris, 1992), pp. 24–88; François Duchêne, *Jean Monnet: The First Statesman of Interdependence* (Norton: New York, 1994), pp. 138–46; Frances M. B. Lynch, 'Resolving the paradox of the Monnet Plan: national and international planning in French reconstruction', *Economic History Review* 37 (1984), pp. 229–43; Wall, *France*, pp. 35–49.

9. Kramer, *West German Economy*, pp. 25, 91–3.

10. *Ibid.*, pp. 45–7. Excerpts of JCS 1067 are reprinted in *ibid.*, pp. 242–6; the unofficial reaction is quoted from *ibid.*, p. 47.

11. George Woodbridge, *UNRRA: The History of the United Nationas Relief and Rehabilitation Administration*, 3 vols (Columbia University Press: New York, 1950), *passim.*

12. Woodbridge, *UNRRA, passim.*

7

The Crisis of 1947

This promising recovery was disrupted in 1947 by severe economic and political crises which culminated in the division of Europe, the Marshall Plan and the Cold War. In mid-1947 many contemporaries were convinced that the recovery had stalled, that American and western European policy had failed, and that only Russia would gain from the disorder. Will Clayton, Marshall's Assistant Secretary of State, noted in a memorandum on 27 May:

> Europe is steadily deteriorating. The political position reflects the economic. One political crisis after another merely denotes the existence of grave economic distress. Millions of people in the cities are slowly starving ... The modern system of division of labor has almost broken down in Europe.

Political historians have often repeated these claims uncritically, effectively setting the scene for Marshall Plan deliverance. Hence, for instance, Isaacson and Thomas, in their respected study of the founding fathers of US foreign policy, *The Wise Men*, introduce their chapter 'Order from Chaos': 'All across Europe, [in early 1947] canals were plugged, bridges broken, rail lines torn up. Farmers were consuming their produce while city workers starved.'[1]

Contemporary analyses and statistics, however, do not support such a dire view of the crisis. By late 1946, in fact, many countries in Europe had achieved a quite remarkable recovery. Most well-informed contemporary observers agreed that the upward trend was inevitably decelerating by early 1947, as many economies had reached full employment. In addition, the severe winter of 1946/7 exacerbated the problems. However, by early 1949 the atmosphere had changed completely, and even gloomy observers now concluded:

> In retrospect, this analysis was not borne out by events. The setback at the beginning of 1947 caused by the severe winter and the fuel crisis was made good by the second quarter of the year, and in the

last quarter of 1947 after a temporary relapse during the summer, progress was resumed with the same momentum as before.[2]

More recently, Alan Milward and other historians have gone even further, arguing that the recovery originated in a postwar European determination to succeed, and that there was hardly any break at all in early 1947. If there was a problem, it was mainly financial. It was the very strength of this recovery, sucking in huge volumes of American resources and causing severe balance of payments deficits, that created short-term tensions. Milward agrees that, had the trade and financial crises run their course without American aid, then the European economies might have been forced to introduce very severe and morale-destroying restrictions. However, he claims that finance was the Achilles' heel; otherwise, the recovery was sound. Even the amount of finance required was relatively small and Marshall Aid did not make a critical difference – saving perhaps only one or two years' growth. Without the additional finance, Europeans would have tightened their belts, worked harder, and would soon have achieved complete recovery.[3]

Contemporaries, however, argued that the weaknesses threatening the recovery were broader than finance alone. The balance of payments problems were symptoms of wider difficulties – not the cause of them. This still seems to be a reasonable conclusion. By late 1946–early 1947, the European economy showed some of the characteristics of the end of a boom. Hence, the levels of employment operating in 1938 had been reached by late 1946 – see Table 7.1 – and the same levels of output by mid-1947. However – and this is critical – even with full employment and production, Europe could not reach its full production potential or finance its overseas import needs. This was the product of long-term structural damage and neglect. The 1930s depression and the war had created many areas in which production could not easily be increased. Output was only just approaching 1938 levels, even though a greater share of a larger workforce was employed. Hence, average productivity must have fallen sharply. Neither capital nor workers were being used to full effect. The market did not clear effectively, either geographically between regions or functionally between farmers, workers and consumers. Only widespread reconstruction and reform of many aspects of European economy and society could achieve this balance. This was the function of the Marshall Plan.[4]

Table 7.1. *European Employment and Inflation, 1946–1948*

	Employment [a]			Inflation (% increase)		
	1946	*1947*	*1948*	*1946–7*	*1947–8*	*1948–9*
Austria	100	119	135	13	148	20
Belgium	92	116	119	14	19	5
Bizone	76	85	95	—	—	—
Britain	103	108	113	5	17	4
Denmark	120	126	133	10	8	8
France	97	106	100	81	69	33
Greece	—	—	—	20	42	23
Holland	105	122	134	13	4	4
Ireland	113	121	—	3	14	−1
Italy	—	118	115	41	43	7
Norway	114	127	137	2	5	1
Sweden	122	122	123	5	6	5

[a] 1938 = 100.
Source: United Nations, *Economic Survey of Europe in 1948* (Geneva: Economic Commission for Europe, 1949), pp. 6, 25.

The evidence for the widespread lack of balance in early 1947 can be found in the severe struggles for resources as well as in the massive European trade deficit. One problem was that bottlenecks were holding up production. Normally, bottlenecks can be evened out by the market, but in 1947 they were unusually widespread and severe. Hence, production increases stopped well short of potential full capacity and there was considerable social unrest. In some countries – in France, for instance – governments fell back on easy money policies – in effect, printing money – permitting serious inflation (see Table 7.1). Elsewhere (e.g. in Britain), tough physical controls limited inflation, but risked the creation of black markets and political opposition. Finally, some governments – Italy, for instance – introduced severe deflationary budgets which reduced inflation at the expense of unemployment and unrest. Everywhere, an increasing proportion of overseas deficits was met by the outflow of gold and dollar reserves.[5]

The struggle for resources was exacerbated by the very slow recovery of European agriculture and by a worldwide grain shortage in 1947. Farm output in Europe fell considerably in 1945/6 as the result of soil depletion, destruction of herds and loss of manpower and machinery (see Table 7.2). Despite the peace, the grain harvests of 1945–7 were far below their 1938 levels. Conditions were made even worse by the harsh winter of 1946/7 and the dry summer in 1947. Only Britain and some neutral countries like Switzerland managed to increase agricultural output in 1938–46. Consequently, food supplies were often worse in 1945/6 than in 1944/5 and only improved a little in 1946/7. Careful management ensured that cereal consumption was about the same as in 1938, except in Germany and Italy, but fat and meat consumption were far below normal. In Germany the average number of calories available per day fell from 3,000 in 1938 to about 1,600 in 1945/6 and 1,800 in 1946/7; the situation only improved very slowly between 1946–1948. In Italy the number of calories available rose from 1,850 in 1945/6 to only 2,000 in 1946/7. Elsewhere in western Europe the number varied between 2,300 in France and 2,900 in Britain in 1946/7. The expectation in late 1947 was that domestic food supplies would fall in 1948 because of the poor harvest in 1947.[6]

Table 7.2. *European Grain and Potato Harvests, 1944–1947 (as % of harvests in 1934–1938)*

	1944/5		1945/6		1946/7	
	Grain	Potatoes	Grain	Potatoes	Grain	Potatoes
Britain	174	186	158	198	156	205
Denmark	104	119	111	134	93	148
France	52	35	80	66	59	101
Germany	58	72	60	68	64	52
Italy	55	83	79	92	68	92

Source: UN, *Economic Report, 1945–47* p. 148.

Averages of 1,800 calories per day for the whole population, including farmers, may suggest that many city dwellers received far less than the minimum amounts required for health and work. Clayton's memorandum to Marshall of 27 May, quoted above, continued: 'Millions of people in the cities are slowly starving. More consumer's goods and restored confidence in the currency are absolutely essential if the peasant is again to supply food in normal quantities to the cities …' This idea – softened a little – was directly transferred into Marshall's Harvard address of 5 June: 'The farmer has always produced the foodstuffs to exchange with the city dweller for the other necessities of life. This division of labor is the basis of modern civilisation. At the present time it is threatened with breakdown …' Milward is correct to argue that 'millions ... slowly starving' is an exaggeration, since infant mortality did not rise in 1947. However, there were indeed severe food shortages in some continental cities and industrial areas which offset the growth of industry. Hence, real wages only crept forwards from their levels in 1945–7, leaving scope for wholesale disillusionment if industrial growth paused or if food shortages worsened.[7]

The French cereal crisis was genuine, but there was little more that the USA could do immediately to help. Clayton's memorandum continued: 'French grain acreage running 20–25% under pre-war, collection of production very unsatisfactory – much of the grain is fed to cattle. The modern system of division of labor has almost broken down in Europe.' French wheat production rose from 4,210,000 metric tons in 1945 to 6,760,000 tons in 1946, but then fell to 3,270,000 tons in 1947 before rising again to 7,630,000 tons in 1948 and 8,080,000 tons in 1949. Short French harvests in 1946 and 1947 were exacerbated by inadequate supplies and high prices on the international markets. Grain prices rose 40% in the USA in 1947; French bread rations were sharply reduced in mid-1947 from 300 grams to 250 a day and then 200 grams a day. Large overseas purchases rapidly absorbed resources intended for industry; French gold and dollar reserves fell rapidly during 1947 and imports even of vital raw materials and machinery were sharply reduced in the autumn. By late 1947 France was at the end of her tether; along with Austria and Italy, she had to be rescued with a special package of interim aid prior to the main Marshall Plan.[8]

Clayton himself had met the Director of the French National Cereal Board in Geneva on 23 April and consequently cabled Dean Acheson, Acting Secretary of State, that 'being convinced of the extreme urgency of this matter I wish to strongly recommend that you go to the President and ask him to request Agriculture to renew procurement of wheat in the north-west ...'. Acheson replied immediately that very large shipments had already been sent, but he promised to meet existing commitments if possible. Marshall added: 'Entire Cabinet and President are of opinion that any additional demands on grain market at this time will simply further inflate grain market and produce no further grain for export.' Clayton had established one of the world's largest commodity-trading firms before entering government and was well equipped to assess the French and international market situation.[9]

The struggle for resources was made worse by the shift in the terms of trade since the 1930s and the shortfall in investment during the depression and the war. In some areas, like machine tools, the war had stimulated investment, but elsewhere, in transport, for instance, there was massive depreciation. This had to be made good if Europe hoped eventually to be able to raise living standards, pay for essential imports and compete with the USA. The main problem was that prices for food and raw materials had risen far more than for manufactured goods since the 1930s. The New Deal programmes for crop limitation and the war-time reorganisation of American industry finally ended the transatlantic food bonanza for Europe, but primary prices had risen everywhere.[10]

Europe had to find extra resources not only for increased exports, but also for more investment – and even then she seemed to be falling further behind America. In 1947 Britain managed about $33 per capita of net investment, France $16, and Italy $9; this was considerably more than in the 1930s, but far less than the American $65. Only Norway and Sweden were anywhere near American levels, and American product-ivity was already several times that of the best European practice. The figures also concealed a qualitative difference. Between the wars the USA had developed a massive additional potential in the new science-based industries – electronics, chemicals, etc. The Germans and the British were also moving into these areas to a certain extent – demonstrated by the potential of their new weapons – but the American commitment of resources was many times higher than the European in both the education of scientific manpower and government and corpor-ate research and development. The Americans seemed to be accelerating down the next technological wave before the Europeans could even catch up on the last – indeed, they might never be able to do so.[11]

The size of investment required, therefore, seemed massive. Yet many contemporaries argued that European programmes were already too large and were drawing too much on American resources. 'Investments in Europe are altogether too large ...', wrote one well-informed Ameri-can economist in 1948, 'and American commentators ... view the vast capital programs as a means of bleeding the American economy. In part, imports are used to support the capital program; and in part the latter robs the export markets.' Yet he agreed that smaller programmes might not be able to restore plant and housing to prewar standards and that such large programmes were necessary to re-establish Europe's viability. 'The price of a truncated capital program may be a series of Marshall Plans.'[12]

Thus, the choices between consumption and investment were

exquisitely difficult for European governments. Socialist egalitarianism and redistribution of income might temporarily raise workers' morale, despite food shortages, but for how long? The difficult calculations are evident in the figures shown in Table 7.3, which compares the distribution of national income in some European countries in 1938 and 1947. Investment rose in all cases, but it was financed either out of consumption or out of the foreign balance or both. In Britain and France the payments deficits were relatively – but not absolutely – small, but Britain put more into social welfare and France put more into new investment. In Italy the fascist state – and its cheap food subsidies – was dismantled, allowing substantial increases in nominal personal consumption as a share of GNP, but a very tight fiscal and monetary policy held employment and total consumption right down. In Norway the government was unable to cut the amount going to personal consumption, and the necessary increases in investment were met by huge balance of payments deficits.[13]

Table 7.3. *Distribution of National Income in Some European Countries, 1938, 1947 (%)*

	France		Britain		Italy		Norway	
	1938	1947	1938	1947	1938	1947	1938	1947
Consumption								
Personal	84	80	78	73	66	86	74	75
Government	13	15	16	24	24	12	11	17
Investment	3	9	7	9	9	13	15	25
G & S[a]	0	−4	−1	−6	1	−11	0	−17
TOTAL	100	100	100	100	100	100	100	100

[a] G & S = balance of payments on current account.
Source: UN, *Economic Survey of Europe in 1948*, p. 45.

Table 7.4 confirms the huge inflow of resources, mostly from the USA, in 1946–7. Europe's balance of payments deficit was covered by US aid, by credits or loans from UN institutions – UNRRA, the IMF and IBRD – and by European sales of dollars and gold. The interesting change from 1946 to 1947 is the increasing proportion of the total deficit that was covered by European sales of dollars and gold. The US congressional elections in November 1946 were won by the Republicans, who were determined to cut overseas costs and not to add to the huge British loan agreed in July 1946. Milward argues that the rising European demand was critical in the financial crisis, but that the sharp reduction in US credits to the Continent was also vital. This forced the Europeans to pay for essential dollar purchases with increasing volumes of their own meagre reserves and to cut imports wherever possible. Hence, foreign gold and dollars poured into the USA and by mid-1947 the Europeans were desperate.[14]

Table 7.4. *Intergovernmental Compensatory Finance, 1946–1947 ($bn.)*

	American aid		UNRRA + IMF + IBRD aid		Foreign gold and dollars	
	1946	*1947*	*1946*	*1947*	*1946*	*1947*
US total	3.4	4.7	1.2	1.1	0.7	2.3
Belgium	0.2	0.0	0.0	0.0	0.1	0.3
Britain	0.8	2.9	0.0	0.2	0.2	0.5
France	1.2	0.7	0.0	0.4	0.1	0.3
Germany (Wt)	0.3	0.4	0.0	0.0	0.0	−0.1
Holland	0.2	0.1	0.0	0.1	0.1	0.2
Italy	0.3	0.3	0.4	0.1	−0.2	0.1
Other	0.4	0.4	0.8	0.3	0.5	0.9
Less Britain	2.6	1.8[a]	1.2	0.9	0.5[a]	1.7

[a] Statistics rounded to one decimal place.
Source: IMF, *Payments Yearbook: 1938, 1946, 1947*, pp. 370–1.

Despite the huge US loan, the financial crisis affected Britain first. Initially, Britain's trade seemed to recover very quickly in 1945–6 (see Table 7.5). Imports from North America (cols 1 and 2) were cut back savagely. Exports to the dominions and Europe (cols 3–4) rose rapidly, but were mostly offset by increased imports diverted from North America. The invisible balance, and hence the overall current balance, moved dramatically towards the black in 1944–8, but only after a sudden reversal in 1946–7. Imports were strictly controlled in 1946 and, by the end of the year, had only risen $28m. over the February estimate of $4300m. However, exports rose from the estimated $2200m. to $3680m. Heavy civil and military expenditure in overseas crisis areas ($1292m.) and lower than anticipated investment and service income ($760m.) meant that Britain remained dependent on the US loan – but to a lesser extent than expected.[15]

In early 1947, however, the recovery died. Imports were pushed up by increases in food and raw material prices, and the severe winter cost

Table 7.5. *British Balance of Trade with Leading Partners, 1944–1948*
($m.)

	USA (1)	Canada (2)	Argentina + Australia + India + New Zealand (3)	France + Germany (4)	Visibles (5)	Invisibles (6)
1944	−5488	−1452	−664	28	−2520	−200
1945	−2364	−1200	−512	104	−1000	−2480
1946	−776	−668	−368	128	−412	−508
1947	−1003	−782	−689	−20	−1455	−81
1948	−468	−600	−572	−68	−604	708

Source: B. R. Mitchell, *European Historical Statistics, 1750–1975* (Macmillan: London, 1980), pp. 600, 867.

more than $800m. in extra fuel and lost exports. This more than offset the reductions in overseas government spending as troops were brought home. It was clear by April 1947 that the US loan would soon be absorbed; government advisers calculated that, even with drastic economies, Britain would be 'completely at risk in 1948'. However, the actual shortfall in the balance of payments was not too drastic; the Bretton Woods and US loan bargain of convertibility and non-discrimination was finally brought to an end by the general world pressure for dollars and the mid-1947 sterling crisis. Despite controls, British expenditure in the USA doubled in early 1947. Simultaneously, sterling-area dollar purchases accelerated. Table 7.6 shows how the loan was spent. A large part was spent on purchases of real and useful, or apparently desirable, dollar goods in late 1946 and early 1947. These rose rapidly in price in early 1947, as demand from all over Europe and the rest of the world focused on North America. Then, once the pound became convertible in July 1947, all holders of sterling, for whatever reason, seized their chance to sell.[16]

Under the loan agreements, only pounds earned in current trade were meant to be convertible, but many overseas holders of wartime sterling balances found ways of getting out. The inevitable result was a run on the pound: by September Britain only had $400m. left of the $3750m. US loan, $500m. of the Canadian loan and $2400m. in gold and dollar reserves – against sterling balance claims of $14,500m. and a dollar outflow rate of $3200m. p. a. so far in 1947. Britain had to default on the obligations assumed in the loan agreement on 20 August. The Americans were informed of the situation late, but tactfully, and recognised

Table 7.6. *How the US Loan was Spent by Britain, 1946–1947 ($m.)*

	1946	1947		
British dollar spending	Jul.– Dec.	Jan.– Mar.	Apr. –Jun.	Jul.– Sept.
In USA				
Food, drink, tobacco	270	156	101	127
Raw materials, oil	150	147	131	128
Machinery, manufactured goods	100	50	73	82
Ships, films	50	24	104	58
Food for Germans	55	66	57	85
Elsewhere in Americas	140	150	323	455
Total dollar spending	765	593	789	935
Other dollar transactions				
British earnings in USA	−245	−66	−57	−60
In Europe and elsewhere	−40	—	35	165
In sterling area	−5	90	248	395
Subscription to IMF	35	0	0	0
Net dollar transactions	510	617	1015	1435
British drawing on US credit	600	500	950	1300

Source: Sir Richard Clarke, *Anglo-American Economic Collaboration in War and Peace* (Oxford University Press: Oxford, 1982), pp. 187–9.

Britain's need to minimise dollar purchases and re-enforce the sterling area. The Bretton Woods dream of multilateralism and convertibility was temporarily over.

None of the other European currencies was exposed to speculation in this way, although most were depreciating fast. Nevertheless, the crisis was real. Milward argues that living standards were still rising in mid-1947, but that any continuance was contingent on further American aid.[17]

With new dollars so hard to find, the continental countries increasingly drew on their gold and dollar reserves and contemplated austerity. In France, US credits of about $2000m. were exhausted by late 1947, and gold holdings fell from $1550m. in 1945 to $872m. in 1946 and $548m. in 1947. There were similar falls in Holland, Norway, Sweden and Italy which could only be met by severe restrictions on dollar purchases and increasing austerity. This trend was clearly visible by early 1947, well before the British financial crisis. In fact, the British decision to introduce convertibility was only justified by unfounded hope and pride. Similarly, faced with new elections and strong communist challenges, most European governments, except Italy, avoided extreme solutions, but had no other plans or revenue with which to meet the oncoming crisis. Ernest Bevin and Georges Bidault, the British and French foreign ministers respectively, therefore seized on General Marshall's famous speech at Harvard on 5 June 1947. It was only a vague outline offering help to Europe, and inviting European suggestions, but Bevin recalled later to the Press, 'I assure you, gentlemen, it was like a lifeline to sinking men. It seemed to bring hope where there was none ... I think you understand why, therefore, we responded with such alacrity, and why we grabbed the lifeline with both hands.'[18]

Yet the lifeline did not materialise into Marshall Plan support for another twelve months while the administration and Congress debated the proposal at length. During this time, conditions in Europe worsened in many respects because the freezing winter of early 1947 was followed by a long dry summer and short harvests. Europe's food imports, therefore, increased even more in late 1947, forcing up North American prices still further, and absorbing the remaining gold and dollar reserves. In addition, many economies in Europe and overseas held substantial inconvertible sterling reserves. Hence, Australia and New Zealand rationed all dollar purchases, and Canada, despite huge wheat sales to Britain and Europe, had to reduce US imports. On the Continent, France, Italy and Norway similarly had large sterling holdings that they could not use to buy dollar goods. Nor could Britain use their even softer currencies to buy essential American imports, and over $400m. had to be sent in gold instead. As a result, in late 1947, many governments curtailed all but essential imports, reduced rations, introduced tough austerity and deflationary budgets and desperately prayed for popular support.[19]

The result was severe strain on the social fabric, especially in countries with strong communist parties such as France and Italy. These parties had successfully built mass movements first by determined opposition to the occupation, and then by responsible support for reconstruction. In France, the weak socialist Ramadier government had ejected the communists in May 1947, and, as a result, faced widespread strikes and riots when it introduced harsh austerity measures in the autumn. Forced out of power, the communists no longer felt that they had to shoulder the responsibility of restraining their supporters. On the right, General

de Gaulle, waiting in the wings, refused to even consider entering
government during such a gloomy period unless the situation deteriorated still further. Fortunately, although the Ramadier government fell
in November, the new Schuman government successfully repressed the
strikes and introduced legislation to stabilise the currency. In Italy,
the centre-right Christian Democrat de Gasperi government which had
expelled the communists in April 1947 met inflation with even tougher
deflationary measures over the summer. These similarly led to widespread strikes and civil disorder during the winter, which the
government defeated. The critical electoral test came in April 1948 when
de Gasperi, supported openly by the Vatican, and covertly by the US,
defeated the communists. In the extreme case of Greece, the civil war
between the communist partisans and the royal government had reached
a critical point by December 1947 when the rebels proclaimed a provi-
sional Greek Democratic government and in the spring were sufficiently
strong to put pressure on Athens.[20]

The US administration, thoroughly alarmed by these developments,
regularly reported by anxious ambassadors, provided considerable extra
finance from a great variety of sources in late 1947. For instance, in
October 1947, the administration found $247m. new dollars for France
in one week. This was composed of $104m. of French gold recovered
from Germany, a new $93m. loan from the Export–Import Bank and
$50m. payment against French claims for wartime costs supplying US
forces. In November, Canada was given an Export–Import Bank loan
of $300m. to enable her to continue purchasing US goods, and thus
indirectly to support her large grain sales in Europe. In October, Britain
was relieved of the responsibility of supplying her German zone, saving
her $65m. in the remainder of 1947 and $150m. in 1948. In December,
she was permitted to draw on the remaining $400m. of the 1946 loan
which had been frozen in August when sterling became inconvertible.
In October, Germany (and Britain) were also assisted by large new
appropriations for the US GARIOA programme and the sale on credit,
for $184m. to the Bizone authority, of $875m. worth (at original cost)
of US military surplus. Italy, in July, received relief supplies worth
$100–125m., and was allowed to purchase $184m. military surplus at
knock-down prices and in August she received $60m. in blocked assets,
28 ships, and cancellation of $540m. Lend-Lease debts. In October, she
received restituted German gold and a $100m. Export–Import Bank
loan, and in November was given control over her large UNRRA

counterpart fund. Finally, from October 1947 to March 1948, the IMF sold nearly $400m. in return for soft currencies, mostly sterling, at the high rate of six dollars to the pound, and the World Bank made available $170m. loans mostly to France, Denmark, Holland, and Luxembourg.[21]

By September 1947, it had become obvious to the administration that the Marshall Plan was too complex to enact before the following spring. The negotiations with the European countries in the Committee of European Economic Cooperation (discussed below, p. 83) had already raised very difficult issues. The continuing economic problems in Europe, and the heterogeneity of the mixed assortment of grants, loans and easements arranged since 1945–7 had also convinced the administration that the Marshall Plan should be far better organised and presented. However, the Europeans had already made it clear they would need substantial allocations in addition to the informal stop gaps listed above to tide them through the winter and spring. Hence, in November and December, during the worst period of French and Italian disorder, the administration secured a large programme of 'Interim Aid' worth $522m. to carry Austria, France and Italy over until Marshall Aid proper arrived. This was not a 'little Marshall Plan', but it was more carefully organised than the previous allocations. It was provided in kind, and supplied through existing American agencies. In the case of France, the administration requested, and mostly received and delivered, $134m. for food, mostly wheat, $147m. for fuel, mostly coal, and $47m. for raw cotton and fertiliser. The legislation consciously allowed the recipients just sufficient resources to keep them going over winter at existing levels. In return, the recipients had to sign bilateral treaties controlling both the direct use of the aid, and the local currency counterpart.[22]

Notes

1. Frederick J. Dobney, *Selected Papers of Will Clayton* (John Hopkins Press: Baltimore, 1971), pp. 201–4; Walter Isaacson and Evan Thomas, *The Wise Men: Six Friends and the World They Made* (Faber and Faber: London, 1986), p. 386.
2. UN, *Economic Survey of Europe in 1948* (Geneva: Economic Commission for Europe, 1949), p. 5. Gunnar Myrdal's preface to the *Survey*, dated April 1949, claims: 'The background against which this SURVEY was written differs considerably from that which existed when the preceding volume was prepared a year ago. Inflation, the shortages of basic materials and many of the other problems which dominated the immediate post-war period have been largely overcome, and Europe's production and trade are now close to their pre-war levels. But, although economic conditions of life have become more normal, the underlying problems of the European

economy do not appear appreciably nearer solution. The progress of the past year would in many cases have been impossible without outside financial assistance ...'

3. Alan S. Milward, *The Reconstruction of Western Europe, 1945–51* (Methuen: London, 1984), pp. 1–55, 91–113.

4. UN, *Economic Report, 1945–47*, pp. 123–37, discuss long-term structural weaknesses.

5. UN, Department of Economic Affairs, *A Survey of the Economic Situation and Prospects of Europe* (Economic Commission for Europe: Geneva, 1948), pp. 75–87, 115–21, discuss bottlenecks and inflation.

6. UN, *Economic Situation and Prospects of Europe*, pp. 10–12; UN, *Economic Report, 1945–47*, pp. 147–57; Alan Kramer, *The West German Economy, 1945–1955* (Berg: New York, 1991), pp. 72–82, discuss food shortages.

7. *FRUS: 1947*, vol. 3, pp. 230–2, reprints Clayton's memorandum; Milward, *Reconstruction*, pp. 17–19.

8. Gérard Bossuat, *La France, L'aide américaine et la construction européenne, 1944–54* (2 vols, Comité pour L'Histoire Économique et Financière de la France: Paris, 1992), pp. 99–139; United States, Department of State, *The Interim Aid Program: Draft Legislation and Background Information* (United States Government Printing Office: Washington, DC, 1947).

9. See Clayton to Acheson, 23 April 1947: *FRUS: 1947*, vol. 3, pp. 701–2, and Acheson and Marshall's replies, *ibid.*, pp. 703–7.

10. United Nations, *Economic Survey of Europe since the War* (Economic Commission for Europe: Geneva, 1953), pp. 11–13 (see p. 12 for a good chart of the industrial countries' terms of trade, 1928–52).

11. UN, *Economic Survey of Europe in 1948*, pp. 224–8; Richard R. Nelson and Gavin Wright, 'The rise and fall of American technological leadership: the postwar era in historical perspective', *Journal of Economic Literature* 30 (1992), pp. 1931–64.

12. Seymour E. Harris, *The European Recovery Program* (Harvard University Press: Cambridge, Mass., 1948), pp. 36, 41.

13. UN, *Economic Survey of Europe in 1948*, pp. 44–55.

14. Milward, *Reconstruction*, pp. 45–8.

15. Clarke, *Collaboration*, pp. 66–85.

16. *Ibid.*, pp. 156–89; Richard N. Gardner, *Sterling–Dollar Diplomacy in Current Perspective* (Columbia University Press: New York, 1980), pp. 306–12. Films and tobacco seemed more essential then than they do now.

17. Sir Alec Cairncross, *Years of Recovery: British Economic Policy, 1945–51* (Methuen: London, 1985), pp. 121–64, and Gardner, *Sterling–Dollar Diplomacy*, pp. 312–47, describe the convertibility crisis.

18. IMF, *Payments Yearbook*, vol. 1 (see statements for individual countries); Milward, *Reconstruction*, pp. 13–19. Bevin's speech of 1 April 1949 is quoted from Alan Bullock, *Ernest Bevin: Foreign Secretary, 1945–1951* (Oxford University Press: Oxford, 1983), p. 405.

19. For a chronology of the main international events in 1947, see United Nations, *Economic Report*, pp. 322–54. For further background, see US Congress, *The Interim European Aid Program: Draft Legislation and Background Information* (80th Congress, 1st session, Senate Document, no. 108 (Government Printing Office: Washington, DC, 1947).

20. For France, see Wall, *The United States and France*, pp. 77–95. For Italy, see James E. Miller, *The United States and Italy, 1940–1950: The Politics and Diplomacy of*

Stabilisation (University of North Carolina Press: Chapel Hill, N.C., 1986). For an overview, and Greece, see David W. Ellwood, *Rebuilding Europe: Western Europe, America, and Postwar Reconstruction* (Longman: London and New York, 1992), *passim*.

21. For an anxious ambassador, see Caffrey's reports from France in *FRUS, 1947*, vol. 3. For lists of loans, see UN, *Economic Report*, op. cit., and US Congress, *Report of the Activities of the National Advisory Council on International Monetary and Financial Problems* (80th Congress, 2nd Session, House Document no. 737, Government Printing Office: Washington, DC, 1948).

22. See US Congress, *Interim European Aid Program, passim*. 'Counterpart' was the term used to describe the local currency receipts from foreign aid sales. See pp. 101–2 below.

8

The Origins and
Intentions of the Marshall Plan

General Marshall introduced his plan in his famous Harvard Commencement address of 5 June 1947. Very broadly, the plan represented the economic counterpart to the Truman Doctrine of March 1947 against communist insurrection. President Truman called it 'two halves of the same walnut', but the exact causes were more complicated than that and have led to a great deal of debate. Marshall's speech was precipitated by several interlocking crises. First, continued lack of agreement over the future of Germany increased tensions between the occupying powers and inhibited German recovery, bearing down the surrounding countries. Secondly, the developing British financial crisis, if allowed to run its course, threatened to disorganise world trade and to end America's multilateral plans. Simultaneously, serious economic crises and strong communist challenges in Austria, France and Italy threatened European stability. Possible outcomes seemed to be a communist takeover of western Europe, or long-run stagnation and a return to 1930s autarchy. These crises became evident in early 1947, when Britain decided to reduce her overseas commitments, leaving serious power vacuums all over the world. It was the British withdrawal from Greece, where she had been opposing communist partisans, that precipitated the Truman Doctrine.[1]

Marshall's decision that the USA should try to help Europe was taken during a difficult meeting of the Council of Foreign Ministers in Moscow in March 1947, at which Marshall became convinced that Stalin was waiting for Europe to fall into communist hands. Hence, on returning home via Germany, he reported on the radio on 28 April: 'We were faced with immediate issues which vitally concerned the impoverished and suffering people of Europe who are crying for help ... Disintegrating forces are becoming evident. The patient is sinking while the doctors deliberate ... action cannot await compromise through exhaustion.' He promised further financial aid for Europe in his Harvard address on 5 June:

Its purpose should be the revival of a working economy in the world so as to permit the emergence of political and social conditions in which free institutions can exist. Such assistance ... must not be on a piece-meal basis as various crises develop ... [it] ... should provide a cure rather than a mere palliative ... The initiative, I think, must come from Europe. The role of this country should consist of friendly aid in the drafting of a European program and of later support for such a program so far as it may be practical for us to do so.[2]

Government officials and informed public opinion in the USA had been worried about the European recovery, and Germany in particular, since late 1946. The harsh winter of 1946/7, growing evidence that Britain was running through the American loan too rapidly, the severe financial problems of other European countries, and the Greek and Turkish crises – all increased administration concern. Britain warned the USA on 21 February 1947 that she would have to leave Greece by the end of March, but Marshall had already told the Senate Committee for Foreign Relations on 14 February that the 'world was in a very critical condition'. These concerns led to several major studies initiated by Marshall, his Under-Secretary of State, Dean Acheson, and other Cabinet officials such as James Forrestal, Secretary of the Navy, and Averell Harriman, Secretary of Commerce. Many of the ideas contained in Marshall's Harvard address and in the Marshall Plan can be traced back to these studies. Outside the administration, leading commentators like the veteran Walter Lippmann argued in April 1947 that the USA should intervene to prevent a catastrophe that could have worldwide consequences.[3]

The most important studies were made by the State–War–Navy Co-ordinating Committee (SWNCC), which was briefed on 5 March and reported on 21 April, and the Policy Planning Staff (PPS), which was formed in February, briefed on 21 March, and made its first report on 23 May 1947. The SWNCC report supported increased foreign aid and listed the countries in need of particular help – Austria, France, Hungary and Italy. It also argued in favour of German recovery and a coordinated coal programme. The PPS reports were written by George Kennan, who had already articulated the containment doctrine against Russia. He argued that an aid programme would have to be large enough and last long enough to convince the Europeans that it would work. The programme should be organised by the Europeans themselves, acting collectively; Germany and Austria should be included; eastern Europe should be invited to join. The long-term aim would be to make Europe so prosperous that communism would have no attractions. The USA should mount a parallel short-term programme to increase German coal output, thereby demonstrating American commitment and breaking a critical bottleneck. These ideas provided the most important creative suggestions in the second part of Marshall's Harvard speech; Marshall's assessment of European problems in the opening portions of his speech was drawn from Will Clayton's analysis, outlined below.[4]

The SWNCC and PPS studies, Clayton's memorandum and Marshall's speech offered no specific 'plan', only a set of principles and a broad invitation to the Europeans to collaborate in a joint programme. In late July 1947 the Assistant Chief of Commercial Policy in the State Department, Ben T. Moore, co-author of the early SWNCC and PPS reports, wrote to a colleague: 'The Marshall Plan has been compared to a flying saucer – nobody knows what it really looks like, how big it is, in what direction it is moving, or whether it really exists. Nevertheless all of us here must cope with this mysterious phenomenon.' However, once Ernest Bevin and Georges Bidault, the British and French Foreign Ministers respectively, grasped the implications of Marshall's speech, they quickly accepted the offer. Initially, the British attempted to present themselves as senior partners with the USA, but Britain clearly no longer had the resources to lead and the administration insisted that Europe be treated collectively in a common programme. The British, however, never abandoned their belief in their special role outside Europe and their special relationship with the USA.[5]

A similar principle of collectivity excluded the Russians and helped to precipitate the Cold War. Initially, it was not clear whether US help would be contingent on Russian participation. Marshall's speech had carefully offered assistance to 'any government' that would help European recovery. Hence Bevin and Bidault invited the Russians to Paris to clarify the situation. Prior to these talks, the USA asked the British to tell the Russians that they could only participate if they would 'permit their satellites to enter fully into economic relations with their Western neighbours'. Accordingly, when the three former allies met on 27 June, Bevin and Bidault argued for a comprehensive European reconstruction programme and suggested that studies be made of the contribution that each European country could make to a general recovery. Faced with the implications of this intrusion on his plans for eastern Europe, Stalin (on 1 July) rejected the proposals and Molotov departed on 2 July. Bevin, apparently satisfied, commented to Jefferson Caffery – the US Ambassador to France – 'I am glad that the cards have been laid on the table and the responsibility will be laid at Moscow's door.' He reported more simply to Attlee: ''e walked out uttering threats'.[6]

Britain and France alone, therefore, called a meeting of the sixteen western European nations on 12 July to plan a solid programme. Collectively, they formed the Committee of European Economic Cooperation (CEEC), which, in July–September 1947, assembled plans to put to Washington. Oliver Franks, the Oxford don who chaired the meetings, secured many mutual concessions, but initially failed to persuade the Europeans to agree to an integrated programme rather than sixteen separate 'shopping lists' which totalled $28bn. The final CEEC report was significantly smaller and more integrated, but the US administration decided that it would have to develop its own administrative system to control the recovery programme. During the autumn and winter there was intense discussion in the USA about how to help Europe, and in December the administration asked for, and Congress agreed to, an emergency programme of interim aid. The administration's long-term plans were put to Congress on 19 December 1947 and, after much bargaining, became law on 3 April 1948. Congress then raised the first year's funds of $5bn. and created the European Cooperation Administration (ECA) to administer the European Recovery Program (ERP) in conjunction with the Organization for European Economic Cooperation (OEEC), the successor to the CEEC. Over the next four years the ECA gave the OEEC $12bn. for distribution in Europe; when the ECA was wound up in December 1951, western Europe seemed to be moving towards improved economic growth and greater economic unity.[7]

It is easy to state this broad factual outline, but more difficult to determine the exact origins and aims of the ERP. There is general agreement that it was meant to prevent the economic and political consequences of the potential failure of the postwar reconstruction plans. The balance of payments figures underlying the oncoming crisis were inexorable and demanded immediate action. It is doubtful whether the British financial crisis alone would have been enough to generate action; the US public felt that they had helped Britain enough since 1941 and were suspicious of the Labour government welfare plans. However, the crises in Greece, Palestine and India intimated how devastating British withdrawal could be in many other parts of the world where the USA had traditionally had little influence. The Canadian dollar crisis outlined above (pp. 38–41) illustrated the North Atlantic implications of the sterling crisis. Canada was Britain's main food supplier, but Britain's other suppliers were also potentially embarrassed by the collapse of sterling.[8]

The sterling collapse was very destabilising, therefore, threatening at the very least to end American dreams of a multilateral trading world. However, a crisis affecting the whole of Europe and weakening its defence against Russian ambitions was even more threatening. Marshall's speech overstressed the gravity of the situation in western Europe – presumably to make the situation quite clear to Congress and American public opinion. However, there is no evidence that he did not mean what he said. His analysis of European problems was mostly drawn from Will Clayton's memorandum of 27 May (quoted above, p. 65), which concentrated on the mainland rather than on Britain. Milward argues that Clayton ignored the rapidly rising industrial output of 1946–7 and helped to create the myth of Europe 'sinking while the doctors deliberate'. However, the focus of Clayton and Marshall's analysis was the failure of European market mechanisms – and the consequent inflation and slow recovery of grain and coal output and manufacturing production. Clayton had seen the evidence at first hand and was clearly convinced that market failure, especially in France, was starving the cities and forcing governments to waste their resources on buying food overseas. He thought that relatively small American inputs could make a large difference to this situation. Hence the emphasis in Marshall's speech on 'restoring a working economy – on a cure not a palliative' – not just on providing relief 'on a piece-meal basis as various crises develop', but on long-term solutions.[9]

Clayton argued in favour of large grants until European agriculture, coal and shipping returned to normal and intra-European trade improved. The aim was 'to break the impasse, to get industry and agriculture moving again, and to restore a sense of confidence in the economic and political system'. Milward derides Clayton as a Houston cotton broker and free-trade ideologue. In fact, as Assistant Secretary of State for Economic Affairs, he was one of the principal architects of American foreign economic policy. In addition, as the founder of the largest US cotton-marketing firm, with branches all over the southern United States, Latin America and Europe, he was especially sensitive to agricultural marketing, movement of crops, transport costs, exchange mechanisms and the integration of natural markets. He often emphasised the assistance that the other primary producers – Canada, Latin America, etc. – could provide, but he was fiercely opposed to multilateral control. His statement, therefore, that 'We must avoid getting into another UNRRA. The United States must run this show', was a realistic appreciation of the fact that the prime requirement was for effective organisation as much as extra resources.[10]

The Marshall Plan was also intended to solve the German problem. By early 1947 the long-run frictions over German policy between the former allies, the surrounding countries, the US military government (OMGUS) and the State Department were reaching boiling point. Table 8.1, derived from tentative contemporary IMF figures, establishes the financial dimensions of the problem. German private trade was minimal in 1946–7; although in surplus, it could not possibly have financed German requirements. Exports were mostly confined to coal and timber, shipped free or at minimal prices to the surrounding countries (see Table 5.7, above). Services like railroad transit across Germany were provided free. The British and American governments, therefore, had to donate much of the food and provisions required for West Germany. In addition, American private institutions and individuals sent substantial gifts. East Germany, with more agriculture and less industry, was far more self-sufficient. Simultaneously, the Russians and the French abstracted large, unquantified amounts of 'war booty', reparations and restitutions. The IMF figures are only approximations, but it is clear that Britain and the USA were pouring resources into Germany from the west while Russia was abstracting them from the east. In addition, all the allies raised very large sums from German sources towards their occupation costs. The Russian figures are IMF estimates, not exact figures.[11]

Table 8.1. *German Trade and Occupation Balances, 1947 ($m.)*

	Private trade	US + UK imports	US gifts	Reparations	Occupation costs
Bizone	98	−624	−100	80	1200
French	4	0	−15	18	200
Russian	13	0	−14	702	2080
TOTAL	115	−624	−129	800	3480

Source: IMF, *Payments Yearbook*, vol. 1, pp. 198–202. The table is based on 'tentative estimates by the Fund'.

The State Department acquiesced in this plunder for the sake of wider US relations and to provide coal and to fund recovery elsewhere, but Clay and the army wanted to limit the quantity of unpaid exports and to rebuild the more peaceful aspects of German industry. Clearly, with no proper incentives, living hand to mouth, and paying very large occupation costs out of local taxes, the German economy recovered slowly, adversely affecting the surrounding dependent economies, such as Belgium, Denmark and Holland. This conflict came to a head in early 1947. In July 1946 Bevin threatened to 'organise' the British zone – including the Ruhr – and to sell coal for export to reduce occupation costs, but he accepted the fusion of the British and American zones into the Bizone in December 1946. This transferred some costs to the USA and made the joint zone more self-sufficient. In January 1947 the military governors agreed to raise coal output further by increasing miners' wages and food allowances – the latter to 4,000 calories a day. However, the State Department still denied them the right to make cash rather than credit sales to Austrian, French and Italian consumers.[12]

The British authorities and the US Army could not give up. After the hard winter of 1946/7, the army persuaded Herbert Hoover to write a report on Germany for Congress. He recommended that German heavy industry (excluding arms) should be revived 'to restore the productivity of Europe', and that proper charges should be made for German exports 'to build a self sustaining economic community in the bizone ...'. Simultaneously, at the Council of Foreign Ministers in Moscow, Bevin persuaded Marshall to raise the Levels of Industry further and to involve the Germans more in management. On his return through Germany, Marshall met Clay, who reminded him: 'We have to recognise that it is not Germany who is paying the penalty today, but rather the tax-payers of the United States and Great Britain and we can unburden ourselves of this expense only by returning Germany to a satisfactory trading position or by abandoning her to chaos.' It was after this harangue that Marshall gave his radio analysis, on 28 April, that 'the patient is sinking ...'.[13]

These suggestions challenged State Department policy, which, since Potsdam, had been to redistribute European heavy industry 'to countries which do not have the German record of aggression'. The White House replied immediately that 'there must be other approaches to these problems than the revival of the German colossus along the lines suggested by Mr Hoover'. The result was the flurry of studies and statements in Washington in the spring and summer of 1947, including Marshall's offer of 'friendly assistance' at Harvard. Marshall refused to give details, but the major problem was whether German revival could be squared with French security. The French themselves, responding sharply to rumours, claimed that a German revival would undercut the Monnet Plan, bring down the government and give power to the left. At the CEEC conferences in August 1947 they opposed the Marshall Plan until they were given promises of the establishment of an international authority for the Ruhr.[14]

The decision to revive Germany, therefore, was partly taken to rectify the anomalous reparations and coal situation and partly to save Anglo-American costs. As Clay argued, the threat from the Soviet Union was only part of the equation. 'In our political warfare with the USSR, we [must] not forget that here in Germany we have 70,000,000 human beings to remember.' This led directly to the Marshall Plan because the State Department knew that, if Germany was to be revived, France and the other neighbouring countries would demand compensation for the loss of reparations and cheap coal. As the general financial crisis deepened in mid-1947, the clamours were bound to become more intense. The change in US policy was evident in a statement of 10 July 1947. The USA, it said, wanted the Bizone to contribute to the European Recovery Program (ERP) and to be represented at the CEEC conference. It promised that Germany would export the goods that other European countries needed for their recovery, that these countries would be compensated for the loss of German raw material exports and helped to pay for the required German goods.[15]

The central role of German production emerged again in September 1947, in the American response to the plans and requests for aid – 'the sixteen shopping lists' – drawn up by the European nations at the CEEC conference. These came to $29.2bn., much more than the USA planned to give, and failed to develop a common regional approach. The USA insisted that they revise their plans. Clearly, their collective deficit with North America would be far smaller if they increased their trade with each other and moderated their more ambitious investment plans. The most glaring example of wasted resources was in Germany, which, before the war, had provided a large share of European coal, steel and machinery. In mid-1947 much of her heavy industry was either damaged and underutilised or subject to reparations claims or dismantling orders. However, the damage was often slight; recommissioning this plant and the associated transport would be the cheapest way of replacing expensive US imports. The alternative course – allowing the Europeans to sell more as well as buy more in the USA – was not immediately practical, either economically or politically. Clearly, though, whatever the economic logic, there would be huge political problems in reintegrating Germany into the European system.[16]

The Marshall Plan also reflected a more general confidence that American methods could revive Europe. American history had convinced leading US businessmen, diplomats and politicians that Europe could become far more efficient and self-sufficient if national rivalries and petty internal barriers on trade, capital movements and migration were whittled away, as in the USA after 1789. Americans were also confident that they had found the right combination of industrial structure and government intervention to achieve high productivity. By the 1920s the USA had produced a modern corporate capitalism. The private, informal attempts to assist Europe in the 1920s were the product of her confidence. The depression had nearly destroyed the system, but the New Deal had introduced new methods of controlling the economy – and they worked. Firms and government had survived the test of war. Now, many of the leaders of American society, from Herbert Hoover through to New Deal social scientists, were convinced that American business and government methods could revolutionise Europe. Their impatience with European bureaucracy and provincialism is evident in many American statements of the period.[17]

'New Left' historians like Gabriel Kolko have argued that the Marshall Plan was motivated by US fears of depression and exclusion from European state trading systems:

> As a capitalist nation unable to expand its own internal market by redistributing its national income to absorb the surplus, the United States would soon plunge again into the depression that only the World War 2 brought to an end. The alternative was to export dollars. ... This time, however, Washington had no intention of operating through an organisation such as UNRRA. By June 1947 what Washington desired was the opportunity not only to subsidise United States exports, but to permanently influence and shape Western Europe's internal economic policies.

Administration officials sometimes made a similar, but not identical point. Hence Will Clayton's memorandum of 27 May argued: 'Aside from the awful implications which this would have for the future peace and security of the world, the immediate effects on our domestic economy would be disastrous: markets for our surplus production gone, unemployment, depression, a heavily unbalanced budget on the background of a mountainous war debt.' Such comments were written partly to persuade, partly from genuine fear.[18]

These fears, however, proved quite ill-founded. American GNP grew rapidly in 1945–55, with only short pauses in 1949 and 1954: see Table 8.2 (col. 1). The table suggests that American credits were granted more readily because the USA could afford them relatively easily at that time. Firstly, in 1947, the US GNP of $231bn. meant that the cost to her, as a percentage of GNP, was less than the benefit to most of the sixteen recipients in terms of their GNPs. US GNP, for instance, was nearly six times that of Britain in 1947, and Britain was by far the largest economy in western Europe at that time. Hence, total American aid and credits, which ran at $5–6bn. per year over the period (see col. 6), were only 2.7% of US GNP in 1946, 2.6% in 1947, 2.1% in 1949, 2.2% in 1950 and 1.5% in the early 1950s.

Europe received most of this in the late 1940s, with far less after 1950. The aid programmes were therefore relatively easy to justify if they satisfied a strong policy objective. Secondly, US government finances in the late 1940s, unlike the 1980s and 1990s, were remarkably healthy. Federal government revenue (col. 2) and expenditure (col. 3) both fell rapidly in 1945–50. The major variable was defence spending, which fell faster than taxation in 1945–6, leaving small surpluses in 1947–9 which were then available for the overseas grants (col. 6). Defence spending rose again in 1950–3 because of the Korean and Cold Wars, and the nature of US foreign aid changed. The sharp fall in defence spending in 1945–7 might have shaken the economy. However, civilian demand for new consumer durables, fuelled by the long period of depression and wartime deprivation and by accumulated wartime savings and the sharp fall in taxes, replaced military demand so rapidly that there was very little unemployment in 1945–55 (col. 7). Despite the gloomy prognostications, therefore, the US economy operated at almost full capacity in 1945–55, with quite serious inflationary outbreaks in 1946–7 and during the Korean War.[19]

Table 8.2. *US GNP, Government Finance, Aid and Employment, 1945–1955*

	GNP ($bn.) (1)	Govt revenue ($bn.) (2)	Govt expend. ($bn.) (3)	Deficit ($bn.) (4)	Defence ($bn.) (5)	Foreign aid ($bn.) (6)	Unem-ployment (%) (7)	Inflation (%) (8)
1945	212	50	95	−45	82	2	2	1
1946	208	43	62	−18	45	6	4	8
1947	231	43	37	7	13	6	4	14
1948	258	45	36	9	13	5	4	6
1949	256	42	41	1	13	6	6	−4
1950	285	41	43	−2	13	4	5	3
1951	328	53	46	8	23	5	3	9
1952	345	68	68	0	44	5	3	−3
1953	364	71	77	−5	50	6	3	−1
1954	365	70	71	−1	47	5	6	0
1955	398	65	68	−3	40	5	4	0

Source: United States, Bureau of the Census, *Historical Statistics of the United States: Colonial Times to 1970* (United States Government Printing Office: Washington, DC, 1975), pp. 135, 199, 224, 874, 1105, 1115.

In 1947/8, therefore, when the Marshall Plan was being organised, most American industries were running at near full capacity and contemporaries were more worried by inflation than depression. It was not necessary to pump up American demand further by subsidising exports. Clayton's remarks were precautionary. A fundamental collapse in Europe would obviously have been extremely serious for America. All businessmen of Clayton's age – especially those from the south – remembered the post-World War I and 1929 depressions. However, exports and aid were a small share of US GNP. The strength of the underlying domestic consumer demand, and the improvement in government management techniques made the immediate economic risks relatively small. In practice, the ERP required a small, but real, diversion of American resources, possibly necessitating higher taxes than might otherwise have been the case. However, at a time of high demand and rapid expansion, it was soon decided that America should provide Europe with the critical goods in short supply rather than with money grants or credits. In the event, domestic demand was so high in the USA in 1948 that a third of the actual supplies (see Table 8.3) were purchased 'off shore' from Canada and Latin America. American purchases also relieved the very serious dollar shortages of suppliers like Canada, which had surpluses with Europe but deficits with the USA.[20]

Table 8.3. *Sourcing of Marshall Plan, April 1948–December 1951*

	Total ($m.)	USA (%)	Canada (%)	South America (%)	OEEC (%)	Others (%)
Food/feed/fertiliser	3209	67	19	12	2	1
Coal	344	71	0	0	25	4
Petroleum	1208	24	0	13	25	39
Raw cotton	1398	100	0	0	0	0
Other raw materials	1883	48	30	15	3	4
Machines/vehicles	1428	97	3	0	0	0
Tobacco	444	99	0	1	0	0
Other commodities	89	86	20	5	2	1
Miscellaneous[b]	778	90	0	4	1	4
Total commodities	10782[a]	70	11	8	5	6
Total commodities	10782	7587	1215	854	513	623
EPU capital and aid	545	—	—	—	—	—
Ocean freight	902	—	—	—	—	—
Technical services	53	98	—	—	2	—
TOTAL	12281	—	—	—	—	—

[a] Statistics have been rounded.
[b] Shipments made but not yet documented.
Source: US, *Statistical Abstract*, 1952, p. 835.

The exact choice and source of goods delivered depended on surpluses and shortages in the USA as well as on OEEC needs and requests. Grain, for instance, was still in short supply in the USA in 1948, and a substantial proportion of ERP grain came from Canada and Argentina. Europe's requests for meat were rejected because supplies in America were tight; US consumption per person was relatively high, but there was no chance of introducing rationing. Coal was delivered as required; the OEEC only wanted 6% of the very large American supply. Oil came from US companies overseas because of high demand and short supply; American oil consumption per head was eleven times higher than European in 1947. The demand for iron and steel scrap was very high in America, so only finished goods were sent. OEEC requests for equipment were reduced because of US shortages and doubts that Europe could absorb so much new machinery; however, only America could provide most of the equipment required. Cotton, tobacco and dairy products, on the other hand, which were in surplus in the USA, were provided freely. The difference between paid and unpaid shipments was the time required to process documents and to pay shippers (the European Payments Union (EPU) is described below, in Chapter 21). Ocean freight and technical services were also provided by the ERP; 50% of the former had to be in American ships to satisfy the American maritime lobby.[21]

The ERP was therefore intended to solve several problems. The common elements were confidence that the USA had the ability and resources to do so and fear of the consequences of failure to address them. The twin related dangers were financial collapse and autarchy in Europe – possibly followed by a new mercantilism – and the looming threat of Russia. Neither had yet materialised, but the dangers were obvious; either could lead to renewed war. At the time that the plan was being formulated, economists calculated that World War II had cost America about $350bn., a future war would cost very much more. The annual cost of the Marshall Plan, about $5bn. on a GNP of about $230bn., was relatively small, therefore. 'It is well to ask', wrote Seymour Harris, a well-known economist who gave evidence to congressional committees, 'whether we should take the prudent risk of spending $25B over ten years (assuming the aid will taper off for five years after 1952) in order to save $1500B (say); on the assumption that the stabilisation of a democratic Europe will contribute substantially to saving us from a war.' He concluded that the USA should do so.[22]

Notes

1. Michael Hogan, *The Marshall Plan: America, Britain, and The Reconstruction of Western Europe, 1947–1952* (Cambridge University Press: Cambridge, 1987), pp. 26–45; Alan S. Milward, *The Reconstruction of Western Europe, 1945–51* (Methuen: London, 1984), pp. 1–55; Melvyn P. Leffler, *A Preponderance of Power: National Security, The Truman Administration and the Cold War* (Stanford University Press: Stanford, Calif., 1992), pp. 141–81.
2. Marshall's radio message is reproduced in the Department of State, *Bulletin*, 11 May 1947, p. 919; the Harvard address is in *FRUS: 1947*, vol. 3, pp. 237–9.
3. Scott Jackson, 'Prologue to the Marshall Plan: the origins of the American commitment for a European Recovery Program', *The Journal of American History* 65 (1979), pp. 1043–68.
4. Wilson D. Miscambleg, CSC, *George F. Kennan and the Making of American Foreign Policy, 1947–1950* (Princeton University Press: Princeton, 1992), pp. 43–74, for the early 1947 State Department studies; many of the critical documents are reprinted in *FRUS: 1947*, vol. 3.

5. Ben T. Moore to Clair Wilcox, Director of the Office of International Trade Policy, Geneva, 28 July 1947: *FRUS: 1947*, vol. 3, pp. 239–41. For the European reaction, see Hogan, *Marshall Plan*, pp. 45–51; Alex Danchev, *Oliver Franks: Founding Father* (Clarendon Press: Oxford, 1993), pp. 57–62.

6. Miscamble, *Kennan*, pp. 55–7; Bevin is quoted in Danchev, *Franks*, p. 63.

7. Danchev, *Franks*, pp. 64–83; Hogan, *Marshall Plan*, pp. 54–87; Harry B. Price, *The Marshall Plan and its Meaning* (Cornell University Press: Ithaca, New York, 1955), pp. 36–70; Leffler, *Preponderance*, pp. 182–219; Milward, *Reconstruction*, pp. 56–89.

8. Alan P. Dobson, *The Politics of the Anglo-American Economic Special Relationship* (Wheatsheaf: Sussex, 1988), pp. 98–138; Gardner, *Sterling–Dollar Diplomacy*, pp. 342–6.

9. Clayton's memorandum is reprinted in Frederick J. Dobney (ed.), *Selected Papers of Will Clayton* (Johns Hopkins Press: Baltimore, 1971), pp. 201–4. For the debate on the ERP as a structural adjustment programme, see Barry Eichengreen (ed.), *Europe's Postwar Recovery* (Cambridge University Press: Cambridge, 1995), pp. 3–35.

10. Gregory A. Fossedal, *Our Finest Hour: Will Clayton, The Marshall Plan and the Triumph of Democracy* (Hoover Institution Press: Stanford, Calif., 1993), pp. 200–54; for Milward on Clayton, see *Reconstruction*, p. 2.

11. IMF, *Payments Yearbook*, vol. 1, pp. 198–202, and John Gimbel, *The Origins of the Marshall Plan* (Stanford University Press: Stanford, California, 1976), pp. 141–75, describe the German economic situation, 1946–7.

12. Gimbel, *Origins, passim*, for US and allied policy on Germany.

13. *Ibid.*, pp. 179–99; Hogan, *Marshall Plan*, pp. 29–39, for pressures to revive Germany.

14. Gimbel, *Origins*, pp. 199–233; Milward, *Reconstruction*, pp. 74–6, for US–French debate on German recovery.

15. Gimbel, *Origins*, pp. 233–80; Milward, *Reconstruction*, pp. 126–67, on France, German recovery and the ERP.

16. Milward, *Reconstruction*, pp. 69–89, for the CEEC and German recovery.

17. Hogan, *Marshall Plan*, pp. 1–25; Charles S. Maier, 'The politics of productivity: foundations of American international economic policy after World War 2', in *idem* (ed.), *In Search of Stability* (Cambridge University Press: Cambridge, 1987), pp. 121–52.

18. Joyce and Gabriel Kolko, *The Limits of Power: The World and United States Foreign Policy, 1945–1954* (Harper and Row: New York, 1972), p. 360. *FRUS: 1947*, vol. 3, pp. 230–2, contains Clayton's views on the ERP as a means of preventing international depression.

19. For analysis of American fiscal policy in the late 1940s, see Herbert Stein, *The Fiscal Revolution in America* (University of Chicago Press: Chicago, 1969), pp. 197–286; for contemporary discussion about the likely effects of the ERP on US inflation or recession, see Jackson, 'Prologue to the Marshall Plan'.

20. For the Canadian financial crisis in late 1947, see above, pp. 38–41.

21. See Seymour E. Harris, *The European Recovery Program* (Harvard University Press: Cambridge, Mass., 1948), pp. 207–37, for analysis of the choice of goods to send to Europe.

22. *Ibid.*, p. 188.

9

The Marshall Plan:
Aims and Achievements

The Marshall Plan became law on 3 April 1948, and the first shipments were made in May and June. As the crisis in Europe worsened in late 1947, the USA granted a substantial package of interim aid – about $520m. – to help Austria, France and Italy until the main Marshall Aid package was decided. Britain was allowed to draw on the remaining $400m. of the American loan in December 1947. Germany continued to receive (GARIOA) relief. After President Truman had signed the Economic Recovery Act which created the ECA and Congress had raised the first year's funds, the USA negotiated bilateral treaties with all the European recipients in which they promised to attempt to reach economic 'viability' within about four years. Each agreed to increase production, control its budgets, limit inflation, expand foreign trade and cooperate with other European countries. The USA hoped that, eventually, an independent and modernised Europe could rejoin the Bretton Woods system. In return, the USA promised to provide aid, mostly in the form of physical supplies of needed goods (raw materials, food, machinery, etc.), rather than loans or credits. However, grants were given for specific purposes – for instance, to the European Payments Union (EPU), to encourage intra-European trade.[1]

Europe was well on the way to achieving these aims when the Marshall Plan ended in December 1951. European GNP and industrial output had risen impressively and, after a pause caused by the Korean War, progressed, as the Americans had hoped, to full recovery by the late 1950s. Foreign and intra-European trade rose rapidly and the dollar gap slowly vanished. By the late 1950s most European controls on trade and currency had ended. Inflation, which had been about to explode in 1947, sank rapidly back in the late 1940s, but revived again temporarily during the Korean War. After numerous currency and tax reforms, European finances were on a much better footing to assist the great expansion of the 1950s. European integration had not developed as the Americans hoped, but, arguably, the ground was laid for future cooperation and unity. Similarly, the Europeans had initially rejected many American industrial and social ideas, only to see them re-emerge after a long dormant period.[2]

European progress was mirrored in the balance of payments figures with the USA: see Table 2.3 and Figure 9.1. The drain on gold and dollar assets in 1947 continued into mid-1948, but then fell rapidly as Marshall Aid began to arrive. European and colonial exports to the USA were still small and were only rising slowly, but in late 1948, together with the aid, they just covered the dollar gap. The situation worsened in early 1949, however, as the US recession reduced demand for imports, causing a second drain on European gold reserves. This precipitated a 30% devaluation of the sterling area and most European currencies, and a rapid fall in dollar imports. Increases in European production and intra-European trade replaced many American goods.[3]

Figure 9.1. *European Dollar Receipts and Payments, 1948–1952 ($bn., current value)*

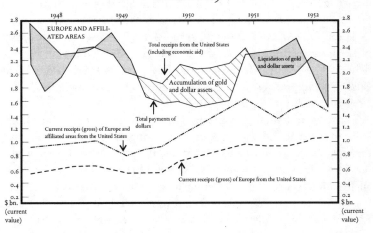

Source: United Nations, *Economic Survey of Europe since the War: A Reappraisal of Problems and Prospects* (Economic Commission for Europe: Geneva, 1953), p. 126.

From late 1949, US recovery, the NATO rearmament programmes and the Korean War created such a large American demand for manufactured goods from Europe and for raw materials from her dependencies that Europe rapidly began to rebuild her gold and dollar reserves. At this point, with growing arms expenditure at home and European viability apparently in sight, the USA cut back on Marshall Plan payments. However, 1950 was a false dawn. In 1951 US (and European) rearmament forced up raw material prices worldwide and plunged Europe back into deficit and financial crisis. The USA met this crisis by passing the Mutual Security Act in October 1951, granting further aid from January 1952. This time the crisis was temporary; although a substantial gap remained, European exports now covered a far greater proportion of dollar purchases and she soon began to regain dollar assets. Even as late as 1953, however, the *Economic Survey of Europe*, while charting the progress made, was still pessimistic about future prospects.[4]

Contemporaries often claimed that the Marshall Plan underlay this recovery. Historians concerned with US–European relations and the origins of the Cold War have also usually accepted these claims. On the other hand, contemporary UN publications and some European economic historians hardly mention it. Recently, some historians have argued in detail that the ERP had little effect because Europe was recovering quickly anyway. They maintain that American aid was small as a proportion of GNP throughout the Marshall Plan period, that most of the infrastructural repairs of war damage and the worst of the bottlenecks had been tackled before and were no longer critical, and that Europe could probably have saved the necessary investment to achieve external viability without American aid.[5]

These criticisms are convincing, but, by concentrating on the dollar value of Marshall Aid, they miss both the continuity of American support throughout the reconstruction period and the many other ways in which the USA tried to supplement physical aid. Table 9.1 confirms that Marshall Aid was small in proportion to GNP, but varied considerably between countries. The table is drawn from several sources, as available. Lack of data, high inflation rates and volatile exchange rates make many of the figures tentative. The 1948–9 column, taken via Milward from the Bank for International Settlements, measures net ERP aid, i.e., after the transfer of conditional aid, which reduced the Belgian and British figures, but increased the French and Dutch. The British (row) figures include the American and Canadian loans. The French figures are merely Milward's 1948–9 figure, but with net government loans added, and prorated using GNP indexes. The Greek figures measure US, but not UNRRA, aid – which in 1946 was almost as much in absolute terms as the later ERP aid. The first set of Italian figures include loans, which were substantial in 1946–7, as well as UNRRA and ERP aid. The second set, taken from Zamagni, exclude loans. The Norwegian figures exclude large early postwar payments, equal to several per cent of GNP, for allied wartime use of Norwegian ships – see Table 11.3. Despite the uncertainty inherent in the figures, it is, however, obvious that for several countries, the earlier aid in 1946–7 was just as important as the later Marshall Aid. Aid declined rapidly after 1950, although its value was increased to a certain extent by the European devaluation of September 1949.

Table 9.1. *Foreign Aid as % National Income, 1946–1951*

	1946	1947	1948	1948–9	1949	1950	1951
Austria	—	—	—	14.0	—	—	—
Belgium/Luxembourg	—	—	—	0.6	—	—	—
Britain	2.8	7.8	2.1	2.4	2.8	1.9	0.5
Denmark	—	—	—	3.3	—	—	—
France	7.7	11.3	10.4	6.5	7.5	1.8	4.3
(West) Germany	—	4.2	5.3	2.9	4.1	2.3	1.6
Greece	—	—	2.9	—	10.9	14.9	11.5
Holland	5.7	4.9	6.8	10.8	4.9	6.9	2.3
Ireland	—	—	—	7.8	—	—	—
Italy (1)	6.8	3.1	3.4	5.3	2.4	1.7	1.4
Italy (2)	4.2	2.0	2.7	2.7	2.6	2.0	1.9
Norway	1.0	1.2	3.1	5.8	5.2	6.3	2.2
Sweden	—	—	—	0.3	—	—	—

Sources: 1948–9 net ERP aid: Alan S. Milward, *The Reconstruction of Western Europe, 1945–51* (Methuen: London, 1984), pp. 95–6. Country rows are taken from country tables in Chapters 10 and 11 below. Italy (1) – as above. Italy (2) – Vera Zamagni, *The Economic History of Italy, 1860–1990* (Clarendon Press: Oxford, 1993), p. 332.

Logistical support and supplies of critical goods helped to remove many crucial bottlenecks during 1945–6. National governments completed repairs quickly in most of the liberated countries, but the allies also helped. In Germany the allied armies undertook a great deal of basic reconstruction, encouraging the first rapid, but partial, recovery. The allies also attempted to ensure the provision of basic supplies such as coal (see Table 9.2). In 1938 British, German and Polish surpluses had supplied much of the rest of Europe. In 1945–6 these surpluses no longer existed and German output was half that of 1938. In July 1945 Truman

decided to distribute a large part of the German output to the surrounding countries at low cost; this helped their early recovery, even if it hurt
Germany. The allies then increased the German supply by paying very
high wages to the miners. Imports from the USA also rose rapidly to
fill the gap in 1946–7. Generally, the Americans did all they could
to ensure adequate coal supplies in countries such as Italy. The first
stage of European recovery then revealed many new bottlenecks which
were only relieved by massive imports from the USA in 1946–7. By
early 1948, when the Marshall Plan began, many of these specific raw
material shortages had been tackled; the problem was a general lack of
finance and modern equipment.[6]

Table 9.2. *Coal Supplies in Western Europe, 1938–1948 (million
metric tons)*

	1935–8	1946	1947	1948
Main producers				
Britain	233	193	200	211
France	46	47	47	56
Germany	136	63	84	91
Poland	61	47	60	—
USA	405[a]	539	613	582
Main importers				
France	23	10	16	12
Italy	12	6	11	8
Source of imports				
Britain	41	5	0	—
Germany	28	13	11	—
Poland	16	15	25	—
USA	—	17	>30	—

[a] Average, 1937–8.
Sources: UN, *Economic Report, 1945–47*, pp. 204–16; United Nations, *Economic Survey
of Europe in 1948* (Economic Commission for Europe: Geneva, 1949), p. 11.

American aid and support was also vital in raising morale and maintaining momentum at critical times. By mid-1947 most European
countries were in increasingly desperate financial circumstances. Several
governments were faced with severe unrest and determined communist
challenges. They also faced widespread hoarding and growing market
failure. The promise of Marshall Aid in June 1947, followed by the

CEEC debates in the autumn and the interim aid in late 1947, were probably just sufficient to prevent them taking extreme and mutually destructive measures to protect their external balance. The critical situation in Austria, France and Italy in late 1947 virtually forced the USA to rush the interim aid legislation through Congress several months before the main Marshall Plan legislation. Milward calculates that, if Europeans had eaten with the same parsimony in 1949 as they had in 1947, there would have been no need for the Marshall Plan and the investment boom could have continued until Europe reached viability without American help. However, the economic and political situation was extremely tense in several European countries and well-informed observers like Kindleberger doubt that they would have been able to survive.[7]

It is likely that had the aid neither been promised nor delivered, the Europeans, as they ran out of dollars, would have cut consumption and investment and then devalued, hoping for a trade boom to save them. Given the massive shift in the terms of trade against manufactured goods since the 1930s, however, and the fact that most European economies were already at full employment, the gains might have been too little and too late. The stronger trading countries – Belgium, Denmark, Norway and Sweden – might have succeeded without too much political strain, but even they depended on buoyant sales in Europe to fund their overseas purchases. Strong, politically cohesive countries like Britain and Holland might have staved off greater economic strain and still won through. Countries like Austria, France and Italy, which were economically and politically weak, might have collapsed in several respects, dragging the whole European system down with them.[8]

The Marshall Plan was vital in establishing financial stability in western Europe. At the end of the war the monetary systems of most European countries were in chaos. The Germans had extracted massive supplies from most dependent countries. They had paid for these by printing local money, but restrained inflation by imposing severe controls. When the Germans left, the liberated populations spent their hoarded notes on the few consumer goods available and prices escalated wildly. In Scandinavia (and Britain) excess wartime liquidity was reined in by strict controls, but in France and Italy inflation accelerated dramatically, and in Germany and Austria there was no viable currency. People lived off meagre coal and food rations and the results of bartering. During 1946 the situation improved as production and US relief increased, thereby reducing competition for goods, and several govern-ments introduced severe currency reforms. In late 1947, however, the continued heavy expenditure on reconstruction, the reduction in US credits, and the near exhaustion of gold and dollar reserves increased inflation. Governments could either keep going by printing money or they could end reconstruction.[9]

The Marshall Plan successfully reduced the pressure on demand by importing fresh stocks in 1948/9. Relatively small additional supplies discouraged hoarding and undermined the black markets. Inflation declined sharply in 1948, therefore, trust in currencies improved, and markets stabilised. Waves of strikes for higher wages diminished, and farmers brought food to market more readily. However, the ECA found it more difficult to persuade governments to solve the underlying problem of their lax fiscal and monetary policies. Britain managed to suppress inflation by tight controls, Italy – after 1946 – was determinedly deflationary, but France, spending heavily on the Monnet Plan, had to be badgered. As Averell Harriman, the US Special Representative in Europe, explained in 1950, the ECA was cautious initially because 'The French feared that we were going to take over their country'; more recently, 'we have put on pressure – a great deal of it aimed at *forcing sound fiscal policies* ...'. The incentives in this case were the Marshall Plan Counterpart Funds (see below), which France needed for Monnet Plan investment. ECA officials threatened to retain the funds until France reformed her finances. However, they were afraid that real severity might undermine the weak but cooperative centrist govern-ments and let in either de Gaulle or the communists. In practice, inflation declined further during 1949–50, only to accelerate again from mid-1950 with Korean War defence spending. The chaos of the 1945–7 period did not return, though, and the devaluation against the dollar in 1949 set parities which, except for France, lasted for fifteen years.[10]

The use that was made of Marshall Plan goods varied considerably by country (see Table 9.3) and over time. Britain had traditionally manufactured her own consumer and producer durables, but imported substantial proportions of her food and raw materials from Canada and the USA. She successfully transferred as many orders as possible to the sterling area, but the ERP financed many vital essentials which could not easily be obtained elsewhere – like advanced machinery, certain foods, and some highly desirable consumer goods such as films and tobacco. The ERP purchases also kept Canada in the British market.

France and Italy, on the other hand, needed a great deal of new machinery and vehicles to supply their industrial recovery. They secured these from the USA, but bought additional food cheaply elsewhere. West Germany, like Britain, received substantial volumes of food, but hardly any machinery and no coal. Before the war Germany had produced a great deal of her own food, but the war and the zonal division had left the British and American zones very dependent on imports. The balance of commodities themselves also changed in 1948–51. In 1948 the emphasis was on food and raw materials, but by 1950 the recovery of German coal exports and better European harvests had changed the balance of imports from food and raw materials to machinery.[11]

Table 9.3. *Composition of Marshall and Mutual Security Administration Aid, 1948–1951*

	Total	Britain	France	Germany	Italy	Others[b]
Authorised shipments ($m.)	12281	2865	2494	1316	1311	4294
By country (%)	100	23	20	11	11	35
By commodity						
Food/feed/fertiliser	26	30	10	43	17	30
Petrol/coal	13	12	23	4	14	10
Raw cotton	11	9	14	19	25	5
Other raw materials	15	25	13	15	6	13
Machines/vehicles	12	6	17	3	15	14
Tobacco	4	8	1	5	0	3
Other commodities	1	0	1	1	0	1
Ocean freight	6	3	12	8	9	4
EPU capital and aid	4	1	0	0	0	11
Miscellaneous[a]	8	4	8	3	13	9

Notes: Statistics have been rounded.
[a] Shipments made but not yet documented + technical services.
[b] Plus EPU.
Source: US, *Statistical Abstract*, 1952, pp. 836–7.

The 'Counterpart Funds' were the local-currency receipt of sales of Marshall Plan supplies. These created special funds which could only be spent with ECA permission. On the whole, the ECA encouraged governments to use the counterpart funds for heavy investment in industry or vital public utilities which might otherwise have been postponed. Some of the weaker continental governments used the American controls to protect worthwhile long-term investments from popular demands for immediate consumption. Generally, private industry on the Continent was able to build new capacity to manufacture consumer goods from profits or from the capital markets. However, basic infrastructure and heavy industrial investment was less easy to finance. In Germany, for instance, the counterpart funds provided a substantial share of new electrical generating capacity; in France they helped to finance the Monnet Plan; in Italy they were used for a variety of industrial projects, for agriculture, the railroads and on public works to absorb surplus labour. Table 9.4 illustrates some of these uses.[12]

Table 9.4. *Use of Counterpart Funds in Europe, 1948–1952*

	Total	Britain	France	Germany	Italy	Others
Total ($m.)	8651	1763	2703	1009	1042	2134
Distribution (%)						
Public debt	29	97	6	0	0	31
Agriculture	7	0	9	7	20	4
Mining	6	0	13	9	0	2
Raw materials	4	0	7	5	2	4
Power	12	0	27	18	0	5
Railroads	6	0	7	1	26	4
Shipping	2	0	3	4	2	2
Other industries	16	0	9	31	29	26
Arms	4	3	8	0	0	5
Miscellaneous	13	0	12	25	21	16

Note: Statistics have been rounded.
Source: Comité pour L'Histoire Économique et Financière de la France, *Le Plan Marshall et le relèvement économique de L'Europe* (Ministère des Finances: Paris, 1993), pp. 162–3 (henceforth CHEFF, *Le Plan Marshall*).

The exceptions to this generalisation were Britain and Norway, which simply used the funds to retire the national debt. In theory, this drained off some of the potential surplus money supply and reduced the danger of inflation. Britain and Norway already had well-developed heavy investment programmes, full employment and well-controlled inflation. Spending the money on further investment would have weakened the controls. In effect, Britain thereby avoided any question of American control of her substantial capital investment programme, which was financed out of general revenues and government borrowing – made relatively easier by the inflow of counterpart funds.[13]

Notes

1. The British loan agreement and the interim aid programme are described in Michael J. Hogan, *The Marshall Plan: America, Britain and the Reconstruction of Western Europe, 1947–1952* (Cambridge University Press: Cambridge, 1987), pp. 82–4; the British bilateral treaty is reprinted in Henry Pelling, *Britain and the Marshall Plan* (Macmillan: Basingstoke, 1988), pp. 153–65. Harry B. Price, *The Marshall Plan and its Meaning* (Cornell University Press: Ithaca, New York, 1955), pp. 305–8, and Imanuel Wexler, *The Marshall Plan Revisited* (Greenwood: Westport, Conn., 1983), pp. 9–54, describe the aims of the ERP.

2. Hogan, *Marshall Plan*, pp. 427–45; Price, *The Marshall Plan and its Meaning*, pp. 223–412; Wexler, *Marshall Plan Revisited*, pp. 249–55, provide simple accounts of ERP achievements.

3. Successive editions of United Nations, Department of Economic Affairs, *Economic Survey of Europe* (Economic Commission for Europe: Geneva, 1948–), describe European trade recovery.

4. United Nations, *Economic Survey of Europe since the War: A Reappraisal of Problems and Prospects* (Economic Commission for Europe: Geneva, 1953), pp. 125–44.

5. Price, *The Marshall Plan and its Meaning*, pp. 394–412; Milward, *Reconstruction*, pp. 91–125; and Barry Eichengreen (ed.), *Europe's Postwar Recovery* (Cambridge University Press: Cambridge, 1995), pp. 3–35, represent three stages in the debate.

6. UN, *Economic Report, 1945–47*, pp. 204–16, on the European coal situation. J. Bradford de Long and Barry Eichengreen, 'The Marshall Plan: history's most successful structural adjustment program', in Rudiger Dornbusch *et al.*, (eds), *Postwar Economic Reconstruction and the Lessons for the East Today* (MIT Press: Cambridge, Mass., 1993), pp. 189–230, argues that coal was not a critical bottleneck in 1948.

7. United States, Department of State, *The Interim Aid Program: Draft Legislation and Background Information* (Document no. 108, 80th Congress, 1st Session; United States Government Printing Office: Washington, DC, 1947); Charles P. Kindleberger, *Marshall Plan Days* (Allen and Unwin: Boston, 1987), pp. 245–65; Milward, *Reconstruction*, pp. 105–13.

8. Harold Van B. Cleveland, 'If there had been no Marshall Plan', in Stanley Hoffman and Charles S. Maier (eds), *The Marshall Plan: A Retrospective* (London and Westview, Conn., 1984), pp. 59–69, explores this counterfactual.

9. UN, *Economic Report, 1945–47*, pp. 157–68; United Nations, Department of Economic Affairs, *A Survey of the Economic Situation and Prospects of Europe* (Economic Commission for Europe: Geneva, 1948), pp. 75–87, are contemporary analyses of European inflation.

10. Wexler, *Marshall Plan Revisited*, pp. 97–117 (Harriman is quoted on p. 100); Gilles Saint-Paul, 'France: real and monetary aspects of French exchange rate policy under the Fourth Republic', in Eichengreen (ed.), *Europe's Postwar Recovery*, pp. 292–319.

11. Milward, *Reconstruction*, pp. 101–7, describes the use made of ERP supplies by country.

12. Hogan, *The Marshall Plan*, pp. 153–5, and Milward, *Reconstruction*, pp. 107–13, discuss the general use of counterparts. The use of counterparts in particular countries is introduced in Chapters 10 and 11.

13. For British and Norwegian use of counterparts, see Pelling, *Britain and the Marshall Plan*, pp. 73, 112, and Wexler, *Marshall Plan Revisited*, pp. 107–12.

10

The Marshall Plan
and the Larger Countries

Britain was the most independent of the major European countries. Table 10.1 (and the following tables for other countries) lays out the most important statistics. The first section provides basic indices and measurements of economic growth and welfare – industrial output, inflation, unemployment, etc. The second section, which sums to zero, provides the essential global foreign trade and payments statistics. All the OEEC countries had substantial trade deficits, but these were offset in different ways by invisibles, capital flows, and various gold and foreign exchange movements. The 'invisibles' included net earnings from transport, insurance, overseas investment, tourism, etc. In the case of Britain, 'miscellaneous donations' covers government development grants to colonies and net private gifts. 'Capital outflow' measures private and government capital investments and loans overseas. 'Aid received' was mostly North American grants and loans. Britain also extended some aid, however, principally the quite substantial 'conditional aid' part of her ERP receipts (see pp. 138–9 below). 'Sterling debts' and 'monetary flows' included offsetting movements of gold and foreign exchange and various IMF, EPU and sterling area transactions. The third section outlines the geography of the current account deficit. This is always negative with the dollar area, but frequently positive with the Third World. Finally, where possible, some assessment is given of the importance of American aid and loans to imports, capital investment and GNP.[1]

British industrial output increased rapidly in 1945–51, unemployment was very low, and inflation was controlled. The Labour government was determined to increase investment and output and to redeem its social pledges. The huge demand for consumer and reconstruction goods from all over the world gave Britain a flying start. Hence, British exports grew rapidly in 1945–50, while imports were held back (see Table 10.1, *Foreign sector*). Invisibles soon recovered their old role, and

Table 10.1. *British Economic Development, 1946–1951*

	1946	1947	1948	1949	1950	1951
Measures and indices						
Industrial output[a]	100	105	114	121	128	132
Unemployment (%)	3	3	2	2	2	1
Inflation[b]	154	169	193	202	230	279
Foreign sector (£m.)						
Trade net	−165	−415	−192	−137	−133	−729
Invisibles net	−56	51	252	216	462	367
Miscellaneous donations	6	−42	−44	−37	−13	−23
Capital outflow	140	−387	−182	−187	−41	−348
Aid + loans	279	842	251	350	259	77
Aid extended	−153	−153	−51	−73	−128	−56
Sterling debts	36	−52	−168	−70	277	85
Monetary flows	−87	156	134	−62	−683	627
Net G & S with						
Dollar area	−304	−504	−241	−288	−88	−447
Europe	80	6	88	−16	117	−198
Sterling area	−32	161	286	322	305	370
Ratios (× 100)						
Aid + loans received : GNP	3	8	2	3	2	1
Aid + loans : imports	26	54	14	18	11	2
Aid + loans : investment	30	70	18	22	15	4

[a] 1937 = 100.
[b] 1929 = 100.
Sources: B. R. Mitchell, *European Historical Statistics, 1750–1975* (Macmillan: London, 1980); IMF, *Payments Yearbook*, vol. 5, 1947–53.

the current account (trade net + invisibles net) became positive in 1948. There was sufficient surplus to make small development grants to the colonies, to finance substantial investments in the dominions and the Middle East, to extend aid to Germany and elsewhere, and to settle some sterling debts. The overseas liquidity provided by these flows assisted British exports, of course. Hence, from 1945 to 1952, Britain moved rapidly towards viability. There were financial crises in 1947, 1949 and 1951, but the country came through each of these with a combination of good luck and American help. The American loan carried Britain through 1947 until much better general trading conditions appeared in 1948. The short crisis in 1949 caused a massive run on the pound and resulted in a 30% devaluation, but it was soon ended by the first stage of US rearmament. Hence, in 1950 Britain was able to increase her gold and dollar reserves, with the inward movement being recorded in 'monetary flows'.[2]

In 1951 British rearmament and increases in food and raw material prices worldwide caused the largest trade deficit since the war. Britain's invisible earnings had improved greatly by this time; the overall deficit was no worse than it had been in 1947 and was less in terms of GNP. As in 1947, the crisis caused an outflow of private capital and gold and dollar reserves, but this was partly offset by assistance from the European Payments Union, recorded in the 'monetary flows' column. The EPU is discussed below, pp. 139–42.) Hence, even though the ERP had ended, the new Conservative government allowed increased consumption as soon as the crisis was over and, from 1953–6, Britain enjoyed rapid expansion. The Suez Crisis in late 1956 again revealed Britain's dependence on the USA, but the government complied with the American terms and the IMF provided the required aid; in 1957 Prime Minister Macmillan was able to tell Britain that 'You've never had it so good!'

The Marshall Aid, at about 2% of GNP, was much smaller than the American loan, and most commentators argue that it was no more than a useful supplement which eased rather than permitted Britain's recovery. However, well-informed officials at the time were still very anxious to receive it. In July 1947, when it was only a hazy idea, Sir Richard Clarke advised the government that, if no aid were given 'in order to make the adjustments quickly enough, drastic action would be needed; it is difficult to see how this could be done without direction of labour and indeed a complete and total national mobilization, as far reaching as that of 1940. It would be only by these means that we could hope to get through.' The main problem, he said, was the large proportion of essential foods, raw materials and machinery coming from the dollar area. He argued that 'Radical cuts in this [import] programme will be extremely difficult to make and if made confront us with the prospect of a decay of industrial activity – a downward spiral towards the plight of Germany today.'[3]

By mid-1948 Britain's trading situation had improved greatly, but the government was still very concerned to receive aid. Hence, the

Chancellor of the Exchequer, Sir Stafford Cripps, warned the Cabinet that, if Britain rejected the terms of the Marshall Plan, there would have to be sharp cuts in American imports and food rationing substantially below prewar levels. Agricultural expansion would have to be halted for lack of feed and industrial expansion would be dislocated by lack of raw materials. Unemployment would possibly increase to 1.5 million. He added:

> These readjustments to the balance of payments would administer a number of violent shocks to the home economy at a number of separate points. The results to the structure of output, exports, investment, consumption and employment are extremely difficult to assess. We should be faced with an abrupt transition from a partially suppressed inflation to something not unlike a slump.[4]

American (and Canadian) supplies seemed so important to contemporaries because, like cereals and meat, they were basic foodstuffs, or, like cotton and oil, they were vital production inputs, or, like films and tobacco, they seemed essential for morale. Table 7.6 (above) shows how the US loan was spent on similar products in 1946–7. In mid-1947 the British government's intended imports from the dollar zone from mid-1947 to mid-1948 were: 75% of Britain's wheat and tobacco (worth $400m. and $100m. respectively), 50% of her maize, barley and oats ($120m.), 40% of her cotton ($100m.), meat and bacon ($475m.), sugar ($100m.) and edible oil and fats ($160m.), and a good deal of her fuel oil and imported machinery and steel. The planned dollar expenditure on oil, oil equipment, and tankers alone was of the order of $350m. –$400m. In total, the government planned to import $3bn.–$3.25bn. worth of goods, against exports of only $0.75bn., leaving a deficit of $2.25bn. –$2.50bn. In the short run, Britain could neither increase her dollar earnings nor find similar supplies elsewhere. The government had already done as much as possible to substitute sterling area supplies for dollar imports. In effect, Marshall Aid was used in the short run to import absolutely vital supplies. In the longer run it provided useful extra resources in several areas, marginally easing restraints on consumption, marginally encouraging new domestic investment, and marginally providing Britain with the extra capital to develop new sources in the sterling area for vital supplies. The effects of this redeployment were delayed by the rearmament crisis, but food and raw material prices fell after 1952, enabling the consumer boom of the mid-1950s.[5]

Other benefits of the aid are suggested by the rearmament crisis of 1950–1. Marshall Aid for Britain was stopped in December 1950, a year earlier than on the Continent, so she paid most of her own rearmament costs. Mutual Security Administration (MSA) Aid, for defence only, partly made up the gap. The result was a substantial diversion of engineering capacity out of exports into defence, with possible long-term effects. These were the years in which Germany, and later Japan – unencumbered by such costs – began to overhaul Britain. More immediately, the arms drive was part of a sequence of events, including the 1951 budget crisis and the division in the Cabinet, that led to the defeat of the Labour government in the 1951 general election. The Cabinet divided over the apparently trifling issue of the imposition of small National Health Service charges. In postwar Britain resources were stretched rubber-band tight. Although relatively small, the ERP aid, prior to 1950, may have enabled the government to avoid taking such destructive decisions earlier – and hence preserved the postwar consensus which, in the short run at least, greatly assisted rapid British recovery.[6]

It has sometimes been argued that Britain wasted much of her Marshall aid. One of the interesting features of Table 10.1 is that such a high proportion of the incoming aid was matched by capital outflows transmitted as 'miscellaneous donations', to the colonies for development, as capital investment to the dominions, and as conditional aid to Europe. Britain had to extend the conditional aid as part of her Marshall Plan agreements. However, Correlli Barnett whose book *Lost Victory* encapsulates these views, argues Marshall Aid and the counterpart funds could have been better used building up Britain's factories and infrastructure in readiness for the industrial battle with Germany and Japan in the 1950s. Instead, he argues, the government wasted too large a proportion of American imports on luxuries such as films and tobacco, and could think of no more imaginative use for the counterpart funds than to reduce the national debt. Most of these points have already been answered. The counterparts were applied differently than on the Continent for good reason – see above, pp. 101–2. The outflow of capital to the sterling area was well justified in terms of the new resources and markets it created, and tobacco and films were vital for morale. Barnett's more general argument is that Labour's social crusade – the welfare state – 'the New Jerusalem' – wasted the victory. In fact, most economic historians agree that Britain's commitment to heavy investment, 1945–51 was so strong that one of the main functions of the Marshall Plan, after providing the vital imports required for industrial regeneration, was to add a little colour to a drab world.[7]

France, too, recovered relatively rapidly in 1945–51, with low unemployment, but high inflation: see Table 10.2. However, the French economy was neither as strong nor as well-organised as the British economy in this period, and by early 1947 the government faced very serious immediate and long-term problems. These were the severe pressure on resources, the backwardness of French industry and agriculture, intractable social and political divisions, the ineffective and inequitable tax system, and the dilemma over the future of Germany. All these issues came to a head in mid-1947, but were either solved or defused over the next few years. First, during 1947–8, North American food shipments and interim aid provided essential supplies. These reduced the pressure on demand and eased the agricultural crisis until Marshall Plan supplies arrived in mid-1948. The crucial foreign-policy decision came in mid-1947, when, after two years of unproductive tussles over loans and the future of Germany, the Socialist Ramadier government finally decided that the USA was more likely than Russia to support French interests. This was the moment that France chose the west. The Marshall Plan confirmed this decision. American assistance gave France a substitute for reparations, and the resources to avoid economic catastrophe. France received about as much Marshall Aid as Britain, but, since the French economy was much smaller than the British at this time, the impact was far greater. In return, France was obliged to accept German recovery. In the short run, the USA guaranteed French security; in the long run, she supported European integration.[8]

The USA supported the French current account throughout this transition. The *Foreign sector* of Table 10.2 gives details of the franc area as a whole with the rest of the world, but, in the French case, the 'territoires d'outre-mer' were relatively small. French trade was severely unbalanced, especially with the dollar area in the late 1940s and early 1950s. She needed massive overseas supplies for her modernisation programme, but had very few exports to send in return. Like Britain, she increased exports to the overseas territories, but the latter were also heavily in deficit with the dollar area. Before the war, France, like Britain, had offset her trade deficits with invisible surpluses, but these were also weak after 1945. Tourists had ceased to visit France, and French foreign investments had been spent. There was a small inflow of private foreign investment, but the major burden was taken first, from

Table 10.2. *French Economic Development, 1946–1951*

	1946	1947	1948	1949	1950	1951
Measures and indices						
Industrial output[a]	90	101	116	129	125	142
Unemployment (000s)	57	46	78	131	153	120
Inflation[a]	604	904	1691	1812	2035	2609
Foreign sector ($m.)						
Trade net	−1527	−1452	−1428	−468	−78	−771
Invisibles net	−225	−61	−102	−72	−37	−200
French colonies[b]	−297	−163	−208	−167	−123	−88
Private capital net	187	95	205	56	160	68
Government loans received	763	1214	451	127	−263	165
Aid received	0	0	754	855	509	478
Monetary flows	1105	368	335	−330	−170	312
Errors + omissions	−5	−1	−7	−1	2	36
Net G & S with						
Dollar area	−1582	−1352	−953	−735	−301	−525
Sterling area	−257	−55	−295	29	39	−106
OEEC (less GB)	−123	2	−72	48	187	−397
Ratios (× 100)						
Aid + loans : imports	39	49	48	48	13	20
Aid + loans : GNP[c]	8	11	10	8	2	4

[a] 1938 = 100.
[b] Balance of colonies with foreign countries.
[c] Calculated from 1948–9 aid : GNP ratio – see Table 9.1, pp. 96–7.
Sources: Warren C. Baum, *The French Economy and the State* (Princeton University Press: Princeton, NJ, 1958), pp. 20, 46, 82–3; Mitchell, *European Historical Statistics*, p. 177; IMF, *Payments Yearbooks*, vols 3, 5; Alan S. Milward, *The Reconstruction of Western Europe, 1945–51* (Methuen: London, 1984), p. 96; Bank for International Settlements, *19th International Report* (Basle, 1949), p. 20.

1945–7, by American loans and by French sales of gold and foreign exchange (see the 'monetary flows' column), and then, from 1948–50, by Marshall Aid. The aid initially provided France with essential food and raw materials, which she could not easily have secured elsewhere, and then with machinery for the Monnet Plan modernisation. By 1950, exports to the franc area and the USA had risen rapidly; imports had been restrained. The rearmament crisis was met by continued US aid and by EPU loans. After some bad years again in the mid-1950s, French trade really recovered and recorded healthy surpluses from 1959 onwards.[9]

Marshall Aid also helped France to address severe domestic issues. The problem (see Table 10.3) was that government revenue, delivered by an inefficient and socially divisive tax system, was far less than expenditure. The latter was increased first, from 1948–50, by the heavy capital expenses of the Monnet Plan, and then, from 1950, by defence. French governments covered the deficit by sales of bonds and by advances from The Bank of France – in effect, by printing money. This caused the severe inflation which, as Clayton and Marshall had observed in early 1947, weakened ordinary market mechanisms and increased social tensions. The counterpart funds helped to offset this deficit, substantially reducing the need to borrow. However, the fiscal difficulties were only symptoms of a more widespread social malaise. The ECA argued in 1948 that the farmers were still hoarding too much food, the rich were keeping too much income, and the state was investing too heavily, at the expense of the urban middle and working classes, the balance of payments, and ERP aid.[10]

Table 10.3. *French Government Finance, 1946–1951 (frbn.)*

	1946	1947	1948	1949	1950	1951
Government budget						
Treasury revenues	427	659	1023	1470	1896	2346
Operating expenses	−345	−444	−681	−842	−1114	−1297
Capital expenses	−165	−239	−578	−828	−832	−755
Military expenses	−171	−231	−332	−377	−463	−857
Treasury deficit[a]	−353	−292	−570	−611	−570	−504
Deficit financed by						
Counterpart funds[b]	143	156	124	289	185	150
Borrowing/advances	210	136	446	322	385	354

[a] Treasury revenues minus main government expenditures did not exactly equal the Treasury deficit.
[b] The counterpart of foreign borrowing and American aid.
Source: Baum, *French Economy*, pp. 52, 56.

Hence, tough ECA Mission Chiefs like David Bruce (who later became the US Ambassador in Paris) threatened to withhold counterpart funds unless the government introduced reforms to improve the tax system and to reduce inflation. American leverage over French policy was increased by the fragmentation of the political system into four centre parties, which formed kaleidoscopic coalitions, and the communists and Gaullists, who opposed the system. To a certain extent, these weak centrist governments secretly welcomed ECA support for unpopular legislation, and many useful reforms were achieved. However, the ECA also found that the French governments were determined to follow their own agenda – completing the Monnet Plan, for instance, and defending Indo-China. They also found that the weak central coalitions could not be pushed too far for fear of letting in the communists or Gaullists. In fact, the ECA released funds regularly in 1948–50 to save French governments from political collapse.[11]

The Monnet Plan was intended to encourage long-term investment in basic industries and essential services – such as agriculture, electricity, coal, gas, railroads, and steel. Light industry and some new industries like cars and electronics were relatively neglected. Similar policies all over Europe at this time laid the base for the prosperity of the 1950s and 1960s. The arguments for modernisation were especially strong in France, which had lagged so far behind Britain and Germany. However, the private capital markets and even the publicly controlled banks were not interested in long-term projects. In Britain the equivalent modernisation was achieved by private firms and nationalised industries, which were often short of raw materials and machinery, but usually had adequate investment funds. In France not even the government, harassed by incessant political pressures and often ill-served by incompetent administration, would have been able to find the required industrial capital without the support of the ECA and the counterpart funds.[12]

The initiative was taken by reformers, led by Jean Monnet, who first convinced the ECA that heavy investment rather than immediate consumption was the best use for US aid. They then persuaded the government to establish a separate Treasury account for modernisation – the Fond de Modernisation et d'Équipement (FME). The government, with ECA support, channelled the counterparts into French heavy industry. The main beneficiaries were the Charbonnages de France, Électricité and Gaz de France, and the SNCF. Large amounts also went into agriculture, oil refineries and steel. After 1951, a far greater proportion was used for rearmament. Bossuat calculates that US aid formed about 15% of French national investment in 1948–51, but a substantial part of this was for reconstruction and housing, which did not use much foreign aid. The counterpart funds, by contrast, provided 52% of the FME budget in 1948–51, 68% in 1948, and 88% in 1949. Overall, Monnet calculated that the counterparts were responsible for a third of the modernisation programme – and for far more than this in the critical years. As a result, one recent commentator records:

> By the end of 1949 France clearly had profited greatly from counterpart funds and the Marshall Plan in general. Spectacular production growth had started, inflation was at least temporarily under control, and the communist left was on the defensive: American aid had helped sustain tottering centrist coalitions and reinforced France's role in the Western anti-communist effort.[13]

Germany had also made a dramatic recovery from the war by 1951, but the accepted effects of American assistance are controversial. Most contemporaries connected the onset of continuous recovery in 1948 with the implementation of the Marshall Plan. However, some, such as Ludwig Erhard, who was head of the Joint Economic Administration of the Bizone in 1948, and German Minister for Economics, 1949–63, criticised the plan and emphasised instead the importance of his currency and economic reforms of 1948. Most debate in the 1960s and 1970s focused on these reforms. More recently, economic historians such as Werner Abelshauser have argued that German recovery was already well under way by late 1948, when the first ERP deliveries arrived, and that the Marshall Plan was not 'the initial spark' for German recovery. Instead, he suggests that West Germany was the 'stepchild' of the Marshall Plan; including GARIOA aid, she only received about $12 per head in 1948, while France received $22, Austria $36, and Holland $45.[14]

Table 10.4 provides the basic statistics. Germany recovered slowly in 1945–7, but industrial output, coal, steel and car production all accelerated from 1948. After the currency reforms in 1948, inflation remained low, except during the Korean War emergency. As Germany recovered, the current account moved rapidly from massive deficit to massive surplus, continuing throughout the 1950s and 1960s. Prior to 1950, however, German imports were covered by large private donations, British and American civilian supplies – principally the GARIOA programme – and the Marshall Plan grants. Before 1950, the largest deficits were with the dollar area, but these rapidly declined as German production increased. By 1952 Germany had once again become the industrial heart of western Europe, earning massive surpluses from sales of machinery and manufactured goods and buying in food and raw materials from her neighbours. The ratios measure the substantial, but rapidly declining, size of American and allied support. The interesting question is the importance of this support in stimulating the recovery.

Table 10.4. *West German Economic Development, 1947–1952*

	1947	1948	1949	1950	1951	1952
Measures and indices						
Industrial output[a]	44	65	88	114	136	145
Unemployment (%)	—	4	8	10	9	8
Inflation[b]	—	90	88	85	100	103
Hard coal (m. tons)	71	87	103	111	119	123
Steel (m. tons)	3	6	9	12	14	16
Cars (000s)	10	30	104	219	277	318
Foreign sector ($m.)						
Current account	−532	−1029	−845	−624	144	557
Private donations	124	126	3	7	11	9
Reparations	−98	−87	−177	0	0	0
Civilian supplies	624	884	536	178	12	0
US grants	17	142	420	303	416	114
Monetary flows	0	−43	182	160	−516	−710
Errors + omissions	−136	17	−25	−34	−66	27
Net G & S with						
Dollar area	—	−1061	−757	−288	−389	−39
Europe (less GB)	—	127	30	−158	581	577
Sterling area	—	−87	−65	−246	−101	−122
Ratios (× 100)						
Aid : imports	80	64	46	19	14	3
Aid : GNP[c]	4	5	4	2	2	0
Aid : investment	—	—	—	9	7	2

[a] 1936 = 100.
[b] 1953 = 100.
[c] GNP, 1949–51, from Helge Berger and Albrecht Ritschl, 'Germany and the political economy of the Marshall Plan', in Barry Eichengreen (ed.), *Europe's Postwar Recovery* (Cambridge University Press: Cambridge, 1995), p. 206. GNP for 1947–8 estimated from Angus Maddison, *Dynamic Forces in Capitalist Development* (Oxford University Press: New York, 1991), pp. 212–13.
Sources: Alan Kramer, *The West German Economy 1945–1955* (Berg: New York, 1991), pp. 164–5; Mitchell, *European Historical Statistics*; IMF, *Payments Yearbooks*, vols 1 and 5.

Abelshauser's thesis, which is now generally accepted, is that, despite the wartime destruction, Germany still had plentiful capital stock and labour in 1946, but was held back by the inter-allied disputes. During 1947 these restraints were removed and in 1948 German output sprang forward. This is consistent with the output statistics in Table 10.4. Abelshauser – somewhat overlooking the importance of the earlier aid – argues that the Marshall Plan deliveries were relatively little and late. Some ECA raw materials, he claims, were of such a low grade that they were sent back. The battle between the army, the State Department and the ECA continued. The State Department still attempted to use German resources for the benefit of the surrounding countries. Abelshauser's views have been contested by Borchardt and Buchheim. They argue that the Marshall Plan supplies and finance removed critical bottlenecks in textiles in 1948–9 and in electricity generation in 1949–51. Without, first, the renewed hope of extra raw cotton supplies in mid-1948, and then the actual deliveries in 1949, the recovery would have ended. Similarly, only effective use of the counterpart funds ensured that sufficient new generating capacity was available during the Korean War boom.[15]

Abelshauser's thesis rests on a distinction between the direct and indirect effects of American policy. He shows that the direct macroeconomic effects of the ERP resources were relatively small, and concludes that the recovery was mostly autonomous. 'The Marshall Plan', he writes, 'did not provide the initial spark for the reconstruction of the West German Economy.' However, he concedes, 'The American policy of stabilisation for Europe ... which had bred the Marshall Plan, stands at the beginning of German reconstruction.' This is a critical point. It is arguable that the ERP deliveries were only one part of a consistent American policy to revive Europe and restore balanced world trade. OMGUS and the British had wanted to include Germany in this recovery since 1946, but were opposed by the State Department and other American policy-makers and the surrounding European countries, who were naturally frightened of reviving 'the German colossus'. Basic German industrial output, aided by British and US supplies, recovered rapidly in 1945–6, therefore, but stalled far below full capacity in late 1946 because of the political uncertainty, critical shortages, currency and transport problems. Steel output even fell below the restrictive allied Levels of Industry allowances.[16]

The Marshall Plan consolidated American policy and solved nearly all these problems during 1947–9. First, in early 1947, the allied govern-- ments really did begin, as Bevin had threatened earlier, to 'organise their zones' for increased production. Extra resources were poured in and incentives applied to widen the critical bottlenecks in food, mining and transport. The Marshall Plan made the Americans the dominant partners in the Bizone and committed them to full recovery. It reconciled the French and other European recipients to the end of reparations and the creation of the Federal Republic. It confirmed the division of Germany and ensured that West German reconstruction meshed closely with general west European recovery. The currency and social market reforms initiated by Erhard in mid-1948 were a product of this certainty.[17]

The currency reform was a straightforward plan, developed in 1946 by American economists, to replace discredited Reichsmarks with new Deutschmarks. It was held on ice until the final division of Germany, because of fear of Russian manipulation of a centrally administered system. The effect of the reform was to unlock hoarded inventories and encourage a massive increase in output. Similarly, American policy transformed Germany's foreign balance from almost complete depend- ence on allied supplies in 1946–7 to a large trade surplus in 1952. The ERP resources and support unleashed the latent German capacity, and the American guarantee reassured Germany's hesitant neighbours. The Korean War demand and rearmament delayed German recovery initially as import prices rose, but then confirmed it as the demand for German machinery and industrial products increased. EPU support during the critical phase of the Korea boom (see below, p. 141) helped to lock Germany into the new western system. Hence, the Marshall Plan established the pattern of intra-European trade that underlay Ger- man export success and western European economic integration in the 1950s and 1960s.[18]

The ECA faced very different problems in Italy. Italy had recovered rapidly in early 1946, with the help of large UNRRA supplies and US loans (see above, pp. 49, 62–3). However, by early 1947 the underly- ing weaknesses in her foreign trade, combined with inadequate domestic supplies, had led to severe inflation and a huge current account deficit. The essential statistics are given in Table 10.5. The deficit was due to the loss of markets in south-eastern Europe, shipping earnings and tourist receipts. US loans and UNRRA aid fell substantially in absolute terms after mid-1946 and even more as a percentage of GNP and imports. Entrepreneurs in foreign trade often retained their dollar-earnings overseas, rather than convert them back into the falling lira. By early 1947 Italy was in a political crisis because of shortages and inflation, and it was clear that a far more severe financial crisis was looming. Much of Italy's foreign reserves were in sterling, which become inconvertible in late 1947. American assistance throughout 1947, the interim aid finance in the winter of 1947/8, and the hope and, finally, the arrival of Marshall Plan resources in mid-1948 assisted Italy over this crisis and indirectly helped to establish the strong centre-right Christian Democrat government.[19]

Table 10.5. *Italian Economic Development, 1946–1951*

	1946	1947	1948	1949	1950	1951
Measures and indices						
Industrial output[a]	71	91	99	109	124	139
Steel (m. tons)	1	2	2	2	2	3
Cars (000s)	11	25	44	65	100	118
Inflation[b]	55	99	104	98	93	106
Unemployment (%)	—	8	9	9	8	9
Foreign sector ($m.)						
Current account	−509	−773	−344	−253	−84	−281
Private gifts	110	65	132	118	111	109
Reparations	—	−4	−28	−8	−37	−63
Add + loans net	666	432	444	341	182	244
Private capital net	−76	184	157	158	−38	174
Monetary flows	−90	84	−358	−387	50	−211
Errors + omissions	−101	14	−3	30	−184	28
Net G & S with						
North America	—	−531	−440	−445	−239	−323
Europe (less GB)	—	—	108	41	58	48
Sterling area	—	—	60	137	128	117
Ratios (× 100)						
Aid + loans : GNP	7	3	3	2	2	1
Aid + loans : imports	72	34	32	26	19	14
Aid + loans : investment	35	13	20	15	10	8

[a] 1937 = 100.

[b] 1953 = 100.

Sources: IMF, *Payments Yearbooks*; Mitchell, *European Historical Statistics*; Vera Zamagni, *The Economic History of Italy, 1860–1990* (Oxford University Press: Oxford, 1993), p. 332.

This government introduced tough conservative monetary and fiscal policies to balance the budget and foreign deficits and to restore Italy's reputation as a sound and respectable country. The majority of Italian academic and intellectual opinion supported orthodox policy. Mussolini's interventionist experiments between the wars had not increased Italian growth. In addition, unlike France, Italy had no foreign policy ambitions other than to win international approval and, therefore, no incentive to develop an equivalent of the Monnet Plan. Hence, Alcide de Gasperi and the Christian Democrats won the critical elections of April 1948, against the strong Italian Communist Party, by promising to provide the Italian upper and middle classes with stability and sound money. The harsh economic budgets that Luigi Einaudi, the Italian Finance Minister, imposed from mid-1947 onwards rapidly curbed inflation and reduced the government and foreign deficits – at the cost, however, of relatively high unemployment (see Table 10.5). Prices actually declined until the rearmament crisis in 1950; the lira stabilised; exports rose far more rapidly than imports, quickly reducing the payments gap and the proportion of imports financed by aid. Marshall Plan supplies were supplemented by private donations, often immigrant remittances, and private capital. Italy had a large but falling deficit with North America, but persistent surpluses with Britain and Europe. The need for Marshall Plan resources was much less than it might have been if Italy had adopted more ambitious policies.

Initially, in 1948, the US government and the ECA were divided between admiration for the stability introduced by the Christian Democrats and concern about the consequent high unemployment. From early 1949 onwards, however, the ECA tried to persuade the Italians to expand investment and output more aggressively, but without success. Instead, the government seemed to ignore Italy's severe social problems and used the counterparts to build up reserves. The ECA was concerned that not only exports, but also unemployed Italian migrants were forced, unnecessarily in their view, on to the European market, annoying Italy's trade partners. If all the OEEC countries had reacted to the dollar gap in this way, the stagnation and social problems of the 1920s and 1930s would soon have returned. The ECA, however, failed to persuade the Italians to develop an investment plan or to expand further. De Gasperi's government knew both its own mind and its electoral possibilities. Fortunately, discontent in southern Italy in 1949–50 and increasing concern among left-wing Christian Democrats led to a more expansionary policy and greater use of ECA resources. Industrial output rose substantially in 1950 and unemployment fell marginally. During the Korean War emergency the government relapsed into fiscal prudence, but from the early 1950s, with stability assured, Italy expanded rapidly. Italy would seem, therefore, to be an example of a country where ECA policies failed to have the intended effects, but it is not clear that de Gasperi or the ECA had much choice. Unlike northern Europe, Italy was too divided geographically and socially to run a balanced, full-employment economy. The ECA could neither easily desert the strong Christian Democratic Party nor lightly risk letting the socialists and communists back into power.[20]

In addition, despite the deflation, Table 10.5 shows that industrial output, steel and car production did grow rapidly in 1946–51. There is also good evidence that the counterparts were used intelligently (the distribution is given in Table 9.4, above). Like France, Italy had a weak capital market. None of the counterparts was used to retire the public debt. Eventually, most were invested in new technologies in engineering, energy, and transport. Large, new strip-steel mills were built, using advanced American machines. These long-term projects did not have much immediate effect on unemployment or southern poverty, but they did create the infrastructure for the remarkable Italian growth in the 1950s and 1960s. Fiat, for instance, relied on the special steel plate for its massive expansion in the 1950s.

The strategic value of the aid was far greater, therefore, than the actual amounts listed in Table 10.5. The ECA also attempted to temper the austerity by encouraging creative spending for industrial reform or in southern agriculture. The wider impact of the ERP, in raising demand generally in Europe and encouraging intra-European trade, assisted Italian exports and gave Italian politicians an important role in supporting European unity. Even deflation had its benefits. After a pause, Italian output did begin to grow rapidly in 1949–50, as entrepreneurs gained confidence in a stable lira, increased their investment and productivity, and squeezed more from their existing workforce and capital resources.[21]

Notes

1. The first division of each table is generally drawn from the relevant sections of Mitchell, *European Historical Statistics*, and the second and third sections from the IMF, *Payments Yearbooks*, usually vol. 1, 1938, 1946, 1947, and vol. 5, 1947–1953. The *IMF Yearbooks* are arranged alphabetically by country. The 1953 *Yearbook*,

which is unpaginated, provides several sets of payments statistics including: (A) In the detailed entry for each country, tables, sometimes in dollars, sometimes in local currency, giving 'Basic Global Data, 1947–52', arranged conventionally in a standard format; (B) 'Summary Balance of Payments Statements'. These provide detailed statements for each country, drawn from the 'Basic Global Data' tables above, but all in dollars, in a compressed standard format. These are intended for international comparison; (C) For most countries, tables giving 'International Transactions, 1946–52', which rearrange the 'Basic Global Data' to highlight the interesting features of each nation's postwar payments position. These tables have been summarised in this text. The final section uses GNP and investment figures from Mitchell, *European Historical Statistics*, and trade and exchange rate figures from the IMF, *Payments Yearbooks*. The introductory sections of successive IMF, *Payments Yearbooks*, discuss the conventions used in presenting international trade and balance of payments accounts.

2. Sir Alec Cairncross, *Years of Recovery: British Economic Policy, 1945–51* (Methuen: London, 1985), and J. Foreman-Peck, 'Trade and the balance of payments', in N. F. R. Crafts and N. W. C. Woodward (eds), *The British Economy since 1945* (Clarendon Press: Oxford, 1991), pp. 141–79, provide overviews of British trade post-1945.

3. N. F. R. Crafts, 'British economic policy and performance, 1945–60', in Eichengreen (ed.), *Europe's Postwar Recovery*, pp. 246–70, argues that ERP funding was too small to have much effect. Sir Richard Clarke is quoted in *idem*, *Anglo-American Collaboration in War and Peace, 1942–1949* (Oxford University Press: Oxford, 1982), pp. 177, 180.

4. Cripps is quoted from Cabinet papers in Cairncross, *Recovery*, pp. 142–3, and Milward, *Reconstruction*, pp. 100–1.

5. Dollar imports as a % of planned British consumption are from Clarke, *Anglo-American Economic Collaboration*, pp. 176–7. Foreman-Peck, in 'Trade and the balance of payments', pp. 171–3, 177–9, argues that North American supplies may have been worth several multiples of their dollar value. See United States, Economic Cooperation Administration, *The Sterling Area: An American Analysis* (ECA: London, 1951), for sterling area trade and investment.

6. See Cairncross, *Recovery*, pp. 212–33, on the rearmament crisis. The general argument that aid eased allocation decisions is in Barry Eichengreen and Marc Uzan, 'The Marshall Plan: economic effects and implications for Eastern Europe and the former USSR', *Economic Policy* 14 (1992), pp. 40–2.

7. Correlli Barnett, *The Lost Victory: British Dreams, British Realities, 1945–1950* (Macmillan, London: 1995); Jim Tomlinson, 'Another Lost Opportunity? Marshall Aid and the British Economy in the 1940s', paper given at conference on the 'Marshall Plan and its Consequences: A 50th Anniversary Conference' at the University of Leeds, May, 1997.

8. Milward, *Reconstruction*, pp. 126–67, and Irwin M. Wall, *The United States and the Making of Postwar France, 1945–1954* (Cambridge University Press: Cambridge, 1991), pp. 63–95, survey French foreign policy.

9. Baum, *The French Economy*, pp. 80–108, analyses French trade.

10. *Ibid.*, pp. 43–79, 111–65, analyses French public finance.

11. Irwin Wall, 'The American Marshall Plan mission in France', in CHEFF, *Le Plan Marshall*, pp. 133–43. Imanuel Wexler, *The Marshall Plan Revisited* (Greenwood: Westport, Conn., 1983), pp. 100–7, describes US policy and French reform.

12. Baum, *French Economy*, pp. 22–8; François Duchêne, *Jean Monnet: The First Statesman of Interdependence* (Norton: New York, 1994), pp. 157–66; Frances M. B. Lynch, 'Resolving the paradox of the Monnet Plan: national and international planning in French reconstruction', *Economic History Review* 37 (1984), pp. 229–43; Milward, *Reconstruction*, pp. 99–100.

13. Gérard Bossuat, *La France, l'aide américaine et la construction européenne, 1944–1954* (2 vols, Ministère des Finances: Paris, 1992), pp. 496–519, provides essential global statistics. For the Marshall Plan and the French aluminium, automobile, coal, electricity, railway and steel industries, see CHEFF, *Le Plan Marshall*, pp. 247–333; see Duchêne, *Monnet*, pp. 166–80, on Monnet's role. Quote is from Chiarella Esposito, 'Influencing aid recipients: Marshall Plan lessons for contemporary aid donors', in Eichengreen (ed.), *Europe's Postwar Recovery*, p. 80.

14. Kramer, *West German Economy*, pp. 148–56, and several essays in Charles S. Maier and Gunter Bischof (eds), *The Marshall Plan and Germany* (Berg: New York and Oxford, 1991), survey the debate.

15. Werner Abelshauser, 'American aid and West German economic recovery: a macroeconomic perspective', in Maier and Bischof (eds), *The Marshall Plan*, pp. 367–409; Knut Borchardt and Christoph Buchheim, 'The Marshall Plan and key economic sectors: a microeconomic perspective', *ibid.*, pp. 410–51; Alan S. Milward, 'The Marshall Plan and German foreign trade', *ibid.*, pp. 452–87.

16. Abelshauser, 'American aid and West German recovery', pp. 405–9 (p. 405).

17. Helge Berger and Albrecht Ritschl, 'Germany and the political economy of the Marshall Plan', in Eichengreen (ed.), *Europe's Postwar Recovery*, pp. 199–245, surveys these points.

18. Charles P. Kindleberger, *Marshall Plan Days* (Allen and Unwin: Boston, 1987), pp. 181–4, treats the currency reform; Milward, 'The Marshall Plan and foreign trade', pp. 452–87, and Peter Temin, 'The "Koreaboom" in West Germany: fact or fiction?', *Economic History Review* 48 (1995), pp. 737–53, survey German trade.

19. John L. Harper, *America and the Reconstruction of Italy, 1945–1948* (Cambridge University Press: New York, 1986), pp. 88–136, and Zamagni, *Economic History of Italy*, pp. 321–36, survey postwar Italy.

20. Italian orthodox policies are described in Marcello de Cecco, 'Italian economic policy in the reconstruction period', in S. J. Woolf (ed.), *The Rebirth of Italy, 1943–50* (Longman: London, 1972), pp. 156–80, and in Harper, *America and the Reconstruction of Italy*, pp. 137–87; Esposito, 'Influencing aid recipients', pp. 81–6, argues that the Italian government consistently deflected ECA plans for faster expansion.

21. For detail, see Ruggero Ranieri, 'The Marshall Plan and the reconstruction of the Italian steel industry, 1947–1954', in CHEFF, *Le Plan Marshall*, pp. 367–85. Zamagni, *Economic History of Italy*, pp. 321–33, makes the general case that the ERP resources were well used (see esp. p. 332). However, her figures for US aid only include UNRRA and ERP funds.

The Marshall Plan
and the Smaller Countries

Many of the smaller countries of Europe had traditionally purchased food and raw materials from North America or eastern Europe and manufactured goods from Britain or Germany. They paid for these by selling specialised goods or services to the major European economies or in international markets. They were hurt badly, therefore, by the tariffs and bilateralism imposed by the larger economies during the depression and, still more, by the war. The great achievement of American policy after the war was, first, to fill the gaps in supply caused by the disappearance of Germany and eastern Europe as sources and markets, and, secondly, to recreate the complex web of trading relationships between the major and minor powers. The administrators of the Marshall Plan were especially adroit at matching their relatively stretched resources to the exact requirements of recipients, with the most useful results.[1]

The degree of dependence on the USA varied according to the local effects of the reconquest of Europe, the temporary disappearance of Germany, the new patterns of European trade and the loss of European empires. Austria's economy, problems and zonal division were somewhat similar to Germany's and made her very dependent on the USA. Belgium and Holland were tied together in the Benelux arrangement from 1944, but whereas Holland had lost both her empire and her main markets, Belgium, a smaller Ruhr in some respects, was well placed to gain from the German collapse. The small Scandinavian countries seemed to be a coherent group, but actually had very different interests; Norway had traditionally relied on her ocean fleet, Denmark on her agricultural exports, and Sweden on her raw materials and industry, each implying a different relationship to the USA. Finally, the smaller Mediterranean nations were all rural and backward, but whereas the eastern Balkan countries, such as Greece, were strategically important and had traditional migrant connections with the USA, Spain and

Portugal were still frozen in fascist autarchy and, therefore, outside the OEEC pale.

The largest amount of aid, in terms of the recipient's national income (see Table 9.1, above), went to Austria. Austria had been closely geared to Germany before the war and had been relatively prosperous. However, she suffered greatly from the disruption of the end of the war and from the division of the country into allied zones. The Americans commented wryly that (as in Germany) the Russians secured the rich (eastern) farmland, the British the cities and industry, and the USA the scenery and the music! Vienna, like Berlin, was also divided into allied zones. It was not clear whether Austria would survive as an independent nation after the war. Her main prewar markets in Germany, Hungary and Italy were either ruined or occupied by Russia. She was desperately short of food, fuel and raw materials and could not manufacture goods for either domestic or export markets. Occupation supplies and UNRRA aid were vital, therefore, from 1945–7. By early 1947 industrial production was still less than 50% of its level in 1938; although Austria had been saved from starvation and the worst of the war damage had been repaired, UNRRA argued that the country was still almost unworkable as an economic entity.[2]

Marshall Aid – 14% of GNP in 1949 – was used to keep Austria going until some of the old links could be restored and to make her more self-sufficient. The aid was used initially to import food – 78% of total imports in 1949 – and then coal and machinery to help restore domestic industry. The counterpart funds helped to finance large investment programmes in electricity, gas, and transport. Austria obviously gained from increased intra-European trade, especially with Germany. Her industrial output recovered quickly, but her economy remained unbalanced until the early 1950s. By the mid-1950s Germany had replaced the USA as her chief trading partner.[3]

Holland also faced a particularly difficult problem of reconstruction in 1945. Before the war, her foreign trade had depended on the export of produce to Germany and Britain and on the triangular trade between the Dutch East Indies, Europe and the United States. The war weakened her European markets and destroyed her colonial power. She attempted to regain the substance of her empire by introducing a liberal constitution and by sending large investments to Indonesia: see Table 11.1. She also embarked upon a substantial investment programme to modernise her industry and agriculture. By 1947, however, her Indonesian policy had led to confrontation with nationalists and a costly war, and in 1949 she was forced to grant formal independence. Both efforts required heavy investment and large government expenditure; taken together, this was sometimes nearly 50% of GNP and led (see Table 11.1) to high taxes, capital levies and huge trade deficits. This inevitably made Holland dependent on the ERP.[4]

Table 11.1. *Dutch Economic Development, 1946–1951*

	1946	*1947*	*1948*	*1949*	*1950*	*1951*
Measures and indices						
Industrial output[a]	77	98	116	129	144	150
Unemployment (%)	—	—	1	1	2	2
Capital formation (%)	—	—	24	23	26	24
Government expenditure: GNP (× 100)	37	36	33	25	26	24
Foreign sector (m. guilders)						
Net G & S	−1312	−1667	−1136	−222	−1066	−90
Private gifts + capital movements	−37	170	127	−41	49	90
Miscellaneous official finance	−47	−242	−91	−206	−327	−174
Finance for empire	−193	−296	−369	−481	−3	−122
Capital levy	306	747	432	205	134	130
Aid and credits	704	701	1072	864	1305	503
Monetary movements	627	587	−35	−87	−77	−187
Errors and omissions	−48	—	—	−32	−15	−150
Net G & S with						
North America	—	−1546	−842	−227	−382	−781
Europe (less GB)	—	—	−282	−7	−348	−505
Sterling area	—	—	55	53	21	1001
Ratios (× 100)						
Aid + loans : imports	33	19	25	18	19	6
Aid + loans : GDP	6	5	7	5	7	2

[a] 1937 = 100.
Sources: IMF, *Payments Yearbooks*; B. R. Mitchell, *European Historical Statistics, 1750–1975* (Macmillan: London, 1980).

Dutch official opinion was that the Marshall Plan came just in time to avoid a disaster. The economy would not have collapsed without the

ERP, but there would have been no increases in consumption for many years. The postwar consensus did accept the need for a long period of restraint to put the economy right, but it is doubtful whether public opinion would have accepted even more privation without radical political change. American assistance was very helpful, therefore, in taking Holland through this difficult period and allowing the recovery to continue. Food comprised about a third of the ERP imports, and machinery about a quarter. The counterpart funds supported heavy investment in agriculture, public services and industry. By the early 1950s this investment was beginning to pay off. The general European revival and removal of trade barriers opened up markets for Dutch produce in Britain and Germany (see Table 11.1), and the trade deficit with America declined.[5]

Belgium, on the other hand, appeared to rely far less on US aid. She recovered very quickly in 1945–6, using her own reserves, private capital and foreign loans to cover her payments deficits (see Table 11.2 and above, p. 49–50). Then, from 1947–9, while Germany was still out of the market, she was able to sell her heavy industrial goods and coal to the surrounding countries. However, as Germany recovered from 1949 onwards, her industrial output stagnated, with relatively high unemployment. Hence, she received little in net US aid and official donations in 1948–51, because her trade was nearly balanced; her European and overseas surpluses nearly covered her dollar deficits. Instead, she received 'conditional aid' – that is, she had to pass on the value of the ECA goods that she received to her trade partners. She did gain from this, of course, both directly, because the goods delivered to her from the ECA might otherwise have been difficult to find, and indirectly, because the credits that she transferred to other countries enabled them to buy her goods and encouraged them to open their markets. Hence, Belgium could have survived the crisis of 1947 without the ERP with no immediate problems. It would eventually have caught up with her, however, as other countries ceased purchasing. Similarly, she gained in 1948–9 as they recovered.[6]

This pattern of deficits and surpluses encouraged Belgium to advocate various intra-European payments schemes. Her problem was that she needed to acquire dollars from her trading partners, not soft currencies like francs or guilders. American policy, however, was to provide ERP recipients with goods and services, which they could control, not dollars. In 1948–9 Belgium and her main trading partners (e.g. Holland) were

Table 11.2. *Belgian Economic Development, 1946–1951*

	1946	1947	1948	1949	1950	1951
Measures and indices						
Industrial output[a]	73	91	100	100	102	115
Unemployment (%)	—	—	4	9	9	8
Inflation[b]	—	—	94	89	93	113
Capital formation (%)	—	—	19	15	17	15
Foreign sector (Belgian frbn.)						
Current account	–16	–16	–6	2	–13	11
Private donations	2	0	1	1	1	1
Aid received	0	0	3	12	9	2
Aid extended	0	0	–3	–11	–9	–1
Private capital	11	13	3	3	–3	–2
Monetary movements	6	2	3	–5	15	–10
Errors + omissions	–2	1	0	0	0	0
Net G & S with						
Dollar area	—	—	—	—	—	–14
EPU area	—	—	—	—	—	20

[a] 1937 = 100.
[b] 1953 = 100.
Sources: Mitchell, *European Historical Statistics*; IMF, *Payments Yearbook*, vol. 5, 1947–53.

able to persuade the USA that some form of dollar-pooling was essential to encourage intra-European trade. The ECA and the OEEC experimented with various payment systems, which led to the European Payments Union, adopted in 1950, and, finally, to full European convertibility in 1958. This complex development is outlined below (pp. 138–41). The practical effect, though, was that it was only through this kind of system that Belgium was able to expand its sales in Europe.[7]

Norway had traditionally relied on her trade with Britain and America and on her commercial fleet, but both had suffered in the depression and the war. However, she did have large claims on the allies – especially Britain – for the use of her ships for wartime freight. In 1945 the Norwegian Labour party was determined to avoid renewed stagnation and to use these claims and her rich natural resources to force through an ambitious, centrally planned programme to rebuild the fleet and to modernise the economy. Table 11.3 shows the very high percentage of GNP being invested in 1946–51 and the consequent current account deficits. During 1946–7 she recovered rapidly, meeting the costs from her reserves (see the large monetary outflow in 1946–7). By mid-1947, however, it was obvious that these would not be enough. Hence, when the British crisis precipitated a run on her reserves, she was forced to seek help. She had originally hoped for political neutrality between Russia and the west, but as the existence of the Cold War became clearer, she gradually opted for the west and joined the OEEC. She hoped initially that American aid would be administered by the UN or a similar neutral organisation, but she soon became an enthusiastic supporter of the ERP and lobbied hard for extra support.[8]

Table 11.3. *Norwegian Economic Development, 1946–1951*

	1946	1947	1948	1949	1950	1951
Measures and indices						
Industrial output[a]	97	115	128	137	150	161
Unemployment (%)	4	3	3	2	3	4
Inflation[b]	—	—	67	68	77	96
Investment:GDP ($\times$ 100)	31	37	37	38	35	35
Foreign sector (m. krone)						
Merchant marine	37	44	65	194	373	1490
Current account net	−926	−1023	−826	−1247	−1254	−1343
Miscellaneous government finance[c]	3	−93	−44	−52	−97	−7
Aid and credits	110	147	435	778	1037	450
Monetary movements	721	782	315	262	8	−312
Errors + omissions	55	143	55	65	−67	−278
Net G & S with						
North America	−350	−668	−482	−546	−403	−663
Europe	—	—	−401	−789	−630	−694
Sterling area	−240	−275	−479	−604	−680	−508
'Unallocated'	3	−214	635	683	926	1938
Ratios ($\times$ 100)						
Aid + loans:GDP	1	1	3	5	6	2
Monetary movements:GDP	7	6	2	2	0	−2

[a] 1937 = 100.
[b] 1953 = 100.
[c] 'Miscellaneous official finance' includes miscellaneous, relatively small payments, such as reparations and subscriptions to international bodies like the IMF.
Sources: IMF, *Payments Yearbooks*; Mitchell, *European Historical Statistics*.

The ERP aid enabled the Norwegian boom to continue after a brief pause in mid-1947. Industry grew rapidly and unemployment remained low (see Table 11.3). By 1950 her shipping earnings had recovered, and by 1955 they were large enough to give her a substantial surplus. Functionally, they offset a consistent goods and services deficit; geographically, the earnings (listed as 'unallocated' in the table) offset deficits with North America, Europe and the sterling area. Norwegian ships did especially well during the Korean War emergency. The Oslo branch of the ECA generally supported the Norwegian growth programme and won over the ECA in Paris and Washington. In 1949, in return, the ECA attempted to persuade the Norwegians to reduce the rate of investment, weaken their controls and admit a European dimension to their plans. To a certain extent, the government agreed to reduce Norway's commitment to socialism in return for continued ECA support. The Korean War pushed Norway further towards the west, but her vital strategic position also obliged the USA to continue to provide aid without too many conditions attached.[9]

Denmark had traditionally relied very heavily on the British market for sales of bacon, butter, eggs, etc. This trade was renewed by bilateral agreement in late 1945, but although Britain took all the Danish output, she only offered low prices – lower than the Germans had done during the war – and irregular supplies of coal and manufactured goods in return. The result was that the Danish farm output grew very slowly until 1948 and she was forced to buy expensive necessities from North America. The ECA helped to balance these purchases and to persuade Britain and Germany to buy Danish provisions on reasonable terms. Improved prices from Britain in 1948 and the German recovery in 1949 had an immediate impact on Danish trade, which expanded rapidly until 1953. Marshall Aid also helped Denmark to embark upon the heavy industrial investment required to supplement this trade, but it took much longer for this to mature and output grew rather slowly in the early 1950s.[10]

Sweden recovered very quickly after the war and required very little aid. This recovery did induce a large payments deficit in 1947, but this was covered by her own resources, and her foreign trade was in surplus after 1949 as her European markets recovered. Sweden was even able almost to balance her US imports with large pulp and timber sales.

The Mediterranean and Balkan periphery was poorer and more severely damaged by the war than the small northern countries. The United States had received millions of immigrants from the area in

1890–1929 and had offered substantial help through UNRRA in 1945–7 (see above, pp. 62–3). However, the Russian rejection of the ERP denied all the Balkans, except Greece, further aid. Before the war Greece had relied on a relatively prosperous foreign trade and shipping industry. She imported essential food and raw materials and exported specialised agricultural exports like tobacco, making up the balance from shipping earnings, emigrant remittances and tourism. She probably suffered more war damage than any other European economy except Russia; her farms, transport infrastructure and shipping were ruined, leaving her very dependent on foreign aid (see Table 11.4). Greece was liberated by Britain in 1944. From 1945–7 she received about $350m. in UNRRA aid, about half of which was food, and the remainder goods like trucks, tractors, fuel, clothing, cotton, etc. Greece received twice as much aid per head of population as any other country. This helped to re-establish her agriculture and rebuilt much of the infrastructure.[11]

Table 11.4. *Greek Economic Development, 1946–1951*

	1946	1947	1948	1949	1950	1951
Measures						
Industry[a]	62	78	85	101	128	148
Inflation[b]	35	42	58	68	71	86
Foreign sector ($m.)						
Current account	−349	−211	−286	−273	−321	−320
Private gifts + capital	28	28	22	26	41	31
Miscellaneous official finance	−6	15	20	4	26	25
UNRRA aid	210	58	8	—	—	—
American aid	—	79	228	253	248	250
Monetary movements	−109	25	−1	3	5	13
Errors + omissions	−2	6	9	−13	2	1
US aid						
As % GNP	—	—	3	11	15	12
As % GFCF	—	—	42	83	76	79
As % balance of payments deficit	—	—	74	100	95	91
As % government deficit[c]	—	100	92	54	92	79

[a] 1937 = 100.
[b] 1953 = 100.
[c] Fiscal years (i.e. 1947 = 1947–8, etc.).
Sources: Mitchell, *European Historical Statistics*; IMF, *Payments Yearbooks*; A. F. Freris, *The Greek Economy in the Twentieth Century* (Croom Helm: London, 1987), pp. 148, 150.

In early 1947, however, many of the essential rail routes were still unusable and the roads were still in a deplorable condition. American analyses described the government as weak, the administration and the middle classes as corrupt, the taxes as uncollectable, and the currency as devalued. Left-wing opposition to the royalist government was leading to open civil war, which Britain was finding too costly to control, precipitating the Truman doctrine and American intervention. The rebellion was finally defeated in 1949, with American economic help and military supplies, but this left a huge developmental problem. Greece was reluctant to join the ERP, because she was already receiving so much aid under other programmes, but the government was eventually persuaded to issue a four-year economic plan for rapid industrialisation to supplement and replace Greece's traditional trade and maritime interests. Under this plan, the ERP provided a very large share of Greek imports, government revenues and investment capital (see Table 11.4) and managed the central banking and currency system. ECA control was inevitably far more direct and visible in Greece, therefore, than it was in Italy or France.[12]

The effect of the American aid was to enable the government to defeat the communists and to restore the essential infrastructure. However, although the 1938 levels of industrial output were reached by 1949, the plan for full-scale industrialisation failed. The intensity of the rebellion and the loss of American support were partly caused by the right-wing Greek government, which would not plan, tax or distribute Marshall Aid fairly and efficiently. The US Porter Mission that investigated Greece in 1947 was shocked by Greek corruption. The American aim had been to re-create a modern industrial state, with a prosperous and stable middle class, but the wealthy elite and a self-interested bourgeoisie weakened these aims.[13]

The aid was reduced in 1949, therefore, when the civil war ended, and again in 1951, when the Korean War began. This ended any hope of being able to continue industrialisation at the same speed, and the remaining US funds were reallocated to defence – since all the surrounding Balkan countries were communist – and to older sectors such as housing and agriculture which could immediately help to raise living standards. The government was also forced to end the complex controls designed to help industrialisation, to devalue the drachma and to introduce a much more conservative economic policy. US development philosophy in the 1950s increasingly stressed the long-run institutional changes required before full-scale industrialisation could begin. Further modernisation in Greece was delayed, therefore, until tourists began to arrive in the late 1950s and Greece joined the EEC in 1962.[14]

Spain under Franco was politically outside the international pale and a model of self-imposed autarchy. She was initially excluded from the UN and the ERP and received no aid except for a loan of $264m. from Argentina, which she used to finance food imports. By about 1950, however, it was becoming increasingly obvious to reformers in Spain that the policy of autarchy was failing as national income fell further behind the rest of western Europe. She received her first small private American loan in 1949, followed by a larger US government loan in 1950. The Cold War increased Spain's strategic value to the USA, and in 1953 she signed a 'bases for aid' defence agreement with the USA. Between 1951 and 1957 the USA sent $625m. in aid, mostly composed of items like raw cotton, olive oil and capital goods.[15]

This aid was part of the mutually reinforcing modernisation which led to the Spanish miracle in the 1960s and 1970s. The strings attached to the aid were, as usual, to set a realistic exchange rate, to stimulate competition and to encourage international trade. Faltering Spanish growth had already persuaded Franco of the need to do something, and he gradually included more reformers and liberal economists in his government. A rapid period of growth in 1951–6 led to crisis in 1957 and further liberalisation. After a pause, Spain joined the World Bank in 1958 and the IMF in 1959. Rapid economic development and political liberalisation continued during the 1960s. As US aid declined, receipts from tourism rose and, by the 1970s, Spain was becoming part of Europe. Portugal, although ruled by the dictator Salazar, had a more open and acceptable economy than Spain. Her large deficits with the USA and Britain in 1946–9 were met from reserves, but in 1950 and 1952 she received substantial ECA/MSA aid. This did not precipitate much development at first, but in the 1960s Spain, like Portugal, benefited from increasing integration with the rest of Europe.[16]

Notes

1. Alan S. Milward, *The Reconstruction of Western Europe, 1945–51* (Methuen: London, 1984), pp. 212–31.
2. UNRRA, Operational Analysis Paper no. 49, *UNRRA in Europe, 1945–1947* (UNRRA: London, 1948), p. 139; Woodbridge, *UNRRA*, pp. 293–320.
3. Milward, *Reconstruction*, pp. 103, 109.

4. Johan De Vries, *The Netherlands Economy in the Twentieth Century* (Van Gorchum: Assen, 1978), pp. 53–5, 63–4, 99–107.

5. Erik Bloemen, 'Technical assistance and productivity in the Netherlands, 1945–1952', in CHEFF, *Le Plan Marshall*, pp. 506–7.

6. Isabelle Cassiers, '"Belgian Miracle" to slow growth', in Barry Eichengreen (ed.), *Europe's Postwar Recovery* (Cambridge University Press: Cambridge, 1995), pp. 271–91; André Mommen, *The Belgian Economy in the Twentieth Century* (Routledge: London, 1994), pp. 75–98.

7. Jef Schram, 'The Netherlands, the Marshall Plan and the European Payments Union, 1947–1950', in CHEFF, *Le Plan Marshall*, pp. 529–48; Imanuel Wexler, *The Marshall Plan Revisited* (Greenwood: Westport, Conn., 1983), pp. 124–7.

8. Helge O. Pharo, 'The Marshall Plan and the modernization of the Norwegian economy', in CHEFF, *Le Plan Marshall*, pp. 591–605.

9. Fritz Hodne, *The Norwegian Economy, 1920–1980* (Croom Helm: London, 1983), pp. 130–79.

10. Hans Christian Johansen, *The Danish Economy in the Twentieth Century* (Croom Helm: London, 1987), pp. 91–103.

11. UNRRA, *UNRRA in Europe, 1945–1947*, pp. 141–4; Freris, *The Greek Economy*, pp. 114–27; Woodbridge, *UNRRA*, pp. 94–137.

12. Wray O. Candilis, *The Economy of Greece: Efforts for Stability and Development* (Praeger: New York, 1968), pp. 1–85.

13. George Stathakis, 'The Marshall Plan in Greece', in CHEFF, *Le Plan Marshall*, pp. 577–89.

14. Candilis, *The Economy of Greece*, pp. 89–100, 124–41; Freris, *The Greek Economy*, pp. 128–54.

15. Joseph Harrison, *The Spanish Economy in the Twentieth Century* (Croom Helm: London, 1985), pp. 120–67.

16. Sima Lieberman, *Growth and Crisis in the Spanish Economy, 1940–93* (Routledge: London, 1995), pp. 17–56.

12

The Marshall Plan
and European Integration

The first steps towards European unity were taken during the operation of the Marshall Plan. It is natural to assume that the inner six – France, Germany, Italy and Benelux – who eventually formed the Common Market in 1956 led the way. However, the USA and the ECA also favoured European integration, and it is interesting to investigate their influence, especially in the early stages. These stages were: the creation of the OEEC in 1948, the establishment of the European Payments Union (EPU) by the OEEC in 1950, the organisation of the European Coal and Steel Community (the ECSC, or Schuman Plan) by the inner six in 1950, and, finally, the signature of the Treaty of Rome by the same inner six in 1957. It is easy to write the history of the origins of the Common Market without reference to the USA; in practice, however, American interest and influence are to be found at all stages.[1]

European unity was first discussed in the USA in September 1942, in a paper by the Council on Foreign Relations entitled 'American Interests in the Economic Unification of Europe with Respect to Trade Barriers'. The USA was still very sensitive about its exclusion from the European trading empires in the 1930s, and the paper concluded:

> The United States would favor economic unification of Europe only if steps are taken to avoid the creation of an autarkic continental economy. Positive American policy should aim at the interpenetration of Europe's economy with that of the rest of the world, as well as lowering economic barriers within Europe. To be successful in this course, the United States must work for the reduction of trade barriers against European goods throughout the world including the United States.

Initially, in 1945–6, the Americans attempted to tackle the universalist aspects of this programme through the UN, IMF, IBRD, UNRRA, etc.; when they realised that European recovery was slower than they had hoped, and when disputes with Russia over Germany increased, they began to search for regional solutions as well. Obviously, a unified Europe was one such solution to these problems.[2]

The first American statements on the Marshall Plan – Clayton's memoranda in early 1947, for instance, and Marshall's speeches – contain simple generalisations in favour of collective European action and European integration. Junior analysts in the State Department were already going much further towards advocating a single market. The famous Cleveland–Moore–Kindleberger memorandum of 12 June 1947, for instance, discussed the costs of the failure to move goods, labour and capital over Europe as a whole because of petty restrictions. Informed political opinion in America knew intuitively how the American market had developed over two centuries of painful constitutional and economic evolution and thought that a similar process should be encouraged in Europe.[3]

American staff papers over the next two years discussed many of the central concepts in European unity. They argued in favour of a continent-wide 'single market', which should be large enough and competitive enough 'to support mass production for mass consumption'. The OEEC would become the legislature of the community, and European equivalents of such American agencies as the Interstate Commerce Commission and the Federal Trade Commission would become the executive. These organisations would harmonise European fiscal and monetary policy and encourage intra-European trade. A European central bank, modelled on the Federal Reserve, would issue a new currency called the ECU. European unity would develop slowly, but the OEEC would gradually create precedents and acquire authority and, ultimately, these would erode national sovereignty. Such a market could compete with the USA, contain Russia, and absorb Germany peacefully.[4]

To envisage the possibilities of unification was relatively easy; to shepherd the Europeans towards actual integration proved far more difficult. Circumstances, however, soon encouraged the idea of a western European bloc. First, Molotov's departure from Paris in July 1947, whether designed by Marshall or not, excluded Russia and eastern Europe from the receipt of Marshall Aid and made western European integration potentially both easier to manage and more important for defence. Then, the need for integration increased in September 1947, when the Europeans in the CEEC produced their 'shopping lists' of requirements for aid, totalling $29bn.; the USA calculated that improved cooperation between them could substantially reduce this amount.[5]

The leading American negotiators at the CEEC, such as Will Clayton and George Kennan, saw Europe in continental terms and tried to encourage the Europeans to act collectively and to reduce their total requirements. These attempts failed and the European request went forward to Washington relatively unintegrated. The Americans then conducted their own detailed investigations and prepared comprehensive legislation over the autumn and winter of 1947–8. The most influential reports envisaged Europe as an integrated unit, and the Americans demanded a 'continuing organisation' – eventually the OEEC – to administer the aid. Unfortunately, the economic crisis in late 1947, as Austria, France and Italy ran out of dollars and civil disorder loomed, forced the US administration to grant interim aid to France, Italy and Greece on an *ad hoc* basis, without integrationist strings attached.[6]

Congress passed the Marshall Plan legislation and created the Economic Cooperation Administration (ECA) to administer the aid in April 1948. The OEEC was created to integrate the national requests in April 1948. During late 1948 the ECA attempted to fashion the OEEC into a supranational agency, with real powers to distribute the aid rationally over the whole Continent. Initially, the USA hoped that the OEEC would be run by a ministerial committee with a powerful director-general who could make quick and authoritative decisions. However, the Europeans refused to nominate an appropriate director and sent only civil servants to the OEEC headquarters in Paris. The USA then attempted to encourage the OEEC to develop a strategy for European recovery and to distribute funds accordingly. Ministers or senior deputies were obliged to attend the committee for the 1948/9 and 1949/50 distributions. However, the political effort of dividing the annual appropriations from Congress proved to be an 'intolerable burden' for the committee, and the last two tranches of aid, in 1950/1 and 1951/2, were distributed by an automatic procedure which related aid to payments deficits. From late 1949, therefore, the OEEC lost its political power and became essentially a research organisation. The name was changed to the OECD in 1961.[7]

The fundamental reason for the failure of the OEEC was the unwillingness of individual European countries to sacrifice their priorities for an ill-defined common interest. The French, for instance, claimed a large share of ERP resources to finance the Monnet Plan. However, the ECA suspected that they needed so much because the French government was afraid of instituting the painful reforms to raise more resources internally. Hence, Averell Harriman, the ECA Special Representative in Europe in 1948–50, commented that France was a sponge 'absorbing these vast resources and giving practically nothing in return to European recovery ... was not this aid that America was giving merely designed to allow French politicians to avoid facing the real issues?' Conversely, the initial OEEC allotment to Germany was so small that the US Army challenged its own government to overthrow the OEEC decision and to provide more. Expansion was needed to reduce German dependence on US and British support, but it obviously had very wide potential effects. An expansionary policy would severely dent French and Belgian exports, but could help Denmark and Holland. The German allocation was increased as a result, but it was never as large per head as it was for most of the other OEEC countries.[8]

Similarly, Italy adopted tough deflationary policies to control inflation and to improve productivity, which it managed to do, but at the cost of exporting underpriced Italian goods and unemployed Italian workers to its neighbours. The ECA also failed to persuade Britain to help France and Norway by buying their wheat and ore instead of relying on her traditional, cheap, empire sources. It soon became evident that the steel production targets of all the major countries were based on national priorities, including defence, not on a European-wide programme with minimum overall costs. Unlike the, generally successful, wartime allocations between the allies, there was less evidence of a technical criterion of efficiency and far less of an imperative to agree. The OEEC negotiations fizzled out in late 1949 with a great deal of mutual recrimination which seemed to retard rather than advance European unity.[9]

As a result, therefore, although Europe recovered rapidly during 1948–9, most nations remained very self-contained – perhaps even more so than in 1947, because of the development of their separate national plans. Britain and France had improved their trade balances, but had done so principally by increasing exports to their old empires overseas. Intra-European trade had grown, but mostly because of increased domestic output. The strict bilateral treaties, which regulated most of the European trade, ensured that minimum requirements were met, but also prevented much further expansion. Hence, Germany was still unable to supply her advanced manufactured goods to her industrial neighbours, or to provide better markets for the raw materials and food of surrounding countries. Belgium could not increase her trade much further. Given the increasing tension with Russia, the whole system was obviously very fragile and far from the universalism advocated at Bretton Woods in 1945.[10]

The failure of the OEEC approach, the general European devaluations against the dollar in September 1949, and the need to prepare a new submission to Congress for spring 1950 forced the ECA to place far more emphasis on the liberalisation of European trade. The result was Paul Hoffmann's famous speech to the OEEC on 31 October 1949, in which he argued that economic integration was essential for European recovery and required:

> the formation of a single large market within which quantitative restrictions on the movement of goods, monetary barriers to the flow of payments, and eventually, all tariffs are permanently swept away. The fact that we have in the United States a single market of 150 million customers has been indispensable to the strength and efficiency of our economy.

The alternative was 'the vicious cycle of economic nationalism ... the cumulative narrowing of markets, the further growth of high cost protected industries, the mushrooming of restrictive practices, and the shrinkage of trade into the primitive pattern of bilateral barter'. Following State Department advice, he omitted references to supranational institutions like a European central bank, which might deter the Europeans. The ECA now hoped that institutional centralisation would develop automatically once intra-European trade had increased. The key institution was to be the European Payments Union, formed in mid-1950, combined with large reductions in restrictions on intra-European trade.[11]

This scheme originated in Belgium's regular trade surplus with her European partners (see above, pp. 126–7). She had been asking, since September 1947, for American assistance for some form of intra-European payments system whereby her debtors could pay her – and continue to buy. Initially, the USA refused to help, so the leading CEEC nations introduced their own scheme in late 1947. The first clearing operation in December 1947 had little effect, because chronic creditors like Belgium and Britain could not, unaided, extend much extra credit to chronic debtors such as Austria, France and Holland. The basic ERP aid went straight to the countries concerned, but did not specifically encourage trade. In early 1948 the Europeans tried to improve their system, and in October 1948 the Americans established a substantial fund to encourage intra-European trade. A proportion of ERP aid, called 'conditional aid', was to be given to creditors in the system as long as they issued equivalent drawing rights to their customers. Hence, in the first year (July 1948– June 1949) Belgium was given $248m. in total aid, but advanced drawing rights of $219m. to her debtors – who then purchased her products. Britain was given $1239m., but advanced $320m. France, on the other hand, received $981m. direct, plus $333m. in drawing rights.[12]

This scheme only encouraged trade between specific pairs of debtors and creditors and, in practice, as the conditional aid was based on forecasts of trade balances, operated randomly. From mid-1949, therefore, the ECA pressed the OEEC to make the drawing rights both multilateral and convertible into dollars. Thus, drawing rights (DRs) advanced by Britain need not be used purely to purchase British goods; Britain would either have to compete for the trade or lose that amount of gold and dollar reserves. Britain and the other creditors were naturally suspicious of this proposal, but in June 1949 they agreed to allow 25% of their drawing rights to become multilateral. The aim of the scheme was gradually to widen European trade and to force the European currencies to become more convertible. The danger was an increased risk of devaluation by former creditors. In fact, Britain, followed by all the European countries, devalued by about 30% against the dollar in September 1949, but this was mostly the result of the American recession of 1949, which reduced British reserves, not of the payments scheme.[13]

The European Payments Union, agreed in 1950, enlarged this scheme. It was initially designed to ease countries towards current-account convertibility, which the USA hoped would be introduced when the Marshall Plan ended in 1952. The ECA and OEEC proposed to increase the 25% DR convertibility to 100%, and thus to make convertible nearly $1bn. of drawing rights on conditional aid. All countries had to agree to reduce trade restrictions, but the EPU, like the IMF, also planned to give debtors sufficient credits to avoid jarring adjustments. Creditors' interests were protected by a $350m. credit from the USA to the union which meant that they did not have to press for immediate payment. The effect was to move Europe nearer to multilateralism and convertibility. Britain responded to the proposal cautiously, fearing that possible runs on sterling might damage her external trade. But she agreed to join in 1950, when her current account moved massively into the black, and she rapidly accumulated gold and dollar reserves (see pp. 106–7). Critics in the USA accused the ECA of creating a soft currency bloc in Europe which would be outside the IMF and would discriminate against the

USA. Nevertheless, the general US policy of aiding European integration overcame these doubts, and the establishment of the EPU was signed in September 1950, with a two-year term.[14]

The EPU was very successful and intra-European trade expanded extremely rapidly (see Table 12.1); by 1951 the volume of trade was far above the levels for 1938 both for western Europe as a whole and for western Europe without Germany. The timing suggests that it was the EPU and the accompanying trade liberalisation that made the difference. From 1938–48 intra-European trade had fallen by 31%. The major element in the initial postwar recovery had been the growth of the British and French empire and oceanic trades, but from 1948 intra-European trade grew much more quickly than extra-European trades. This trend continued, despite some serious relapses (for instance, in 1951–3), in the 1950s and 1960s, with dramatic political consequences. Britain and France had attempted to re-create their old Third World trading dependencies immediately after the war. By 1955 it was obvious that this was failing. The real growth of trade was within Europe. France, forced to choose between France *outre-mer* and France in Europe, settled for Europe in 1957. Britain, with a larger and older commitment to the extra-European world, was peripheralised in Europe; ultimately, when the relative weakness of her old extra-European trades had been truly revealed, she had to sue for entry into the Common Market in 1962 and 1972.[15]

Table 12.1. *Intra-European Exports, 1938–1951 (% change)*

% change in exports	European countries, including Germany		European countries, excluding Germany	
	1938–48 (1)	1948–51 (2)	1938–48 (3)	1948–51 (4)
Commodity group				
Raw materials	−50	53	−52	56
Food, drink, tobacco	−36	138	−36	131
Machinery, chemicals	−13	94	66	38
Other capital goods	−9	87	33	42
Consumer goods	−38	102	−18	88
TOTAL (including unspecified)	−31	89	−15	67

Source: United Nations, *Economic Survey of Europe since the War* (Economic Commission for Europe: Geneva, 1953), p. 122.

The growth of the intra-European trade in effect locked Germany and France and the smaller European nations into the postwar settlement. The post-1945 years were so much more peaceful and productive than the post-1919 years because both capital and labour made major compromises – the first to invest heavily in new plant and machinery, the second to moderate wage claims for long enough for the heavy investments to produce real economic and social dividends. (An outline of the 'politics of productivity' is given in Chapter 14, below.) Obviously, both the ERP itself and the EPU were vital ingredients in this settlement. As far as the intra-European trade is concerned, once the leading European countries had committed themselves – by making the appropriate liberalisation concessions (reducing tariffs, quotas, etc.) and investing heavily in the appropriate commercial organisation and industrial infrastructure – then there was no turning back without very heavy costs and the breakdown of the social bargain between capital and labour. Moreover, the continued growth of the intra-European trade promised further large increases in profits and wages.[16]

Germany in particular gained from the operation of the EPU. She had traditionally provided Europe with machinery, chemicals, transport and other capital goods (see Table 12.1). These exports collapsed after the war, and Europe had to rely on American and British capital goods for reconstruction. Imports of these goods rose more than any other item after 1938, causing the huge transatlantic payments deficits and the rapid British recovery. The EPU encouraged this trade in general, and the displacement of these imports in particular, by giving credits to the deficit economies in Europe to enable them to continue importing long after they would normally have had to stop. Germany herself was the first to gain from this when, in 1950, her rapid expansion was threatened by the Korean emergency. Food and raw material prices rose sharply and put her into a heavy payments deficit. The EPU mechanism covered the deficit until the consequent demand for capital equipment carried Germany into surplus again. After 1952, German surpluses increased steadily as the surrounding countries purchased her heavy equipment. This time the EPU credits helped to carry the smaller countries – and the German exporters – through until equilibrium returned. These EPU operations in the early 1950s helped to confirm West Germany's west European orientation and to cement her into the postwar settlement.[17]

France also was guided by the EPU mechanism towards European integration. Initially, the French questioned the value of the intra-European trade and feared that trade liberalisation would expose them to German competition. Some ministries argued that it would be better to rely on trade with the French colonies and eastern Europe. However, the EPU carried France, like Germany, through the Korean War emergency and covered heavy French deficits in 1951–4. During this period France discovered that, although her imports from Germany rose by leaps and bounds, so also did her exports to Germany of food and raw materials. Meanwhile, the weakness and costs of her overseas territories were exposed. The great French fort at Dien Bien Phu in Vietnam was lost in 1954. In addition, by 1954 Britain was moving towards – and, in fact, had nearly adopted – convertibility, and the OEEC was extending its liberalisation to include the dollar area. Both these events potentially exposed the French export trade to increased British, German and North American competition. By 1955 the OEEC was pressing France to open its domestic market. In 1955 France had an unexpectedly large surplus in the EPU, but in 1956 she was once again in heavy deficit. The logic of further defensive integration with Germany was obvious.[18]

The United States also encouraged and supported formal European moves towards regional integration. In 1947 a natural reaction to the war, the critical economic situation, and pressure from the USA had persuaded many Europeans to consider the possible solutions that lay in integration. The subregional Benelux Union had been progressing slowly since 1944. At the CEEC conference in August 1947 the Italians suggested a European union, and the CEEC set up a European Union Study Group. In 1949–50 the recovery, the continued pressure from the USA, the break with Russia, and the success of the EPU all increased the number of suggestions coming forward. In January 1949 France and Italy signed a customs-union treaty, but it came to nothing. In late 1949 France, Italy and the Benelux countries again considered a limited customs union, but they could not agree on whether to include Germany. Simultaneously, several European statesmen, such as Dirk Stikker, Chairman and 'Political Conciliator' of the OEEC in 1950, Giuseppe Pella and Maurice Petsche, produced various integration plans.[19]

The decisive proposal was the French Schuman Plan of 1950 to establish the European Coal and Steel Community as an explicit fore-runner to a wider common market. France had wanted to match Germany's dominance in heavy industry by neutralising the Ruhr in some way ever since the 1920s. After the war the Monnet Plan had built up French heavy industry, but the French were frustrated in their hopes to control the Ruhr. At the CEEC conference they had persuaded the Americans to create an International Authority for the Ruhr, but when the British and Americans decided to encourage German recovery, this proved toothless. When German recovery became obvious in late 1949 and Britain continued to limit its involvement in Europe, France changed tack. The Schuman Plan proposed to pool the French and German markets for coal and steel in friendly cooperation under an international high authority. Many commentators see the plan as a daring French solution to the age-old European problem of Franco-German rivalry and a courageous assertion of French independence.[20]

However, plans to link the French and German coal and steel industries had been around since the 1920s. What was surprising was the French decision – so soon after the war – to combine with Germany and to exclude Britain. This was only possible because the American guarantee to western Europe in NATO, signed in April 1949, not only contained Russia, but also controlled Germany. In effect, NATO gave France a strong American military guarantee in place of a weak and hesitant British one. 'We waited on you for a decision when Hitler entered the Rhineland in 1936', Monnet told Cripps, 'and the results were disastrous. We shall not make that mistake again.' NATO enabled France to transfer allegiance from Britain to Germany with less real risk. The plan was still a bold leap in the dark. Germany was bound to recover. The French could only hope that the Germans would become good Europeans. Ernest Bevin, who had initiated NATO, was at first furious at the unforeseen consequences. Dean Acheson initially denounced the plan as 'the damndest cartel', but the Americans also wanted European unity, and Acheson wrote later: 'The more we studied the plan, the more we were impressed.' In addition, the plan itself, although named after Robert Schuman, the French Foreign Minister who took political charge of it, was in fact the brainchild of Jean Monnet, who had spent many years in the United States and had absorbed federal ideas. The plan was essentially a daring federal experiment. Furthermore, the State Department continuously monitored the negotiations. American officials commented that: 'Although the articles as finally agreed ... are all somewhat more qualified than American officials in touch with the negotiations would have wished, they are almost revolutionary in terms of the traditional European approach to these basic industries.'[21]

The Schuman Plan did not become reality without considerable

American help. The French and German invitation to the other Europeans to join the ECSC was accepted by Benelux and Italy, but not by Britain. This was the first time that the 'Europe of the six' acted collectively. The minimum French requirement was that Germany join the international organisation and end its own traditional steel and coal cartels. The Germans wanted to reduce the burden of occupation controls with as little change in industrial structure as possible; their hand was progressively strengthened after the outbreak of the Korean War in June 1950, when their industry became vital to American defence plans. The American High Commissioner in Germany, John McCloy, worked very hard over the winter of 1950/1 to make sure that the French conditions were met and that a truly international industrial organisation emerged; the ECSC contained Europe's first strong anti-trust law, later to be copied in the Treaty of Rome. Thus, the ECSC was initiated by the French and met French purposes, but it concealed strong American influence both in its concepts and their execution.[22]

The Americans continued to support European integration until the Treaty of Rome was signed by the six in 1957. The High Authority of the ECSC was treated as a sovereign state by the USA; ambassadors were exchanged and a substantial loan was granted to the ECSC under the Mutual Defence Act. The USA smoothed the way for the ECSC at GATT. The USA also encouraged other European developments after 1950 – it supported the first stages of the Common Agricultural Policy, for instance, because of its wider interest in European union, even though it feared, as with the ECSC, the long-run effects of regional protectionism. The USA therefore had a substantial influence on European integration. The effects of the war, the international trade situation, and the break with Russia gave it an obvious interest. It helped to establish the arena – a divided western Europe – and to create the conditions – a flourishing intra-European trade – in which integration was possible. Even some of the ideas and instruments behind European integration reveal American ideology and influence. The US federal experience proved a prescient predictor of the long-run future of Europe and, therefore, gave weight to its short-run policies.[23]

Notes

1. For views on US policy and European unity, see Michael J. Hogan, *The Marshall Plan: America, Britain, and the Reconstruction of Western Europe, 1947–1952* (Cambridge University Press: Cambridge, 1987), pp. 427–45; Alan S. Milward, *The Reconstruction of Western Europe, 1945–51* (Methuen: London, 1984), pp. 466–77;

Imanuel Wexler, *The Marshall Plan Revisited* (Greenwood: Westport, Conn., 1983), pp. 205–48; Max Beloff, *The United States and the Unity of Europe* (Brookings Institution: Washington, DC, 1963), *passim*.

2. Beloff, *Unity of Europe*, p. 2.
3. For instance, see Clayton's memorandum of 27 May 1947, point 9, in Frederick J. Dobney (ed.), *Selected Papers of Will Clayton* (Johns Hopkins Press: Baltimore, 1971), p. 203; Charles P. Kindleberger, *Marshall Plan Days* (Allen and Unwin: Boston, 1987), pp. 1–24; Hogan, *Marshall Plan*, pp. 35–53.
4. Beloff, *Unity of Europe*, pp. 29–48; Milward, *Reconstruction*, pp. 232–98.
5. Alex Danchev, *Oliver Franks: Founding Father* (Clarendon Press: Oxford, 1993), pp. 57–83, and Milward, *Reconstruction*, pp. 56–89, discuss the CEEC meetings.
6. Dobney (ed.), *Clayton*, pp. 219–22; Wilson D. Miscamble, CSC, *George F. Kennan and the Making of American Foreign Policy, 1947–1950* (Princeton University Press: Princeton, 1992), pp. 61–5.
7. Milward, *Reconstruction*, pp. 168–211.
8. See Hogan, *Marshall Plan*, pp. 161–74; Milward, *Reconstruction*, pp. 180–211 (Harriman is quoted on p. 189).
9. On European steel and colonies, see United States, Senate, 81st Congress, 2nd Session, Document no. 142, 'An Analysis of the ECA Program' (United States Government Printing Office: Washington, 1950), pp. 1–8. On the failure of the OEEC, see Wexler, *Marshall Plan Revisited*, pp. 205–23.
10. Barry Eichengreen, *Reconstructing Europe's Trade and Payments: The European Payments Union* (Manchester University Press: Manchester, 1993), pp. 10–27; Milward, *Reconstruction*, pp. 212–31, 282–3; UN, *Economic Survey of Europe in 1948* (Economic Commission for Europe: Geneva, 1949), pp. 134–64.
11. Paul Hoffmann is quoted in Hogan, *Marshall Plan*, p. 274, and Beloff, *Unity of Europe*, p. 44.
12. Eichengreen, *Trade and Payments*, pp. 10–27, and Jef Schram, 'The Netherlands, the Marshall Plan and the European Payments Union, 1947–1950', in CHEFF, *Le Plan Marshall*, pp. 529–48, discuss the origins of the EPU; Wexler, *Marshall Plan Revisited*, p. 139, provides figures of conditional aid.
13. Wexler, *Marshall Plan Revisited*, pp. 135–53.
14. *Ibid.*, pp. 155–75, describes the origins of the EPU.
15. UN, *Economic Survey of Europe since the War* (Economic Commission for Europe: Geneva, 1953), pp. 121–4, analyses rapid growth of the intra-European trade; Milward, *Reconstruction*, pp. 335–61, describes the differential growth of intra- and extra-European trade.
16. Eichengreen, *Trade and Payments*, pp. 81–97, 121–6.
17. Alan S. Milward, 'The Marshall Plan and Europe's foreign trade', in CHEFF, *Le Plan Marshall*, pp. 641–50; Peter Temin, 'The "Koreaboom" in West Germany: fact or fiction?', *Economic History Review* 48 (1995), pp. 735–53.
18. Frances Lynch, 'France and the European Payments Union', in CHEFF, *Le Plan Marshall*, pp. 237–43.
19. Milward, *Reconstruction*, pp. 233–55, 421–61.
20. *Ibid.*, pp. 362–420.
21. Acheson is quoted in Wexler, *Marshall Plan Revisited*, p. 239. Acheson was naturally more restrained in his autobiography: see Dean Acheson, *Present at the Creation: My Years in the State Department* (Norton: New York, 1969), pp. 498–507; François

Duchêne, *Jean Monnet* (Norton: New York, 1994), pp. 181–225. The State Department official, Miriam Camps, is quoted in Duchêne, *Monnet*, p. 215.

22. Volker Berghahn, *The Americanization of West German Industry, 1945–1973* (Berg: Leamington Spa, 1986), pp. 111–54; for another view, see John Gillingham, 'The European Coal and Steel Community: an object lesson?', in Barry Eichengreen (ed.), *Europe's Postwar Recovery* (Cambridge University Press: Cambridge, 1995), pp. 151–68.

23. Frederico Romero, 'Independence and integration in American eyes – from the Marshall Plan to currency convertibility', in Alan S. Milward, *The Frontier of National Sovereignty: History and Theory, 1945–92* (Routledge: London, 1993), pp. 155–81.

13

The United States, Britain and European Unity

American strategies at Bretton Woods and in the Marshall Plan gradually forced Britain to choose between her traditional relationships with North America, the Commonwealth and western Europe. At first, in 1945–6, she sought to use American help to re-create her old trading patterns as rapidly as possible. Then the crisis of mid-1947 forced a new appraisal. The USA, via the Marshall Plan, hoped that Britain and France would help to lead the OEEC and respond to America's offer of friendly assistance. British attitudes evolved from a desire to lead and a willingness to cooperate in late 1947 and early 1948, when the need for dollars was greatest, to a tougher attitude in late 1948 and early 1949, when the full implications of American plans became clearer. By 1950 Britain had decided to cooperate fully both in a North Atlantic union for defence and with Europe, North America and the Commonwealth for trade, but not to join a narrower European combination, which threatened her traditional interests. In the 1950s, therefore, Britain emphasised her role outside Europe and her 'special relationship' with the USA as a partial alternative to integration in Europe.[1]

The last years of the war naturally focused Britain's attention on Europe and established her occupation commitments in Germany. The collapse of Germany produced good markets for British manufactured goods on the Continent, and she purchased as much cheap grain and timber as possible from eastern Europe. However, her major postwar expansion in exports was in her traditional oceanic trades; the European proportion did not increase at all, and her imports were even more concentrated on North America than they had been before the war. Britain's problem was to continue the expansion in trade, maintain domestic investment and full employment, and meet the Labour government's social commitments, all on tiny reserves of gold and dollars. She pressed the USA to make resources available around the world so that her traditional customers had the credit to buy British goods. Her financial situation was too weak to extend the credit herself. In the event, the US loan provided the necessary credit direct to Britain, and British trade expanded rapidly from 1945 until the crisis of mid-1947.[2]

The British government did consider the establishment of closer ties with Europe in the summer of 1945, in case the US loan failed. An alternative to the American loan (Plan 1) and Keynes's 'Austerity' was worked out by senior civil servants. This was 'Plan 2', reported here in Sir Richard (Otto) Clarke's edited papers:

> the essence of which was to create as big a multilateral group as we could (sterling area, French, Belgian, and Dutch areas, Scandinavians etc.), to trade freely between themselves – about 75% of pre-war world trade – and to pool and allocate their dollars. The group could have associates: Canada might be prepared to be paid 50% in sterling and 50% in dollars if they could see a multilateral group taking shape, and with no alternative markets anyway: it could borrow from the USA ...

This might have been similar to the trade and payments arrangements set up by the OEEC in 1948–9, but would have included the European empires and discriminated against the USA. There was a good chance that the other countries would have accepted British leadership, but in 1946 Keynes and the government decided to opt for the American connection.[3]

British trade expanded very rapidly until the crisis of mid-1947. As the crisis loomed, the government considered alternative strategies, but they did not expect to receive much help from Europe. The major emphasis in early 1947, as economists watched the loan melt away ever faster, was to cut back imports, to expand domestic output of coal and food, and to attempt to increase exports. The crisis was seen as far more than a domestic financial crisis, which Britain could solve unilaterally by repudiation of the loan agreement. Officials feared that the dollar shortage would dry up economic activity all over the non-dollar world and would cause a permanent reduction in British living standards.[4]

By July 1947 Marshall's speech had raised hopes in Britain, but officials argued that the most useful US aid would be assistance in the area from Suez to Singapore and in the Far East, which would enable Britain to earn dollars. However substantial the dollar flow to western Europe, it would be a long time before the European countries would pay gold or dollars for British exports or would supply Britain's basic imports. If no aid was forthcoming, Britain would have rapidly to strengthen her bilateral treaties, especially with strong countries with complementary trading interests like Canada, Australia, New Zealand, Eire and Denmark. Britain ended dollar convertibility in August 1947, and henceforth ran the sterling area as a sealed system in which dollar earnings, purchases and balances were very carefully controlled.[5]

The American insistence on giving aid to Europe as a whole and on cooperation between the European countries seemed to require a new British policy. Nevertheless, as the paramount need was to earn dollars, the British were initially prepared – within limits – to lead and to cooperate in Europe. Hence, Bevin and Bidault brought the European nations together and organised the CEEC conference; when the OEEC was formed in early 1948, however, they were careful to limit its potential power and activities. There were significant differences in attitude between the Foreign Office and the various economic ministries in Britain. The Board of Trade and the Treasury thought that the OEEC should work with European countries on a commodity by commodity basis, in low-key pragmatic cooperation, to purchase dollar supplies in the cheapest possible way. A commodity approach would also allow consideration of Commonwealth interests. However, they recognised that, in principle, even this could lead to 'very far reaching pooling of financial resources. Such a pooling would be equivalent to complete economic union. It would obviously be quite impossible to embark upon this without far reaching measures of political and military union as well.' In practice, they were reluctant to sacrifice British or Commonwealth interests. Thus, Britain continued to buy cheap Canadian wheat and ore rather than French wheat and Norwegian ore, despite the French and Norwegian national plans.[6]

The Foreign Office, meanwhile, led by Ernest Bevin, had been exploring the idea of a much more adventurous policy to preserve an important world role for Britain by integrating the sterling area with Europe. This would create a supranational European *system*, led by Britain and including all the OEEC countries and their empires, which could both contain Germany and stand between Russia and America. Cautious trading and currency agreements would be too weak to have the desired effect. In March 1948 what was called the 'London Committee' of senior British officials reached a compromise between the Treasury and the Foreign Office views. The aims and outcome of policy should be a permanent European organisation with real interventionist and countervailing powers; the steps towards it should be gradual and pragmatic. The committee recognised that this would be a risky endeavour for Britain, potentially involving some loss of sovereignty, danger to sterling, major structural changes, and friction with the Commonwealth, but equivalent dangers threatened anyway. The alternative policy was to sink back as a permanent pensioner and satellite of the USA, which would end Britain's world role. This was the nearest that Britain came to Europe before 1962.[7]

By mid-1948 it was becoming clearer that the Americans wanted a strong federal Europe, with a large open market regulated by strong supranational institutions. Simultaneously, relations with Russia had worsened, the Berlin airlift had begun, and several European nations had revealed their chronic political instability. The American enthusiasm and the rush of events pulled the continental Europeans closer together as they looked for strong allies and a stable continental structure. Hence, a powerful European movement began in early 1948, with appeals for a European government and assembly etc. The British, however, having encouraged the idea at first, were now repelled by the instability on the Continent and preferred to pursue their traditional connections with North America and the Commonwealth.[8]

British ministers recognised that substantial support for Europe was vital because of the Russian threat, and in January 1948 Ernest Bevin initiated the negotiations that were to lead to the formation of NATO a year later. But they thought that the American plans and the enthusiasm of the European movement for an integrated Europe were going too far. Contemporary government papers stressed that the movement towards European federation was gathering so much strength that ministers' hands might be forced. Hence, Otto Clarke wrote in September 1949:

> Before very long Ministers will have to take a decision which if favourable to Federation will be substantially committing. We cannot continue for long without a European policy ... At one time, I thought this decision could be postponed for a long period, and that we could proceed pragmatically; an Open Conspiracy of bureaucrats and business men would link the affairs of the Western European countries closer and closer together [until we] had the substance of Western European Government without its form. But little progress has been made so far ... I am now inclined to think the political steps have to be taken first ...[9]

Clarke continued: 'The idea of a Western European Federation derives from the search for a "Third Force" to stand between the USA and Russia ... A Federation ... could be decisive in stopping war, by establishing with the USA a decisive preponderance of power.' It might be necessary, he argued, for Britain to sacrifice her independence to a federation to secure this peace. There were great constitutional and political problems in forming a western European federation. Britain, he concluded, must sacrifice her independence 'in the most effective way. We have seen the difficulties of European Federation ... more certain and favourable results to this country would be secured by Union between the USA and the British Commonwealth ... this is a much less fantastic notion than the Western European Federation.' Clarke's views were representative of government thinking; the North Atlantic Treaty went forward, but western European union did not.[10]

The reluctance to enhance British exposure to some form of European unity was increased by adverse balance of payments movements in 1949–50, which deteriorated into a sterling crisis in September 1949 and were followed by a 30% devaluation of the pound from $4.03 to $2.80. The crisis was caused partly by rapid internal British growth and overheating, and partly by the American recession of 1949, which cut British and Commonwealth exports to the USA drastically. Meanwhile, the reciprocal and overseas trade of the European countries continued, growing rapidly throughout the recession and revealing the potential benefits of further European integration. The dependence of the British economy on demand from the Third World and the USA was also demonstrated in the dramatic recovery of British exports in early 1950, which was caused partly by the devaluation itself, partly by the US recovery. Heavy expenditures in rearmament pulled the USA out of recession in early 1950 and required increasing volumes of Commonwealth goods, such as rubber and tin, which in turn increased British exports to the Far East.[11]

The initial British response to the payments crisis was to resist devaluation and to cut dollar imports by 25%. Britain also persuaded other OEEC countries to replace purchases from North America with goods from the sterling area. This sort of discrimination would have been totally unacceptable under the Bretton Woods system, of course, but the Americans were not able to complain, because they were still running a very large payments surplus and dollars were scarce. Nevertheless, as usual, they urged the Europeans to reduce internal restrictions and to achieve balance by improving productivity, integrating their markets and, possibly, devaluing. They pushed hard against persistent British and European opposition to improve the European payments mechanism and to create a freer internal market. This produced the second currency agreement in June 1949. Britain, of course, was afraid that the right of the European countries to convert weak currencies like the franc into sterling and sterling into dollars would threaten her reserves and, therefore, her markets in the sterling area.[12]

By July 1949 the recession and the sterling crisis had convinced Britain of the dangers of too close a link with Europe. Instead, she proposed a 'constructive compromise' with the USA, according to which, implicitly, the USA would support Britain and the sterling area at critical times, and Britain would assist the USA by maintaining stability in the old imperial areas, where she still had valuable influence. The communist conquest of China in 1949 underlined the potential value of British support east of Suez. These ideas were developed in trilateral talks between Britain, the USA and Canada in London in July 1949 and in Washington in September, and established the idea of a special relationship between Britain and the USA, from which the Europeans were excluded. As part of the deal, the British devalued the pound and the Americans agreed both to open up the US market and to increase expenditure in the Third World to generate British exports.[13]

The corollary of British exceptionalism was the American hope that they could now push harder for European unity without British opposition. Hence, Hoffmann's speech of 31 October 1949, quoted above, voiced even more explicit aims. The Americans were horrified in late 1949, therefore, when Britain opposed the strengthening of the OEEC, the extension of the European payments mechanism, and the development of tighter continental groupings. British policy, as Cripps explained in a speech to the OEEC on 1 November, was to sustain 'the largest multilateral trading area in the world, for which [she was] banker'. She was at the conjunction of three trading circuits – the Atlantic economy, Europe and the Commonwealth – and was anxious to expand trade and unity in each, but not at the expense of one another. The essential factor was the type of organisation in each; she could go so far with enthusiasm, but not beyond a certain critical point. However, the Americans were now faced with French fears of a rapidly recovering Germany. Everyone, except perhaps the French, agreed that this recovery was vital for European revival and defence; the problem was one of containment.

The NATO agreements, which Britain supported, integrated Germany into western European defence, but the Americans and the other Europeans had also hoped, with British help, to balance Germany economically.[14]

British opposition was critical in delaying or weakening the first US and European proposals for unification. The most important debate was on the European Payments Union (see above, pp. 138–42). Britain had opposed any serious extension of currency convertibility in Europe, although she supported trade liberalisation. The Washington agreements persuaded her to go rather further – and Cripps's speech broadly supported Hoffmann's proposals – but she delayed her approval throughout early 1950. Britain finally agreed to the EPU because of American pressure and promises, European threats to proceed without her, and because her payments situation had improved dramatically since mid-1949. She also ignored the first European attempts to forge customs unions – the Finebel, Pella, Petsche and Stikker Plans – thus contributing to their failure. The Finebel Plan, for instance, aimed to unite the Benelux countries, France and Italy in a customs union, but only British membership could have reconciled France to German participation, a *sine qua non* for Holland.[15]

In the end, France had to act alone. The creation of the Federal Republic and the process of rearmament had accelerated German recovery and by 1950 the allies were having to bid for German support. The Schuman Plan was a last chance for France and it only succeeded because of heavy American diplomatic pressure. Britain rejected the plan because of its supranational implications for the defence industry and because it seemed to endanger socialist planning for growth and full employment. 'It's no good. We can't do it, the Durham miners won't wear it', commented Herbert Morrison, the Deputy Prime Minister. The French rejected British pleas for entry in a 'special capacity'. Hence, while the six came together for the first time, Britain banked on the Commonwealth and the Atlantic economy, both attractive assets at the time, but possibly less effective in the long run. Quite unexpectedly, it was the intra-European trade, even though between broadly similar countries, that flourished most in the 1950s and 1960s, while Britain's traditional and more complementary Third World trade declined in relative terms, or was eaten into by the recovery of Japan. Similarly, even though the American market grew massively post-1950, Britain had no exclusive hold on it, and the traditional raw material and food

imports from North America were gradually devalued by technical change.[16]

Notes

1. Alan P. Dobson, *The Politics of the Anglo-American Special Relationship, 1940–1987* (Wheatsheaf: Sussex, 1988), pp. 98–138; Henry Pelling, *Britain and the Marshall Plan* (Macmillan: Basingstoke, 1988), *passim*.
2. C. S. S. Newton, 'The sterling crisis of 1947 and the British response to the Marshall Plan', *Economic History Review* 37 (1984), pp. 391–408.
3. Sir Richard Clarke, *Anglo-American Collaboration in War and Peace, 1942–1949* (Oxford University Press: Oxford, 1982), pp. 57–9, 126–36.
4. *Ibid.*, pp. 156–74 (see p. 172 for Clarke's opinion that US aid to Europe would not help Britain).
5. *Ibid.*, pp. 175–80.
6. *Ibid.*, pp. 191–4.
7. *Ibid.*, pp. 194–201; Michael J. Hogan, *The Marshall Plan: America, Britain and the Reconstruction of Western Europe, 1947–52* (Cambridge University Press: Cambridge, 1987), pp. 109–19.
8. Hogan, *Marshall Plan*, pp. 135–6, 174–88; Alan S. Milward, *The Reconstruction of Western Europe, 1945–51* (Metheun: London, 1984), pp. 233–55.
9. Clarke, *Collaboration*, pp. 201–2.
10. *Ibid.*, pp. 202–8. For Bevin and NATO, see Alex Danchev, *Oliver Franks* (Clarendon Press: Oxford, 1993), pp. 84–108, and Wilson D. Miscamble, CSC, *George F. Kennan* (Princeton University Press: Princeton, New Jersey, 1992), pp. 113–40.
11. Milward, *Reconstruction*, pp. 335–61.
12. Sir Alec Cairncross, *Years of Recovery: British Economic Policy, 1945–51* (Metheun: London, 1985), pp. 165–211; Milward, *Reconstruction*, pp. 299–334.
13. Hogan, *Marshall Plan*, pp. 238–68.
14. *Ibid.*, pp. 268–92.
15. *Ibid.*, pp. 293–335.
16. *Ibid.*, pp. 364–79; Milward, *Reconstruction*, pp. 335–61, 362–420; Alan S. Milward, *The European Rescue of the Nation State* (Routledge: London, 1992), pp. 396–433.

The Marshall Plan and European Society, 1945–1960

There have been great changes in methods of production, social structure and public attitudes in America and Europe since 1945. These were driven by rapid technical change and produced new styles of consumption, organisation and government on both sides of the Atlantic. Society in 1990 would hardly have been recognisable to citizens of 1945. However, although developments in each region have, to a certain extent, been autonomous, there have also been massive flows of information, capital and personnel across the Atlantic which have produced convergence. Most of these flows were, inevitably, from America to Europe. In 1945 America already had the most advanced technology, large industrial firms, a fluid consumer society and a large, well-organised interstate trade. In 1945 European technology was relatively backward, firms were small, society and consumption were class-based, and most economic and social life was organised around narrow national markets.[1]

Since 1945, the European economy has developed many characteristic American features. For instance, huge increases in intra-European trade, encouraged by improved transport and EC legislation, have produced large-scale industrial restructuring and many firms now operate throughout Europe. These new corporations are organised more like American oligopolies than traditional British or German firms: their managers use American methods, often learned in American-style management schools; their products and services are advertised in American-style media and are marketed in American-type stores. This market is kept far closer to full employment than in the 1930s by the use of relatively active and coordinated fiscal and monetary policies – which were developed, in key respects, in the USA. The market is policed by European adaptations of American anti-trust legislation and regulatory agencies. Developments now occur almost simultaneously on both sides of the Atlantic. For instance, changes in technology and the effects of public policy, including anti-trust, deregulation and privatisation, have enabled smaller, more flexible firms to compete with the giants in both the USA and Europe.[2]

At the same time, European trade unions, which were very strong in 1945, have generally been edged into a limited collective bargaining role similar to that of the unions in the USA. Trade-union law, like anti-trust law, has also developed on American lines. The left in Europe has been weakened since 1945. American ideas have produced a meritocratic society. Similarly, European national planning methods which developed after the war have generally been discredited. Many national institutions in Europe have been, or are in the process of being, weakened. European social services are now being pared down to American levels. As national institutions and identities weaken, a certain sense of European identity is emerging. Finally, the Maastricht Treaty, marginally analogous to the US constitution, has started to address the legal and financial problems of European federalism.[3]

The interesting question is to ask to what extent these developments can be traced back to the ideas and policies of the Marshall Plan. Many of them would have happened without American influence and, in many ways, Europe remains quite unlike the USA. There is a long tradition of anti-Americanism in Europe, projected by interests determined to preserve special national and distinctively European values. In 1945 the aristocratic right opposed Americanisation because it seemed to threaten standards and quality; the left opposed America because it was the home of capitalism. Nationalists were afraid of the multicultural and multiracial nature of American society. The governing élites in the major European countries were concerned by the anti-imperial and federal ideas of the Americans. America was so dominant in 1945 that its ideas could not be ignored – but they were often rejected at the time. In the long run, however, many American social ideas have been copied in Europe.

The administrators of the Marshall Plan approached Europe with clear ideas about the way in which economic and industrial life should be organised. Many of the leading administrators were enlightened liberal businessmen, like Paul Hoffmann, the first administrator of the ECA, who had made his name and his fortune as President of Studebaker, a leading American car manufacturer, or Averell Harriman, who was originally a railroad executive and Wall Street banker. A second large group comprised academics and government servants who had developed their ideas during the depression and the New Deal and believed that well-informed government intervention was needed to make the market work. These two groups had often been at odds in the 1920s and 1930s, but American success in World War II had brought them together and convinced them that American methods could help to save Europe.[4]

They argued, that the modern corporation, operating over a continental market, had been the source of advanced technology in America since the 1920s. Social policy and price controls should provide a safety net for the unfortunate; modern fiscal, monetary and welfare policies should prevent depression; anti-trust laws should ensure fair competition. Large, rationally organised trade unions were required to protect vital labour interests without challenging management prerogatives. Union leadership and participation were rational calculations, not a class duty. The product of modernised institutions was far higher productivity and living standards. In Europe, by contrast, many of the Marshall Plan administrators thought that industrial and social structures and policies were still bound by inherited class attitudes and narrow national markets. They hoped that both could be shattered by American leadership and experience. European recovery would not be permanent unless it was accompanied by great changes in public policy and attitudes to competition, technology, and labour–management relations.[5]

They hoped to persuade the Europeans to restructure their industry on the American pattern; Volker Berghahn goes so far as to claim that World War II itself was about which model of capitalism would survive. They argued that all the European countries – especially Germany – had developed cartels and restrictive practices in the late nineteenth century as a result of limited European markets and the great depression. European imperialism and international rivalry were products of these developments. In the 1920s temporary prosperity and the spread of new American industries had reduced the power of European cartels, but they had returned with greater force in the depression. In 1945 European governments seemed determined to use trade organisations and state planning as they had used trade controls. The administrators of the Marshall Plan argued that these combinations and restrictive practices reduced welfare and retarded recovery. Hence, the bilateral treaties of the Marshall Plan all contained commitments by the recipient countries to restrict discriminatory practices or arrangements by private or public enterprises which prejudiced the recovery programme.[6]

These ideas had major effects on the future direction of European policy, both immediately and over the next forty years. The first of these was the breakdown in the broad left anti-fascist coalition which had controlled most European governments and collective union movements in 1945. This collapse began in 1945–6; although the communists generally supported plans for national reconstruction and acted responsibly, the socialists remembered their prewar tactics and suspected their long-run aims. When the first rush of recovery petered out in late 1946, the coalition began to dissolve as the pressure for resources increased and labour became more desperate. However, the critical break came in late 1947 and early 1948 and was caused by different attitudes to the Marshall Plan. Following the Russian lead, the communists generally opposed the acceptance of American aid; despite complaints about the various strings attached the socialists, generally, took it willingly.[7]

The parallel division in the European trade-union movement came in early 1948, when the TUC and other moderate union organisations challenged the communist-dominated World Federation of Trade Unions (WFTU), which had been formed in 1945 by the American Congress of Industrial Organizations (CIO), the British Trades Union Congress (TUC) and the Russian union organisation, to debate the Marshall Plan. The communists refused, so the moderate labour unions organised their own conference to discuss the plan and walked out of the WFTU in January 1949. The moderate left flirted briefly with the idea of some sort of pan-European neutralism – a sort of United Socialist States of Europe – but this proved impractical, forcing them into the arms of the Americans. The growing Cold War quickly confirmed this division and generally committed the moderate European left to the Atlantic Alliance and the Marshall Plan vision of liberal capitalism.[8]

The breakdown in the left affected each European country differently. In Britain the Attlee government had a broad popular mandate to extend the welfare state, nationalise the transport, power and steel industries, and maintain the sterling area. The major impetus for this was obviously British, although Marshall Aid may have eased the finance. By 1950 the government had enacted much of its programme, but had lost impetus for further change. In 1951 it lost power to the Conservatives, who freed the economy along liberal capitalist lines. The pattern of industrial control and consumerism that developed in the 1950s was broadly American; there has been no fundamental change since then, despite the temporary radicalism of the 1960s and 1970s.

To what extent was the Marshall Plan responsible for the victory of

Atlanticism? It is not possible to identify the conditions that had this effect. Indeed, while leading administrators of the Marshall Plan frequently criticised the priorities of the Labour government, the USA generally supported Britain and its government as valuable allies and recognised that they were enacting popular democratic decisions which they should not contest. Hence, Paul Hoffmann argued in the Harriman Committee that 'Aid from this country should not be conditioned on the methods used to reach these goals so long as they are consistent with basic democratic principles.' The ambivalence of Labour's position is suggested by Churchill's famous quip in the 1950 general election:

> Fancy the Socialist Government in England keeping themselves alive, economically and politically by these large annual dollops of dollars from capitalist America. They seek the dollars, they beg the dollars, they bluster for the dollars, they gobble the dollars, but in the whole of their 8000-word manifesto they cannot say 'thank you' for the dollars.[9]

In the long run, the Labour government collapsed for two reasons. First, obviously, when the Cold War threatened, it, along with the other west European democracies, threw in its hand with the United States. There was no other viable middle way. Then the Atlantic Alliance brought with it the huge rearmament costs of 1950–1 and loss of popularity. The Labour government recognised the costs and the implications, but was afraid that, if it did not demonstrate its commitment to western unity, the USA might leave Britain alone to face Russia across a defenceless Europe. Secondly, Carew thinks that 'Marshall Plan values' sapped the viability of the labour movement. 'By the end of the 1950s organised labour in Britain and elsewhere in Europe had been steered away from some of the more radical objectives it had briefly and vaguely harboured in 1945 ...' These were the results of the politics of consumerism and productivity, which are discussed below.[10]

Both France and Italy had powerful communist parties which were thrown out of postwar coalitions in 1947 because of the Marshall Plan, thus establishing centre-right governments that chose the west and liberal capitalist economic policies. In both cases, in 1945–7 the communists had supported constructive social reform, but, on Russian directives, had baulked at Marshall Aid. There were no 'American orders' to exclude the communists, but the Ramadier government in France and the de Gasperi government in Italy calculated that the provision of aid probably depended on creating 'homogeneous' centrist governments which were acceptable to the Americans. The alternative, in the economic situation of early 1947, was increasing social breakdown and left–right confrontation – for instance, in France, between de Gaulle and the communists. American aid allowed the élite to avoid this unpleasant choice. Having been excluded from power, the communists, on Russian orders, attempted to exploit the economic crises of late 1947 to regain their position by calling violent strikes. However, aid arrived just in time to defeat these strikes, and public opinion and governments swung to the right.[11]

The Italian government introduced conservative fiscal and monetary polices to reduce inflation and increase exports which meant that ECA allocations were sometimes not used in full. In each case, the USA would have preferred more effective centre-left governments, but the residual strength of the communists made this impossible. Clumsy US attempts to split the left in Italy generally strengthened the communists at the expense of the socialists, confirming kaleidoscopic coalitions of the centre-right in power; it was not until prosperity increased in the mid-1950s that more moderate governments were formed. The German left was also potentially strong immediately after the war, but had no power under the military government, of course. With the advent of the Cold War, and as the military government released control, the left was isolated, as in France and Italy, and the centre-right governments of Adenauer and Erhard imposed tough, but successful, liberal conservative policies.[12]

The administrators of the Marshall Plan hoped that increased productivity and rising standards of living would not only help the European balance of payments, but also divert attention from the traditional European distributional struggles, which had always been so much worse than in the USA. Europe had been borrowing American ideas since the late nineteenth century, but American technology advanced dramatically during the war, and postwar surveys in Britain and elsewhere in Europe revealed huge differences in output per capita. The surveys suggested that the causes were not just technical, but reflected deep-rooted differences in cultural and workplace attitudes between Europe and America. In the prosperous 1920s and 1960s US multinationals were the normal methods of diffusion, but American corporations showed very little interest in Europe immediately after the war, except in scavenging Germany's wartime secrets. However, the ECA attempted to educate European employers and unionists by sending productivity teams to the USA and by establishing productivity centres in Europe which demonstrated American ideas. In the short run, European productivity increased rapidly over the ERP period and there was great admiration – at least on the surface – for American technical methods.[13]

However, European managers and workers, used to narrow markets, low volumes, craft skills, labour solidarity, lack of price competition and government controls, took time to adapt to a more open mass-production system. This was especially true in Britain, where many employers who were doing well in the postwar boom did not think that American methods could be applied in British conditions. Surprisingly, the Labour government and the trade unions were more receptive to good American managerial ideas than the employers were, but British trade unions often had more power to block ideas that they did not like than their continental colleagues. Ultimately, they did learn, but there was a long delay and the connection with Marshall Plan activities was not clear.[14]

In France, on the other hand, the economic and political pressures to modernise were far greater; improved productivity and 'Americanisation' seemed to offer the hope of defusing traditional French social divisions. Hence, France sent 450 missions to the USA, whereas Britain only sent 66. Nonetheless, most French employers were even more conservative than the British and it was not until the mid-1950s that French productivity really began to accelerate. In Germany, too, once recovery had begun, there was great interest in what the USA had to offer, but only a belated general acceptance of Marshall Plan ideas. In Italy high unemployment and cheap labour limited employers' interest in the conciliation aspect of productivity, but the leading firms, such as Fiat, did import the first production-line technology under the ERP. Hence, physical productivity rose very rapidly in the 1950s and, by the early 1960s, such major firms as Olivetti were beginning to modify labour relations. As in Britain, the messages of the Marshall Plan were well-diffused and productivity did begin to rise rapidly in the 1950s. However, the detailed linkages between the propaganda and the results were obscure.[15]

The administrators of the Marshall Plan began the process of restructuring European industry, but met with only modest success at first. In Germany the occupation forces agreed to remove the leading Nazi administrators and to decommission the largest arms factories. The

Americans then went on to insist on mild decartelisation and recon-struction in heavy industry. Their first clash was with the British occupation forces, who, following Labour party doctrine, attempted to transfer control of the Ruhr mines to the new Social Democratic *Land* government, which planned to create 'a communal economy in coal, steel, iron and chemicals; an economy managed by business professionals with the participation of the state, the cities, the unions, and the cooper-atives'. The Americans criticised both the production record of the vital mines in the British zone and the potential for nationalised mines to concentrate their benefits in Germany (or even in North Rhine-West-phalia) and not throughout Europe. They insisted on a coal management plan, according to which ownership was vested with private trustees for five years.[16]

The Americans were able to impose more of their own ideas after the merger of the zones. New independent companies were created in chemicals, coal and steel which were large enough to be efficient pro-ducers in the European and world economy. The most decisive American action came with the discussion of the Schuman Plan in 1950, when the US High Commissioner, John McCloy, insisted that the Ger-man mines be separated from their traditional cartel partners in heavy industry, thus creating a much more open industrial structure that was less threatening to France. However, these reforms only won grudging acceptance from German businessmen and administrators. A surprising proportion of the less conspicuous middle-rank employers and civil servants survived the anti-Nazi purges. They had begun their careers in the 1920s and had lived through the depression, the Nazis and the war; they were reluctant to lose the close ties and arrangements between cartel firms. It was not until this generation retired and then died in the 1950s and 1960s, and the new managerial class found that they could compete effectively outside Germany, that managers accepted American methods.[17]

While negotiating the US loan, the USA had persuaded Britain to commit herself to discuss decartelisation. This led to the abortive Havana International Conference, but she committed herself again in the Marshall Plan bilateral treaty and in 1948 introduced the Monopoly Act 'to make a good impression on the Americans'. Moreover, there were strong internal reasons to support the development of an anti-cartel policy. The cartels, which had been introduced in the 1930s to manage depressed trades, had grown even stronger during the war and had become very unpopular. In addition, academic and government debates about postwar reconstruction included discussions about cartels and restrictive practices, and by 1944 a consensus was emerging that was much nearer to the American position. Hence, all parties in the general election of July 1945 committed themselves to limit cartel powers; Labour, for instance, argued for a mixed policy of nationalisation, strong state supervision and strong enforcement of competition.[18]

Labour won the election, but, once in power, found that the organisation of their desperately needed export drives depended on the trade associations that arranged cartels. There was no chance of long-run reform of industrial structure immediately after the war. In addition, as in Germany, most businessmen and senior civil servants had lived through the depression and believed that industrial controls and planning were essential. Hence, the Monopoly Act of 1948 established the Monopoly Commission as a weak organisation; restrictive practices were not made illegal *per se* and the commissions's role went no further than investigating monopoly situations. It was not even allowed to use 'the pitiless publicity' which Theodore Roosevelt's somewhat similar Bureau of Corporations had been given in 1902, and its reports were wrapped in typical British discretion. In the long run, however, as in Germany, the ideas planted in 1948 had their effect. In the more expansive 1950s and 1960s, as the older generation died away, as firm size increased, and as the European market widened, so British views on anti-trust changed. The Restrictive Practices Act was passed in 1956, and there has been further legislation since then. Similarly, at the European level, the Treaty of Rome of 1957 contained a section (Article 86) on 'Competition Policy', but this was hardly used until the early 1990s.[19]

By the mid-1950s most European governments had adopted much of the liberal consensus of the New Deal, but the various components had been added at different speeds and in different ways. Keynesian fiscal policy had been used by America and Britain to manage demand during the war, but did not become the generally accepted instrument of employment policy, either there or in Europe, until the 1950s and 1960s. This was partly because, during reconstruction and the long European boom, employment was very full in most economies without the need for artificial stimulus, partly because of the initial importance of planning, and partly because the cautious officials who had been appointed in the 1930s lingered on in many governments and it took time for younger personnel to take over. However, the ECA and the OEEC, which temporarily employed a surprising number of the leading names in American and European economics, played an important part in this process by establishing full employment and maximum production as the norm for government policy and by attempting to persuade fiscally conservative governments – the German and Italian, for instance – to reduce unemployment.[20]

The defeat and weakening of postwar governments on the left in Europe ensured that the use of controls and planning would decline once the difficult transitional problems had been solved. This implied an increasing reliance on the market and, therefore, on market rules. The American influence on the development of European anti-trust and productivity policy has already been explained. The development of an important but limited role for trade unions in the new market-place was partly a result of long-term changes in the external environment and in generations, as discussed above, but it was also partly due to the fracturing of left-wing politics in the late 1940s, and wider Marshall Plan influences. The Marshall Planners were certain that, in order to improve living standards, European capital and labour would have to learn to work together much more effectively, increasing productivity and salaries. This implied an improved system of industrial relations and a definite role for labour, ultimately based on the American experience of labour relations.

In the USA, trade unions had traditionally placed more faith in wage bargaining than on government policy because of the difficulty of capturing political power over a continental area. At first they were only successful in craft trades and, in the 1920s, entrepreneurs such as Henry Ford excluded unions. In the 1930s, however, new more radical unions successfully organised the mass-production industries. By 1950 a relatively orderly system of collective bargaining at firm and plant level had become the central mechanism of US labour relations, successfully negotiating improved productivity and higher wages. The Wagner (1935) and Taft Hartley (1946) Acts codified the practices involved. By the early 1950s, it had become accepted academic doctrine in America and Europe, supported by ECA and Ford Foundation research into labour problems, that the role of managers was to generally manage their firms, and the main role of unions was to secure a better deal for their members by detailed collective bargaining, in limited but vital areas.[21]

The influence of the Marshall Planners, in their attempts to transfer these ideas to Europe, varied considerably from country to country. In

Britain, the leading trade unions and the TUC were already firmly established and powerful organisations. They were well connected with the government, and could afford to accept or reject American ideas. Gradually, however, the academic consensus affected public opinion, and after long periods of more difficult labour relations in the 1950s and 1960s, British legislation moved nearer the American model. In France, the stronger unions were traditionally further to the left than in Britain, and less willing to conduct orderly collective bargaining. The many small employers were also strongly opposed to ceding rights to unions. The Marshall Plan staff in Paris, therefore, had to work hard to introduce American bargaining ideas. The first major collective bargaining agreement was with Renault in 1955 – but it was not widely copied, until larger and more modern firms appeared in the 1970s and 1980s.[22]

In Germany, the allies had the chance to impose their own system, but did not agree on aims. The British, and the Germans in the Ruhr, were in favour of socialist control and co-determination in which labour representatives sat on the boards of companies. The Americans wanted a freer market, without cartels and state controls, but with collective bargaining. For a long time there was no real consensus. In the long run American management ideas triumphed, but they have had to co-exist with British and native German influences stressing corporatism and co-determination. In Italy, Marshall Plan advice to introduce a high productivity, high wage, high consumption economy was initially ignored. Italian productivity advanced by leaps and bounds, but on a low wage sweat-shop basis. Sufficient new labour was always arriving from the South. Even advanced firms like Fiat achieved high productivity, not only by introducing improved machinery, but also by emulating 1920s style Ford labour relations. The once powerful communist led trade-union movement declined all through the 1950s. However, in the late 1960s the mass of ordinary Italians did begin to enjoy the consumer revolution, and to claim their rights as workers. Then the unions recovered rapidly, and modern collective bargaining appeared.[23]

Perhaps the greatest contrast between the USA and Europe throughout the postwar period was the relatively generous European policy on welfare. European governments built on domestic traditions and political pressures that took them far beyond American practice. For instance, the British National Health Service seemed to be not only fairer but also more effective and cheaper than the mixed state and privately organised American equivalents. Curiously however, Marshall Plan economists, who were often old New Dealers, or young idealists, had some expansionary influence in Europe even in welfare legislation. For instance, they attempted to introduce New Deal social welfare ideas in Germany and Italy, that they knew were not politically possible in America. In general however, by the late 1950s the academic consensus – as described in the leading economics textbooks – which in Britain at that time were often American – was remarkably confident and uniform. Much the same New Deal liberal consensus was portrayed in America and Europe, although it may have seemed rather to the left in America and to the right in Europe. The immediate impact of the Marshall Plan was therefore only part of a much longer process of cultural assimilation which has introduced much more uniform economic and social policies around the whole Atlantic basin.[24]

These governmental contrasts were less important for most Europeans than the growth of the consumer society based on the mass-produced consumer durables that had first appeared in America in the 1920s. The most important new products were cars in which Europe reached 1920s levels of American market penetration in the 1950s and 1960s – see Table 14.1. European cars were custom-built in the 1920s, and it was not until the 1950s that true American mass-production methods were introduced and prices were reduced to levels that most ordinary consumers could afford. Many other consumer durables such as televisions and washing machines developed the same way. Similarly, American casual clothing and mass entertainment were copied and adapted, especially among the young.

Table 14.1. *Diffusion of Cars in the USA and Europe, 1920–1970 (cars in millions, and population per car)*

	USA		Britain		France		Germany		Italy	
	Cars	Pop.	Cars	Pop.	Cars	Pop.	Cars	Pop.	Cars	Pop.
1910	<1	202	<1	579	<1	731	<1	2018	—	—
1920	8	13	<1	179	<1	248	<1	998	<1	1259
1930	23	5	1	43	1	38	<1	133	<1	223
1940	27	5	2	24	2	23	1	49	<1	165
1950	40	4	2	21	2	25	1	90	<1	135
1960	62	3	6	9	6	8	4	12	2	25
1970	89	2	12	5	13	4	14	4	10	5

Sources: United States, *Historical Statistics*, pp. 8, 716; Mitchell, *European Historical Statistics*, pp. 30–4, 668–70; Svennilson, *Growth and Stagnation*, p. 236.

The Americanisation and democratisation of European society went beyond simple consumption, and eventually involved new styles of life and personal relationships. Europe had at last reached Rostow's 'Era of High Mass Consumption', emulating American developments a generation earlier. According to David Ellwood, Americanisation was a special form of modernisation driven by two forces. On the demand side, development was driven by the 'revolution of rising expectations' – a phrase coined at the time by Harlan Cleveland – a leading Marshall Planner – the expectations fuelled by mass observation of the 'American Dream'. On the supply side, the development was enabled by the new machinery and organisation of production introduced from the USA during the Marshall Plan period and shortly after. The precise technical means by which the technology was transferred was another matter.[25]

The interesting question is the responsibility of the Marshall Plan for increased European interest in the American model. Marshall Plan administrators, such as Paul Hoffmann, frequently advocated mass production for mass consumption in a single European market – that is, an American vision of the European future. However, probably the single most important force projecting American values was American performance in World War II, and the invasion of Europe. A longer-term influence creating the desire to emulate American consumption patterns was the image of America portrayed in the media, especially Hollywood, which in the 1950s generally presented the smiling side of American life. Magazines like the National Geographic, which were widely available in Europe, also encapsulated the American dream in their attractive colour advertising of American homes, gardens and recreations. Similar productions had seductively presented American living standards to the 1920s generation of Europeans, but in the depressed 1930s and the troubled 1960s, the American dream faded.[26]

The productivity and welfare gap between America and Europe, however, was also greatest about 1950, and the Marshall Planners were far more confident than previous American missionaries that they knew what to do. 'The Americans want an integrated Europe looking like the United States of America – God's own country', wrote Robert Hall of the British Treasury. Far more aggressively than before or since, the ECA argued through every documentary media possible that if Europe adopted American methods and attitudes, especially the latter, then she, too, could prosper. Paul Hoffmann wrote, 'Even more important than what (visiting) Europeans learn about lathes and ploughs is what they learn about America. They learned that this is the land of full shelves and bulging shops, made possible by high productivity and good wages, and that this prosperity may be emulated elsewhere by those who will work towards it.' The entertainment media and the educational propaganda to a considerable extent acted together, collectively projecting the same text. The consequent increased demand for consumer goods and improved life-styles then operated together with the new technology, and improved organisation to revolutionise European production and living standards.[27]

Notes

1. André Siegfried, *America Comes of Age: A French Analysis* (Jonathan Cape: London, 1927), and Jean-Jacques Servan-Schreiber, *The American Challenge* (Hamish Hamilton: London, 1968), provide interesting transatlantic contrasts from the French perspective in the 1920s and post-1945 respectively.
2. Volker Berghahn, *The Americanization of West German Industry, 1945–1973* (Berg: Leamington Spa, 1986), pp. 326–33; Helen V. Milner, *Resisting Protectionism: Global Industries and the Politics of International Trade* (Princeton University Press: Princeton, NJ, 1988), pp. 264–301; Michael J. Piore and Charles F. Sabel, *The Second Industrial Divide: Possibilities for Prosperity* (Basic Books: New York, 1984).
3. Anthony Carew, *Labour under the Marshall Plan* (Manchester University Press: Manchester, 1987), pp. 240–50.
4. Michael J. Hogan, *The Marshall Plan* (Cambridge University Press: Cambridge, 1987), pp. 1–25; Alan R. Raucher, *Paul G. Hoffmann: Architect of Foreign Aid* (University Press of Kentucky: Lexington, 1985), *passim*; Rudy Abramson, *Spanning the Century: The Life of W. Averell Harriman, 1891–1986* (Morrow: New York, 1992), *passim*.
5. Charles S. Maier, 'The politics of productivity: foundations of American international economic policy after World War 2', in *idem* (ed.), *In Search of Stability* (Cambridge University Press: Cambridge, 1987), pp. 121–52.
6. Berghahn, *Americanization of West German Industry*, pp. 26–39; for American analyses of European development, see Max Beloff, *The United States and the Unity of Europe* (Brookings Institution: Washington, DC, 1963), pp. 38–43; for the US–British bilateral treaty, see Henry Pelling, *Britain and the Marshall Plan* (Macmillan: Basingstoke, 1988), pp. 153–65.
7. Carew, *Labour under the Marshall Plan*, pp. 18–39; Melvyn P. Leffler, *A Preponderance of Power* (Stanford University Press: Stanford, 1992), pp. 183–219.
8. Carew, *Labour under the Marshall Plan*, pp. 70–9.
9. Hoffmann is quoted in *ibid.*, p. 12; Churchill is quoted in Alex Danchev, *Oliver Franks* (Clarendon Press: Oxford, 1993), p. 61, from *The Times*, 10 Feb. 1950.
10. Carew, *Labour under the Marshall Plan*, pp. 224–50. The costs and motives of British rearmament are discussed in Sir Alec Cairncross, *Years of Recovery* (Methuen: London, 1983), pp. 212–33.
11. Irwin M. Wall, *The United States and the Making of Postwar France* (Cambridge University Press: Cambridge, 1991), pp. 63–95.
12. US–Italian politics are discussed in James Miller, *The United States and Italy,*

1940–1950 (University of North Carolina Press: Chapel Hill, NC, 1986), pp. 223–70; US–German politics are discussed in essays by Schwartz, Schwabe and Link in Charles S. Maier and Gunter Bischof (eds), *The Marshall Plan and Germany* (Berg: Oxford, 1991), pp. 171–330.

13. Carew, *Labour under the Marshall Plan*, pp. 131–223.

14. Jim Tomlinson, 'The failure of the Anglo-American Council on Productivity', *Business History* 33 (1991), pp. 82–92.

15. Carew, *Labour under the Marshall Plan*, pp. 158–223; Richard F. Kuisel, 'The Marshall Plan in action: politics, labor, industry and the programme of technical assistance', in CHEFF, *Le Plan Marshall*, pp. 335–58; Werner Link, 'Building coalitions: non-governmental German–American linkages', in Maier and Bischof (eds), *The Marshall Plan and Germany*, pp. 282–330; Erik Bloemen, 'Technical assistance and productivity in the Netherlands, 1945–1952', in CHEFF, *Le Plan Marshall*, pp. 503–13.

16. John Gimbel, *The Origins of the Marshall Plan* (Stanford University Press: Stanford, 1976), pp. 203–19.

17. Berghahn, *Americanization of West German Industry*, *passim*.

18. Helen Mercer, 'Anti-monopoly policy', in H. Mercer, N. Rollings and J. D. Tomlinson (eds), *The Labour Governments and Private Industry: The Experience of 1945–1951* (Edinburgh University Press: Edinburgh, 1992), pp. 55–73.

19. Tony Allan Freyer, *Regulating Big Business: Antitrust in Great Britain and America, 1880–1990* (Cambridge University Press: Cambridge, 1992), *passim*.

20. Herbert Stein, *The Fiscal Revolution in America* (University of Chicago Press: Chicago, 1969), pp. 3–5, 454–68; for Britain, see J. D. Tomlinson, 'A "Keynesian revolution" in the making', and Alan Booth, 'Defining a "Keynesian Revolution"', both in *Economic History Review* 37 (1984), pp. 258–67; for France and Italy, see Chiarella Esposito, 'Influencing aid recipients: Marshall Plan lessons for contemporary aid donors', in Barry Eichengreen (ed.), *Europe's Postwar Recovery* (Cambridge University Press: Cambridge, 1995), pp. 77–86; for Germany, see Thomas Schwartz, 'European integration and the "Special Relationship": implementing the Marshall Plan in the Federal Republic', in Maier and Bischof (eds), *The Marshall Plan and Germany*, pp. 171–215.

21. See Henry Pelling, *American Labour* (Macmillan: Basingstoke, 1988), *passim* for a simple history of American labour. For the ECA research, see Carew, *Labour under the Marshall Plan*, pp. 194–200.

22. Carew, *Labour*, pp. 201–17.

23. Carew, *Labour*, pp. 107–110, 217–23; Federico Romero, 'Where the Marshall Plan fell short: Industrial Relations in Italy', paper given at a conference on 'The Marshall Plan and its Consequences: a 50th Anniversary Conference' in Leeds, England, May 1997.

24. For instance, see Paul Samuelson, *Economics: An Introductory Analysis* (McGraw-Hill: New York, 1st edition, 1948; 5th edition, 1961).

25. Walt Rostow, *The Stages of Economic Growth: A Non-Communist Manifesto* (Cambridge, 1960); Ellwood, *Rebuilding Europe*, pp. 222–8.

26. Ellwood, *Rebuilding Europe*, *passim*. For Americanisation in the 1920s, see Frank Costigliola, *Awkward Dominion: American Political, Economic and Cultural Relations with Europe, 1919–1933* (Cornell University Press: Ithaca, New York, 1984), *passim*. For Americanisation in Britain, see David Reynolds and David Dimbleby, *An Ocean Apart: The Relationship between Britain and America in the Twentieth Century* (Hodder

and Stoughton: London, 1988), pp. 96–115, 267–86. For Americanisation in Germany, see Ralph Willett, *The Americanisation of Germany, 1945–1949* (Routledge: London, 1989).

27. Hall is quoted in Hogan, *The Marshall Plan*, p. 427; Paul Hoffmann, *Peace Can be Won* (Michael Joseph: London, 1951), p. 91.

15

The End of the
Dollar Gap, 1950–1970

Western European exports to the United States recovered dramatically in 1950–1960; by 1970 it was the dollar, rather than European currencies, that was in serious trouble. The international financial crises of the early 1970s, the most serious since the war, devalued the dollar and destroyed the Bretton Woods system. Table 15.1 details the essential changes in US–European trade and the financial flows between 1947 and 1970. The major elements were: (a) the current account – composed of the trade balance, US military expenditure in Europe and the balance on services; (b) the capital account – composed of US government grants to European countries, such as the Marshall Plan, and US private and government capital flows to Europe; and (c) the residual monetary flows. These offset the balances of the current and capital accounts and comprised the transactions in currencies, mostly dollars, which foreign banks held as reserves, gold and company and government securities. In 1947 the need for US supplies made European countries desperate to increase their gold and dollars reserves. By 1970 the persistent US trade deficit had resulted in a worldwide surplus of dollars, and the stronger European central banks were seeking ways of reducing their holdings.[1]

Transatlantic current accounts were transformed in 1947–71. European trade was massively in deficit with the United States in the late 1940s, but improved progressively during the 1950s. Despite European hopes, the improvement was halting, with frequent relapses in 1951–4, 1956–7 and in the early 1960s, but the trend towards a more reasonable balance was clear. This result was the product of a dramatic change in US trade. American exports to Europe did not overtake their 1947 level ($5.3bn.) until 1953, and grew slowly to $7.4bn. in 1960 and to $14.8bn. in 1970. Meanwhile, European exports to the USA grew far more rapidly: by 1955 they had reached $2.5bn., by 1960 they had risen to $4.3bn., and by 1970 to $11.4bn. Hence, a significant gap remained – and was filled by service and capital items – but the proportions had been trans-

Table 15.1. *US Balances with Western Europe, 1947–1970 ($m.)*

	1947	Annual average, 1948–55	Annual average, 1956–8	Annual average, 1960–5	Annual average, 1966–9
Trade balance	4892	2002	2223	2814	1317
Military	−164	−771	−1640	−1101	−814
Services	299	−242	−464	−567	−1045
Current account	5027	989	119	1146	−542
Government grants	−672	−2041	−375	−169	−38
US capital outflow	3746	−299	−699	−1109	−1313
US private	−78	−127	−545	−1359	−1135
US government	−3668	−172	−154	250	−178
Capital account	−4418	−2340	−1074	−239	−1278
Residual covered by					
Foreign long term	−184	107	255	320	2661
Short term	−784	553	572	472	2429
Official reserves	−1447	141	726	765	−150
Errors	1806	550	−598	−1425	−3047
Monetary movements	609	−1351	−955	−132	−1893

Source: UN, *Economic Survey of Europe in 1971* (Economic Commission for Europe: New York, 1972), p. 35.

formed. The westward flow was only 17% of the eastward flow in 1947, but had reached 50% by 1958 and 83% in the, for Europe, unusually good year of 1959. The gap widened again temporarily in the early 1960s, but western Europe had clearly reached viability.[2]

US exports to Europe grew more slowly after 1947, partly as normal European supplies recovered, partly because of long-term trends, and partly because of government policy. The short-term recovery of European agriculture and industry in the late 1940s is discussed above. However, long-term trends, concealed by the war and postwar emergencies, but dating from at least the 1920s (if not earlier), were also suddenly revealed in the mid-1950s. These affected US exports of food, which could increasingly be provided by Europe itself, and raw materials like cotton, which could either be purchased more cheaply in the Third World or could be replaced by synthetics. Technical and demographic developments were gradually eroding America's traditional role as the 'garden of the world', the greatest exterior source of Europe's supplies.[3]

In particular, the surprisingly large sums that Britain, France and

Holland had diverted from Marshall Aid to alternative suppliers in the dominions, the colonies and the Third World began to pay off in the mid-1950s. For instance, Europe received increasing amounts of crude oil from the Middle East, while the USA herself began to move from being a surplus supplier to a deficit importer as her own consumption rose and domestic resources declined. By the mid-1950s it was possible to use the commodity composition of the leading American exports to calculate that the long-run US trade surplus over Europe was bound to end by the mid-1970s. The immediate sign of this in the mid-1950s was a substantial shift in the terms of trade in Europe's favour as the effects of the Korean War emergency wore off and food and raw material prices fell. Suddenly, what had frequently appeared to be a hopeless position *vis-à-vis* North America was in fact manageable.[4]

Nature was supported by artifice, however. A major element of US policy in the Marshall Plan was to allow the Europeans to improve their trade balances by discriminating against American goods; this kept them in the (open) international market and on the US side in the Cold War. By the mid-1950s the European recovery convinced the Americans, with some pleasure, that their policy had been successful. Europe was not seen as a threat, and even the Treaty of Rome, which contained overtly protectionist measures and did raise some alarm, was generally accepted as valuable integration. It was not until the early 1960s that the USA began to complain strongly about EEC discrimination, but by this time the machinery was well-established. The major instrument of discrimination against US goods was the devaluation of all European currencies against the dollar in 1949, which left the dollar overvalued until the early 1970s. In addition, the European economies, and the EEC and EFTA collectively, discriminated against all non-essential US imports with a barrage of quotas, import licences and exchange controls.[5]

For instance: the USA had enjoyed a lively European trade in the latest consumer durables – radios, gramophones, cameras, etc. – in the 1930s, but these were all excluded to encourage local production. Consequently, US cars and many other consumer durables, which were still very good value in the 1950s, were never seen in Europe. The beneficiaries of this discrimination were, of course, the new industries in many European countries, particularly in Germany, whose competitive products moved into the vacuum. Hence, there was a curious paradox in the 1950s that non-commercial items – the military, popular culture, etc. – America and Americanisation were to be seen everywhere in Europe, but American goods were relatively scarce and increasingly excluded. The corollary of this was that, for trade in many new capital and consumer durables and in the more luxurious food products, Germany and, to a lesser extent, France and Italy became pivots of the European system.[6]

Meanwhile, European exports to the USA mounted more rapidly than at any time since 1918–21, by 70%, in volume terms, from 1952–6. Europeans, often aided by technical advice and machinery from the Marshall Plan, soon copied the essentials of American consumer durable design and, helped by cheaper labour and the favourable exchange rate, began exporting to the USA. Spurred on by dollar export drives, exports of European consumer goods to the USA doubled in 1952–6. In 1920–1 the equivalent export surge had been curtailed by new US tariffs, but this time, while the USA did not reduce her tariffs much, she did not increase them either. Small US firms lobbied the administration for protection, as in 1921, but the larger multinationals, with increasing interests in Europe, were less concerned. The US government was prepared to accept substantial economic costs in order to preserve European prosperity, confirm the Franco-German settlement, and contain Russia. Hence, they did not oppose the European export drive. The most important and visible new European imports were cars, particularly, by the late 1950s, the Volkswagen Beetle, the first really successful small foreign car to sell in the USA.[7]

The major new item in the current account was American military expenditure in Europe, which was running at about $1.5bn. a year in the late 1950s, an obvious result of the Cold War. However, the Europeans began to recover their traditional surplus in services. In shipping, this was explicitly helped in some instances, e.g. the Norwegian fleet, by Marshall Plan dollars. In US travel and tourism, the key factor was the transformation of the European image, accurately caught by Hollywood, from postwar austerity to 1950s prosperity. In finance, the City of London was gradually restored to prosperity by the painful re-establishment of convertibility and rapidly increasing monetary flows. Finally, the opportunity for Europe to increase her traditional earnings via the Third World and Latin America developed as the US overseas purchases of raw materials increased. The long-run threat to this balance was that, even though the Third World increased its exports to the USA, Europe would not be able to recapture the consequent dollar earnings either because of decolonisation or American and Japanese competition.[8]

Marshall Plan Aid – listed under US 'government grants' in Table 15.1 – was replaced by Mutual Security Aid from 1 January 1951, administered under the Mutual Security Act of October 1951 by the MSA. The MSA continued to provide important civilian and military supplies for the allies. The civilian element – listed under 'government grants' – contained many of the same goods provided under the Marshall Plan, but fell rapidly in the 1950s. A considerable volume of military goods were sold to the allies by the USA for cash or credit in the 1950s and 1960s and are therefore listed in the 'current account'. The military goods and services that were provided under the Mutual Security Act are not listed in the table. These were worth about $1.5bn. per annum throughout the 1950s, but gradually fell in the 1960s.[9]

The American capital account was transformed in the 1950s. In 1945–7 US government loans – principally the British loan of 1946–7 – were the mainstay of European finance. From 1948 these were replaced by the Marshall Plan and MSA grants. However, as the value of these dropped in the 1950s and even began to be repaid, producing a small net inflow into the USA in the early 1960s, they were replaced by a very large private capital outflow. This was primarily an outflow of direct investment – that is, investment by American companies in European branches – such as the expansion of Ford at Dagenham. US private capital had not been attracted by the dour statism of the late 1940s, but began to revive in the early 1950s as the future of Europe became more secure, and expanded to a flood in the early 1960s. After 1965, the US administration began to place controls on the outflow, which reduced it slightly, but the US multinational companies were now so well-established that they were able instead to raise money for expansion in Europe.[10]

The cause of this increase in American direct investment in Europe has been debated endlessly. American companies had been attracted to Europe since the late nineteenth century, of course, and most of the large American firms specialising in advanced consumer goods had established themselves in Europe between the wars. Ford, for instance, had built the Dagenham factory in 1927 and GM had purchased Vauxhall and Opel at about the same time and had bid for Fiat. The logic of these purchases had been the attraction of the local market, the need to build European-style models (for instance, in cars), and the need to provide a local service. In addition, it had been important for American firms in the 1930s to get inside the European tariff barriers. During the war these firms had either closed down or they had been forced to cooperate with the belligerents.[11]

The special attraction after 1950 was the recovery and integration of the European market, combined with the difficulty of supplying goods direct from America in the face of European discrimination and the overpriced dollar. At first, most American companies went to Britain, which had a common language and institutions and could be used as a springboard not only for her own large market, but also for Europe and the Commonwealth. After 1957, however, an increasing proportion of American companies went to Europe to take advantage of the Common Market. These companies were often experienced at operating in several foreign jurisdictions and soon became, in some respects, more European than their various British, German, French and Italian competitors.[12]

These American multinationals were usually more efficient than their domestic competitors, operated in the most modern section of the market, employed the most advanced technology, offered the best wages and conditions, and earned the best returns. As a result, the American commercial presence in Europe, often quite heavily disguised, was represented by her multinational companies and not by US imports. The sales of US multinationals were about twice as high as US exports to the EEC in 1957 and had risen to six times as high by 1987. These companies had become so dominant by the mid-1960s that they seemed likely to take over all the advanced production in Europe; this naturally generated a chauvinistic reaction. The cult book, *Le Défi américain*, by Jean-Jacques Servan-Schreiber, a French bestseller in the 1960s, sounded the alarm, but urged the French to adopt the best American methods. In most respects, the American companies seem to have been good citizens, though, introducing the best American practices and setting an example to European companies.[13]

The net residual of the balances on the current, government and capital accounts was covered by the monetary movements listed in Table 15.1 – sometimes called collectively the 'transfer gap'. In 1946–7 US exports were needed so desperately that European governments and private investors sold their American shares, raised credits and raided their gold and dollar reserves to find the resources to pay for them. By contrast, the central banks and private companies in Europe and Japan were awash with dollars by 1970 and were seeking ways of diversifying their reserves into stronger currencies like the mark or the yen, or demanding gold from the US Federal Reserve. The major components of the transfer gap were European purchases of US government and corporate securities, European short-term credits to the USA, and changes in official reserves. European investment in America was initially much slower than US investment in Europe, but European purchases of American assets were becoming substantial by the mid-1960s. Unlike US investment in Europe in the 1950s and 1960s, most European investment in America was in American companies, not in branch plants of European companies. The European establishment of branch plants across the Atlantic did not really begin until the 1970s and 1980s.[14]

Bretton Woods made the dollar a key currency after the war, and European dollar holdings rose quickly in the 1950s and 1960s. European central banks continued to hold dollars as reserves even when their own economic position had improved, because, apart from sterling, it was the universally accepted unit of account and store of value. A large advantage of this central role was that, to whatever extent other countries were willing to hold dollars, the USA was able to increase imports or expand direct investment overseas without immediate payment. The costs, however, were that, after the general European devaluation of 1949 and given that European inflation was generally faster than American in the 1950s, the dollar became relatively overvalued and US exports were increasingly discriminated against in world markets. Other countries – apart from Britain – were not prepared to take over this key currency role, because, as long as the dollar was at the centre of the system, the mark and the yen could remain relatively soft currencies, to the advantage of German and Japanese exports.[15]

The enlarged European reserves increased world liquidity and encouraged international trade and growth. In 1947 the danger had been that dollars would become so scarce that the British and Europeans would be forced to establish their own autarchic currency systems. The growing flood of dollars to Europe ended this fear and made convertibility and multilateral trade easier. The process was encouraged by the development of the Eurodollar markets in the late 1950s. These traded in the dollar and the leading European currencies. They came to be centred on London rather than on New York because of the controls on capital outflow that the USA had introduced in the mid-1960s.

The volume of Euro-currency handled on the markets increased from about $7bn. in 1963 to $57bn. by 1970. These markets helped the USA to finance her deficit, but also, after a delay, encouraged inflation, speculation and hot-money movements. It was too easy for hard-pressed governments to ignore deficits and overheat their economies. Once a run had started on even the strongest currency, it was extraordinarily difficult to contain. Speculators such as multinational companies, oil-rich sheiks and the 'gnomes of Zurich' had little to lose. Hence, these institutional developments began to degrade the relatively stable monetary system that had been envisaged by Keynes and White at Bretton Woods into a sort of 'Casino Capitalism', destabilised by huge unchecked financial flows.[16]

The outflow of US dollars rapidly changed the USA's net debt position to Europe. In 1950 US assets in Europe were about $12bn., compared to European holdings of American assets of about $9bn. By 1969 US holdings had grown to $41bn., but European holdings of American assets were about $55bn. The American holdings were mostly long-term assets, of course, such as the factories, plant and machinery of their multinationals; the European holdings were portfolio investments and short-term dollar holdings, etc. It was not for another ten years that European direct investments in America began to approach the American level in Europe.[17]

Notes

1. Developments in American trade are surveyed in United Nations, *Economic Survey of Europe in 1971: The European Economy from the 1950s to the 1970s* (Economic Commission for Europe: New York, 1972), pp. 23–41, and Fred Block, *The Origins of International Economic Disorder: A Study of United States International Monetary Policy from World War 2 to the Present* (University of California Press: Berkeley, 1977), pp. 140–63.
2. The changing trade ratios are calculated from US, Bureau of the Census, *Historical Statistics of the United States: Colonial Times to 1970* (United States Government Printing Office: Washington, DC, 1975), pp. 903–5.
3. UN, *Economic Survey of Europe in 1957* (Economic Commission for Europe: Geneva, 1958), Chapters 4 and 5.
4. *Ibid.*
5. Alan S. Milward, 'The Marshall Plan and German foreign trade', in Charles S. Maier and Gunter Bischof (eds), *The Marshall Plan and Germany* (Berg: Oxford, 1991), pp. 452–87.
6. *Ibid.*, pp. 481–7.
7. Helen V. Milner, *Resisting Protectionism* (Princeton University Press: Princeton, NJ, 1988), pp. 18–44, analyses the change in US tariff policy; Alan S. Milward, *The European Rescue of the Nation State* (Routledge: London, 1992), pp. 408–24, analyses British and German car exports.

8. Successive annual issues of UN, *Economic Survey of Europe* (Economic Commission for Europe: Geneva, 1948–), analyse European trade; Block, *United States International Monetary Policy*, pp. 140–63, examines the US trade deficit.

9. UN, *Economic Survey of Europe in 1971*, p. 35.

10. Block, *United States International Monetary Policy*, pp. 146–7.

11. Mira Wilkins, *The Maturing of Multinational Enterprise: American Business Abroad from 1914 to 1970* (Harvard University Press: Cambridge, Mass., 1974), pp. 49–260.

12. *Ibid.*, pp. 284–408.

13. John H. Dunning, 'European integration and transatlantic foreign direct investment: the record assessed', in George N. Yannoupoulos (ed.), *Europe and America, 1992: US–EC Economic Relations and the Single European Market* (Manchester University Press: Manchester, 1991), pp. 153–76; Jean-Jacques Servan-Schreiber, *The American Challenge* (Hamish Hamilton: London, 1968), *passim*.

14. Block, *United States International Monetary Policy*, pp. 164–202; UN, *Economic Survey of Europe in 1971*, pp. 33–9.

15. Robert Gilpin, *US Power and the Multinational Corporation: The Political Economy of Foreign Direct Investment* (Macmillan: London, 1975), pp. 150–6.

16. Andrew Shonfield (ed.), *International Economic Relations of the Western World, 1959–1971*, 2 vols (Oxford University Press: London, 1976), vol. 1, pp. 1–140, surveys international economic relations over the whole period. The growth of the Eurodollar market is described in UN, *Economic Survey of Europe in 1971*, p. 37. Susan Strange, *Casino Capitalism* (Basil Blackwell: Oxford, 1986), pp. 1–24, originated this phrase.

17. UN, *Economic Survey of Europe in 1971*, pp. 33–9.

16

Conclusion:
Prosperity and Convergence

The major aim of the postwar American recovery plans was to restore the prosperity and viability of western Europe. In addition, the USA wished to integrate the individual economies both among themselves and with the wider international economy. The ERP, together with the parallel American recovery policy in the Far East, it has been argued, laid the foundations for the European and international boom of 1948–73. They also led to a marked convergence in incomes and living standards in the leading OECD industrial economies as productivity and lifestyles in the western European and Far Eastern countries caught up with those in North America.[1]

On the other hand, President Truman's Point Four programmes of American economic and technical assistance to the Third World, worked less well. Hence, incomes in large parts of the Third World have fallen behind the OECD norm. Also, the eastern bloc was excluded, or excluded itself, from the European recovery plans, did not share to the same extent in the boom of the 1950s–1970s, and then fell disastrously behind in the 1980s. The collapse of the Russian empire in eastern Europe in the late 1980s was in part a consequence of this. While containment and deterrence held the frontiers, the domestic economies of the west were transformed. Ultimately, by the late 1980s the impossible task of matching the industrial power and prosperity of the west and the growth and dynamism of east Asia helped to destroy the legitimacy and morale of the communist order.[2]

The European recovery programmes were introduced at a crucial moment in international development, when several outcomes were possible. Obviously, the potential for rapid growth was already present in all these societies, but it had to be activated and directed into viable channels. The long boom of the 1950s and 1960s started in most countries in the late 1940s, when American influence was greatest. Some of the ideas of the Marshall Plan continued to have delayed effects into the 1970s and 1980s. However, there were also long-term reasons why Europe and Japan could have been expected to start growing more rapidly and catching up with the United States at this time. The difficulty is to isolate the significance of the long-term from the catalytic elements in the expansion that occurred. The argument of this book has been that American policy was very important in European reform and development. It now remains to put the effect of the policies in their long-term context.

The long-term convergence of the leading powers has been the subject of much recent discussion. It was generated by the observation that the great surge in productivity and welfare that has been enjoyed by the industrial countries in the twenty-five years after the war was initiated by western Europe and Japan when they brought into production the large arsenal of unexploited technology and commercial methods initiated in the United States in the 1920s and 1930s. In some important respects – for instance, in the degree of penetration of the major consumer durables like cars – the Europe of the 1950s relived the American boom of the 1920s. The waning of the European industrial boom in the mid-1970s and the stagnation in the 1980s came when the backlog of innovations had been exploited.[3]

Economists generalised from this episode, arguing that, if the conditions were right, the following countries had a good chance of catching up with the leaders. Abramowitz, who wrote the lead article in 1986, argued that:

> being backward in the level of productivity carries a *potential* for rapid advance. Stated more definitely the proposition is that in any comparisons across countries, the growth rates of productivity in any long period tend to be inversely related to the initial levels of productivity.

Any country contains a portfolio of up-to-date and old equipment, but the average varies. Other things being equal, a large new investment will have a much greater effect on the average in a backward economy than in a modern one. Hence, the followers have scope for more rapid advance. This idea was sharpened in American minds by the obsessive 1980s literature about American decline that exploited the fear that not just convergence, but overtaking might also be involved.[4]

The statistical backing for convergence can be measured in several ways. America's share of world GNP was about the same as the major

European nations individually in 1860, had almost equalled their total by 1914, peaked in the 1920s and mid-1940s, and has declined sharply since then. Her share of world manufacturing overtook Britain's between 1865 and 1880, peaked in the 1920s and 1940s, and then declined sharply (see Figure 1.1 above). These measures are an indication of gross size and industrial and military power, but welfare and productivity can be measured more fairly and precisely as output per head, either of the whole economy or of manufacturing: see Table 16.1.

Table 16.1. *Comparative Levels of Productivity, 1870–1987, US levels compared to 15 other countries, Britain and Germany*

	15 countries		GDP[a]		Manufacturing[b]	
	Mean GDP[a]	Variation	Britain	Germany	Britain	Germany
	(1)	*(2)*	*(3)*	*(4)*	*(5)*	*(6)*
1870	130	0.51	95	198	204	204
1890	147	0.48	98	188	195	205
1913	164	0.33	128	203	213	179
1929	175	0.29	154	244	250	238
1938	164	0.22	143	196	208	208
1950	217	0.36	167	269	263	274
1960	192	0.29	168	191	250	225
1973	145	0.14	152	148	208	156
1979	133	0.15	—	—	193	138
1987	—	—	129	124	189	175

[a] GDP per capita.
[b] Output per capita.
Sources: Moses Abramowitz, 'Catching up, forging ahead and falling behind', *Journal of Economic History* 46 (1986), pp. 385–486; Stephen Broadberry, 'Manufacturing and the convergence hypothesis', Centre for Economic Policy Research, Discussion Paper no. 708 (1992), pp. 1–38. Some dates are approximate.

The overall lead of US productivity (col. 1) over the fifteen other major industrial countries, like US shares of world GNP and manufacturing, developed in the late nineteenth century, peaked about 1950, and has declined sharply since then. Interestingly, the variation in productivity (col. 2) between the major industrial countries has also declined sharply, suggesting the development of common production methods and styles of consumption. These averages conceal a huge range of local differences, but with a recent long-run tendency towards the mean.

American GDP per capita, for instance (col. 3), was slightly lower than British GDP in 1870, but grew much more rapidly until 1960. Since 1960, though, Britain has caught up with the United States. American (and British) GDP per capita (col. 4) was initially much higher than German GDP per capita, and maintained or increased that differential until 1950; since 1950, however, Germany also has caught up with the United States. Within each economy, structural shifts between major activities sometimes had as much influence on the overall average as improvements in productivity in particular occupations. For instance, the final decline of agriculture in both America in, say, 1940–70 and in Germany in, say, 1950–70 came later than in Britain, giving large opportunities to improve average productivity.[5]

American manufacturing output per head (col. 5) was always much higher than GDP per head. In 1870 it was already twice as much as the British and German levels, when the US GDP as a whole was only marginally more productive. This is probably because, at that time, GDP per capita encompassed not only the 'American system' workers of the industrial north-east, but also the desperately poor and inefficient ex-slaves and sharecroppers of the defeated south. American manufacturing output advanced even more as full-scale Ford-style mass production took hold in 1890–1929. During and after World War II many US firms added more advanced scientific methods to their arsenal – for instance, in chemicals and electronics – increasing their advantage still further. Since about 1950, however, first the capacity for simple mass production and then scientific production has diffused to their competitors. Hence, both German and British manufacturing output have gained rapidly since 1945, although there still remains a considerable gap.[6]

The critical factors that resulted in American productivity being so much higher than European in the early twentieth century were probably the massive, uniform, protected market, the economies of scale, the existence of large corporations, and better commercial organisation and natural resources. Since the early nineteenth century there had been an extremely favourable interaction between agriculture and industry, increasingly linked by effective transport. All this helped the mass-production technology of the early twentieth century to go much further in America than in Europe. The European countries were hindered by narrow geographical and class markets, small-scale, less effective commercial organisation, and more costly natural resources. The result was that mass-produced goods such as cars could be manufactured on a far greater scale and far more cheaply in America than in Europe.[7]

On the other hand, 'social capability', or human capital, which is always one of the key elements in permitting rapid advance, was no more developed in the United States than in Europe. In the early and mid-nineteenth century the education and human capital levels in north-eastern America (and Britain) may have justified the relatively high income levels per capita, but this was no longer so by the 1930s. While America produced far more university graduates than the European countries, the technical capacity of the general workforce – many of whom had come from backward European countries or from farming in the American south and west – was not much higher than its European equivalent – and certainly not in the ratio of two or three to one.[8]

Since 1960 or so, many of the critical American advantages have been either weakened or even reversed. The United States now has to import many of her natural resources at world prices, although food remains much cheaper in America than in Europe. Raw materials and food now represent a far smaller share of final consumption than previously, in any case. The decline in oceanic transport rates *vis-à-vis* inland rates, and the removal of most restrictions on international trade, have elimin-ated the advantage that the huge American market once gave to its domestic manufacturers. New technology and public policy have reduced many of the advantages of economies of scale. Hence, small firms in small countries can now gain access to raw materials and sell their products on almost equal terms on the international market. The giant American corporations no longer enjoy such significant advant-ages. Social capability and human capital therefore become much larger factors in comparative productivity.[9]

America's postwar economic policy towards Europe (and Japan) was clearly an important catalyst in these developments. They may or may not have happened anyway. What were the alternatives? Clearly, a continuation of the European autarchy of the 1930s could not have yielded such high international incomes, because of the narrowness and class stratification of European markets. The wartime Axis and Japanese visions of empire, leaving aside the moral costs, would presumably have created large regional markets, but they would have been organised by a cartelised and restricted capitalism, without the potential benefits of the transatlantic and trans-Pacific trades. A revitalisation of the old European empires after the war, if possible, would have created large international markets, but would have left Europe disintegrated, Ger-many detached and America potentially isolated. Furthermore, technical development has tended to reduce the value of the old colonial trades in favour of more general interactions.

The policy of the Marshall Plan, therefore, was probably aimed at the best possible outcome, with, as it turned out, the most favourable potential for future economic growth. US policy and the Marshall Plan pushed Europe towards an integrated and multilateral future, created mechanisms to transfer the best of US commercial organisation, social patterns and technology, and attempted to create an open and unified international market. Clearly, as Milward has demonstrated, the Europeans instinctively opposed many of the American plans. The war and postwar reorganisation, even in Germany, did not create a *tabula rasa*. The Luftwaffe failed, as Keynes had noted wryly, to destroy sufficient British industrial capital to necessitate a new beginning. Each of the European countries had their own particular plans and style of capitalism, but there was a tendency in the long run to converge on the American norm.

The administrators of the Marshall Plan adopted a liberal policy, aimed at restoring European viability, American trade and international peace. This was not altruism, but enlightened self-interest. What were the long-run costs and benefits? Obviously, most countries gained greatly from the general prosperity – but the USA lost relatively. The Marshall Plan did not foresee that, after twenty years of rapid growth, the long-run effects of encouraging European and Far Eastern recovery and of permitting discrimination against American exports would be that European and Japanese industry would displace American industry not only overseas, but also in her own backyard. Nor, probably, did it expect such a marked convergence in OECD incomes, or that, after 1973, America would have to endure long run the stagnation of real wages for a generation. In this sense, therefore, was the Marshall Plan wise? Would an isolationist policy have preserved the advantages that America enjoyed in 1945 for longer? Obviously, this is an impossible question to answer. All one can say is that a relatively liberal policy, as well as long-run costs, had many favourable effects.

The analogy with the shift in British policy from mercantilism to liberalism almost exactly a century earlier is instructive. Britain moved to free trade in the mid-1840s, when she thought that her industry was unassailable and when there were strong domestic and international reasons for doing so. For twenty years or so, during the mid-Victorian boom, the policy earned obvious rewards as free trade was reciprocated

186 THE UNITED STATES AND EUROPEAN RECONSTRUCTION

and British exports to America and Germany rose. Then, after 1873, the costs increased as foreign competition developed and cheap food imports undermined British agriculture. From 1873 to the late 1890s, during the 'Great Depression', the old staple trades stagnated and America and Germany overtook Britain in the new industries.[10]

However, Britain also enjoyed major benefits from her liberal policy. Although incomes were stagnant, cheap food increased real wages and created a margin for many new styles of consumption. Just as important was the huge increase in commercial and financial contacts with the outside world, which created a network of clients and friendships that became vital in 1914. Similarly, despite the parallel stagnation in American incomes since 1973, the US liberal policy has resulted in cheap imports, improving the overall standards of American consumption and creating the network of allies that won the Cold War. Furthermore, the very long dénouement was not complete disaster in the British case – Britain is still a very rich nation – and the long-run results in the American case, with its far greater resource base, may be even more favourable.[11]

Notes

1. Barry Eichengreen, 'Mainsprings of economic recovery in post-war Europe', in *idem* (ed.), *Europe's Postwar Recovery* (Cambridge University Press: Cambridge, 1995), pp. 3–35, includes a recent review of the literature.
2. Peter G. Boyle, *American–Soviet Relations* (Routledge: London, 1993), pp. 249–81. George Kennan was an architect of both policies. See Wilson D. Miscamble, CSC, *George F. Kennan* (Princeton University Press: Princeton, NJ, 1992), *passim*.
3. N. F. R. Crafts, 'The golden age of economic growth in Western Europe, 1950–1973', *Economic History Review* 48 (1995), pp. 429–47, surveys the recent literature on convergence.
4. Moses Abramowitz, 'Catching up, forging ahead and falling behind', *Journal of Economic History* 46 (1986), pp. 385–406.
5. Stephen Broadberry, 'Manufacturing and the convergence hypothesis: what the long run data show', Centre for Economic Policy Research, Discussion Paper no. 708 (1992), pp. 1–38, provides a different view.
6. Richard R. Nelson and Gavin Wright, 'The rise and fall of American technological leadership', *Journal of Economic Literature* 30 (1992), pp. 1931–64.
7. H. J. Habakkuk, *American and British Technology in the Nineteenth Century* (Cambridge University Press: Cambridge, 1962), *passim*; David A. Hounshell, *From the American System to Mass Production, 1800–1932: The Development of Manufacturing Technology in the United States* (Johns Hopkins University Press: Baltimore, 1984), *passim*.
8. Nelson and Wright, 'The rise and fall of American technological leadership', pp. 1946–50.

9. *Ibid.*, pp. 1955–62; Michael J. Piore and Charles F. Sabel, *The Second Industrial Divide* (Basic Books: USA, 1984), *passim*.

10. Ernest Bevin told the US Chargé in London on 16 June 1947: 'that the US was in the position today where Britain was at the end of the Napoleonic wars. When those wars ended Britain held about 30 percent of the world's wealth. The US today holds about 50 percent. Britain for 18 years after Waterloo "practically gave away her exports", but this resulted in stability and a hundred years of peace.' This was reported to General Marshall: *FRUS: 1947*, vol. 3, p. 255.

11. Michael A. Bernstein and David E. Adler (eds), *Understanding American Economic Decline* (Cambridge University Press: Cambridge, 1994), and Paul Kennedy, *The Rise and Fall of the Great Powers: Economic Change and Military Conflict from 1500 to 2000* (Fontana: London, 1989), discuss American decline.

Suggestions for Further Reading

There is a vast diplomatic and political literature on the American role in postwar Europe, but no single good economic history text. A good, short, general overview is by David Ellwood, *Rebuilding Europe: Western Europe, America and Postwar Reconstruction* (Longman: London and New York, 1992). The Marshall Plan generated considerable interest among leading contemporary economists, such as Thomas Balogh, *The Dollar Crisis: Causes and Cure* (Blackwell: Oxford, 1949); Seymour E. Harris, *The European Recovery Program* (Harvard University Press: Cambridge, Mass., 1948); and Roy Harrod, *Are these Hardships Necessary* (Hart-Davis: London, 1947). These were followed in the early 1950s by much heavier celebrations and appreciations of the Marshall Plan. Examples are: Howard S. Ellis, *The Economics of Freedom: The Progress and Future of Aid to Europe* (Harper: New York, 1950); Harry B. Price, *The Marshall Plan and its Meaning* (Cornell University Press: Ithaca, 1955) – the official ECA history of the Marshall Plan; William Diebold, *Trade and Payments in Western Europe: A Study in Economic Cooperation, 1947–1951* (Harper: New York, 1952); and W. A. Brown, Jr., and R. Opie, *American Foreign Assistance* (Brookings Institution: Washington, DC, 1953).

Economists, however, lost interest after Europe recovered, leaving the field to diplomatic and political historians, who often avoided economic issues and concentrated on the Cold War. Some exceptions were the New Left historians, such as Joyce and Gabriel Kolko, *The Limits of Power: The World and United States Foreign Policy, 1945–1954* (Harper and Row: New York, 1972). Similarly, from the other ideological quarter, Raymond Aron, *The Imperial Republic: The United States and the World, 1945–1973* (Prentice-Hall: Englewood Cliffs, New Jersey, 1974), emphasised the success of the Marshall Plan. Both these studies, however, were concerned with the political economy of the Marshall Plan, not with the detailed economic history. A good modern political history, aware of economic issues, is Melvyn P. Leffler, *A Preponderance of Power:*

National Security, the Truman Administration and the Cold War (Stanford University Press: Stanford, 1992).

In the mid-1980s economic historians began to rediscover the period, perhaps in order to understand the nature of the 1948–73 boom or the origins of the modern European movement. The most influential study was by Alan S. Milward, *The Reconstruction of Western Europe, 1945–51* (Methuen: London, 1984); this generally discounted American influence both in the recovery and in European integration. Michael J. Hogan, *The Marshall Plan: America, Britain, and the Reconstruction of Western Europe, 1947–1952* (Cambridge University Press: Cambridge, 1987), on the other hand, argued that the United States endeavoured, with some success, to recast western Europe in the American image; Michael J. Hogan, 'American Marshall Planners and the search for a European neocapitalism', *American Historical Review* 90 (1985), pp. 44–72, is a briefer version; Imanuel Wexler, *The Marshall Plan Revisited: The European Recovery Program in Economic Perspective* (Greenwood: Westport, Conn., 1983), covers similar ground. All these books convey a clear message. Milward writes good, traditional economic history, with accessible economic analysis; Hogan and Wexler are political economists, with a different aim and style; Hogan and Milward can both be confusing and heavy going at times (see Diebold, below, for detailed reviews).

The 1980s were the first time that academics could reasonably hold anniversary conferences and the last chance for some administrators of the Marshall Plan to record their assessments. Charles P. Kindleberger, an influential young economist in Germany and the State Department in 1947, wrote *Marshall Plan Days* (Allen and Unwin: Boston, 1987). This includes some fascinating contemporary departmental and personal papers on the origin of the Marshall Plan and an important critical review of Milward. A useful review article on the work of Hogan, Kindleberger and Milward is William Diebold, Jr., 'The Marshall Plan in retrospect: a review of recent scholarship', *Journal of International Affairs* 41 (1988), pp. 421–35. A good selection of essays based on a conference which included some key participants is Stanley Hoffman and Charles Maier (eds), *The Marshall Plan: A Retrospective* (Westview Press: London, 1984). Robert J. Donovan, *The Second Victory: The Marshall Plan and the Postwar Revival of Europe* (Madison Books: New York, 1987), is a useful coffee-table picture book of the leading personalities and incidents.

In the mid-1990s – approaching the 50th anniversary of the Marshall
Plan – scholarship has apparently moved into a third stage, with econ-
omic historians as well as political economists somewhat qualifying
Milward's views. An example is Barry Eichengreen (ed.), *Europe's
Postwar Recovery* (Cambridge University Press: Cambridge, 1995). This
is a selection of essays which claims to bring 'international institutions
back into the analysis of post-war Europe's growth'. See also Barry
Eichengreen and Marc Uzan, 'The Marshall Plan: economic effects and
implications for Eastern Europe and the former USSR', in *Economic
Policy* 14 (1992), pp. 13–76. A recent useful anthology of articles, some
of which are in English, is contained in CHEFF, *Le Plan Marshall*.
French history naturally attracts most of the articles here, but every
European recovery country is included – except Britain! The preface is
by Jacques Delors, the former President of the European Commission.

The most useful works on American (and British) plans for postwar
Europe are Richard N. Gardner, *Sterling–Dollar Diplomacy in Current
Perspective: The Origins and Prospects of our International Economic Order*
(Columbia University Press: New York, 1980), and Fred L. Block, *The
Origins of International Economic Disorder: A Study of United States
International Monetary Policy from World War 2 to the Present* (University
of California Press: Berkeley, 1977). Keynes's ideas about the postwar
world are summarised in Sir Roy F. Harrod, *The Life of John Maynard
Keynes* (Macmillan: London, 1951). Alan P. Dobson, *The Politics of the
Anglo-American Economic Special Relationship, 1940–1987* (Wheatsheaf:
Sussex, 1988), and Robert M. Hathaway, *Ambiguous Partnership: Britain
and America, 1944–1947* (Columbia University Press: New York, 1981),
describe the Anglo-American relationship. German plans for the postwar
world are indicated in Alan S. Milward, *The New Order and the French
Economy* (Oxford University Press: London, 1970).

Sir Alec Cairncross, *Years of Recovery: British Economic Policy,
1945–51* (Methuen: London, 1985), contains useful chapters on the
external economic relationship between Britain and the United States
and on the American loan, but less about the impact of Marshall Aid
on Britain. Leslie S. Presnell, *External Economic Policy since the War,
vol. 1: The Post War Financial Settlement* (HMSO: London, 1986), is an
official British history of the postwar settlements. Sir Richard Clarke,
Anglo-American Collaboration in War and Peace, 1942–1949 (Oxford
University Press: Oxford, 1982), is the edited (by Sir Alec Cairncross)
papers, including important documents, of a leading British civil servant.

Henry Pelling, *Britain and the Marshall Plan* (Macmillan: Basingstoke, 1988), is a short general study, with good photographs of the participants and useful reprints of the US Economic Cooperation Act, 1948, and the bilateral Economic Cooperation Agreement between Britain and the USA, but no real economic analysis of the impact.

A specialist literature on the American economic relationship with the various European countries is only just emerging, and readers will sometimes have to use general or foreign language studies. France, however, is quite well served. The best recent study is Gérard Bossuat, *La France, l'aide américaine et la construction européenne, 1944–1954*, 2 vols (Ministère des Finances: Paris, 1992); voluminous sub-headings will help poor linguists (Gérard Bossuat, 'L'Aide américaine et la France après la Seconde Guerre Mondiale', *Vingtième Siècle* 9 (1986), pp. 17–35, is a short version). Frances M. B. Lynch, 'Resolving the paradox of the Monnet Plan: national and international planning in French reconstruction', *Economic History Review* 37 (1984), pp. 229–43, is useful. Warren C. Baum, *The French Economy and the State* (Princeton University Press: Princeton, New Jersey, 1958), contains helpful chapters on the modernisation plans and the French balance of payments. Irwin M. Wall, *The United States and the Making of Postwar France, 1945–1954* (Cambridge University Press: Cambridge, 1991), is a detailed political history.

American influence on Germany is controversial. Alan Kramer, *The West German Economy, 1945–1955* (Berg: New York, 1991), is a good short introduction. John Gimbel, *The Origins of the Marshall Plan* (Stanford University Press: Stanford, 1976), explains how the German problem in American diplomacy led to the Marshall Plan. Gerd Hardach, 'The Marshall Plan in Germany, 1948–1952', *Journal of European Economic History* 16 (1987), pp. 433–86, is a long article on the impact of the plan. Charles S. Maier and Gunter Bischof (eds), *The Marshall Plan and Germany: West German Development within the Framework of the European Recovery Program* (Berg: Oxford, 1991), contains several good articles debating the US influence on Germany. The CHEFF, *Le Plan Marshall*, anthology contains some of the most recent views on the debate. Peter Temin, 'The "Koreaboom" in West Germany: fact or fiction?', *Economic History Review* 48 (1995), pp. 737–53, challenges the impact of the Korean War boom on Germany and, thereby, somewhat re-establishes the importance of earlier US and European initiatives.

Vera Zamagni, *The Economic History of Italy, 1860–1990* (Oxford University Press: Oxford, 1993), contains a good chapter on Italian reconstruction, emphasising the role of the counterpart funds. George H. Hildebrand, *Growth and Structure in the Economy of Modern Italy* (Harvard University Press: Cambridge, Mass., 1965), is an earlier study. Marcello de Cecco, 'Economic policy in the reconstruction period', in Stuart J. Woolf (ed.), *The Rebirth of Italy, 1943–50* (Longman: London, 1972), pp. 156–80, records ECA opposition to the tight Italian fiscal and monetary policy. Several articles in CHEFF, *Le Plan Marshall*, discuss the ERP and Italy. John L. Harper, *America and the Reconstruction of Italy, 1945–1948* (Cambridge University Press: New York, 1986), and James E. Miller, *The United States and Italy, 1940–1950: The Politics and Diplomacy of Stabilisation* (University of North Carolina Press: Chapel Hill, NC, 1986), are detailed political studies of the American–Italian relationship.

The smaller European countries are less well served, usually only receiving snippets in general texts. For Belgium, see Isabelle Cassiers, ' "Belgian Miracle" to slow growth: the impact of the Marshall Plan and the European Payments Union', in Eichengreen (ed.), *Europe's Postwar Recovery*, pp. 271–91; Kindleberger, *Marshall Plan Days*, pp. 230–44; and André Mommen, *The Belgian Economy in the Twentieth Century* (Routledge: London, 1994), pp. 75–98. For Denmark, see Hans Christian Johansen, *The Danish Economy in the Twentieth Century* (Croom Helm: London, 1987). On Greece, see A. F. Freris, *The Greek Economy in the Twentieth Century* (Croom Helm: London, 1986), and George Stathakis, in CHEFF, *Le Plan Marshall*, pp. 577–89. For Holland, see Johan De Vries, *The Netherlands Economy in the Twentieth Century* (Van Gorchum: Assen, 1978). For Norway, see Fritz Hodne, *The Norwegian Economy, 1920–1980* (Croom Helm: London, 1983), or Helge Pharo, in CHEFF, *Le Plan Marshall*, pp. 591–605. Basic information on Spain, which was excluded from the Marshall Plan but did start to change, partly under American influence, in the 1950s, is provided in Joseph R. Harrison, *The Spanish Economy in the Twentieth Century* (Croom Helm: London, 1985), and Sima Lieberman, *Growth and Crisis in the Spanish Economy, 1940–93* (Routledge: London, 1995). Switzerland and Turkey are covered in CHEFF, *Le Plan Marshall*, by, respectively, Antoine Fleury, pp. 549–75, and Jacques Thobie, pp. 565–75.

The crisis of 1947, and the origins and macroeconomic effects of the Marshall Plan are treated in the general and country studies cited above. At one extreme, Milward, *Reconstruction*, pp. 1–55, and *idem*, 'Was the Marshall Plan necessary?', *Diplomatic History* 18 (1989), pp. 231–53, minimise both the crisis and its effects. The counterfactuals, 'Did dollars save the world?', and 'If there had been no Marshall Plan?', are addressed respectively by Kindleberger, *Marshall Plan Days*, pp. 246–65, and Harold Van B. Cleveland, in Stanley Hoffman and Charles Maier (eds), *The Marshall Plan: A Retrospective* (Westview, Conn., 1984), pp. 59–69. For the crisis in Britain, see also C. S. S. Newton, 'The Sterling crisis of 1947, and the British response to the Marshall Plan', *Economic History Review* 37 (1984), pp. 391–408, and Alex J. Robertson, *The Bleak Mid Winter (1947)* (Manchester University Press: Manchester, 1987). For what it actually felt like to be in Europe that summer, see the edited travel notes of the diplomatic historian Thomas A. Bailey, *Marshall Plan Summer* (Hoover Institution Press: Stanford, California, 1977).

James Foreman-Peck, in N. F. R. Crafts and N. W. C. Woodward (eds), *The British Economy since 1945* (Clarendon Press: Oxford, 1991), argues in a small aside, pp. 171–3, 177–9, that the effects in Britain may have been much greater than Milward suggests. J. B. De Long and Barry Eichengreen, 'The Marshall Plan: history's most successful structural adjustment program', in Rudiger Dornbush, R. Layard and W. Nolling (eds), *Postwar Economic Reconstruction and Lessons for the East Today* (MIT Press: Cambridge, Mass., 1993), pp. 189–230, argue that the effects of the direct transfer of resources under the ERP may have been small, but that the programme did help to create the postwar social contract. Several articles in Eichengreen (ed.), *Europe's Postwar Recovery*, accept Milward's case about the minimal quantitative effects, but argue that the indirect effects were greater. Eichengreen and Uzan, 'The Marshall Plan', makes a similar point.

The origins of European integration have generated a similar range of views: Hogan, Milward and Wexler all have useful sections; Max Beloff, *The United States and the Unity of Europe* (Brookings Institution: Washington, DC, 1963), provides the political background; Gimbel and Kindleberger show the central role of German trade. Jef Schram, in CHEFF, *Le Plan Marshall*, pp. 529–48, analyses the Low Countries and the origins of the European Payments Union. Barry Eichengreen, *Reconstructing Europe's Trade and Payments: The European Payments Union* (Manchester University Press: Manchester, 1993), shows how the EPU cemented Germany into the European system. François Duchêne, *Jean Monnet* (Norton: New York, 1994), and John Gillingham, in Eichengreen (ed.), *Europe's Postwar Recovery*, pp. 151–68, interpret the Schuman Plan in different ways. Hogan discusses British opposition to entry into

Europe. Alan S. Milward, *The European Rescue of the Nation State* (Routledge: London, 1992), contains good accounts of European integration
and British exceptionalism.

The theory that, behind the immediate aims of the Marshall Plan lay
reforming and stabilising neo-capitalist aims, is best expressed in Hogan,
The Marshall Plan, and Charles S. Maier, 'The politics of productivity:
foundations of American international economic policy after World War
2', *International Organisation* 21 (1977), pp. 607–33. The greater American success post-World War II than post-World War I is analysed in
Charles S. Maier, 'The two postwar eras and the conditions for stability
in twentieth-century western Europe', *American Historical Review* 86
(1981), pp. 327–52. Both of Maier's essays are reprinted in Charles
S. Maier (ed.), *In Search of Stability: Explorations in Historical Political
Economy* (Cambridge University Press: Cambridge, 1987).

The American attempt to restructure German capitalism is analysed
in Volker Berghahn, *The Americanization of West German Industry, 1945–
1973* (Berg: Leamington Spa, 1986). Tony Allan Freyer, *Regulating Big
Business: Antitrust in Great Britain and America, 1880–1990* (Cambridge
University Press: Cambridge, 1992), describes the milder pressure in
Britain, as does Helen J. Mercer, *Constructing a Competitive Order: The
Hidden History of British Anti-Trust Policies* (Cambridge University
Press: Cambridge, 1995). Anthony Carew discusses the parallel American attempt to reorganise the left and labour relations in Europe, in
*Labour under the Marshall Plan: The Politics of Productivity and the
Marketing of Management Science* (Manchester University Press: Manchester, 1987). The narrower American aim, to improve European
productivity by introducing American machinery and attitudes, is discussed in Jim Tomlinson, 'The failure of the Anglo–American Council
on Productivity', *Business History* 33 (1991), pp. 82–92, and in several
articles in CHEFF, *Le Plan Marshall*.

The American leaders 'Present at the Creation' are surveyed as a
group in Walter Isaacson and Evan Thomas, *The Wise Men: Six Friends
and the World They Made: Acheson, Bohlen, Harriman, Kennan, Lovett
and McCloy* (Faber: London, 1986). On individuals, see Forrest Pogue,
'George C. Marshall and the Marshall Plan', in Maier and Bischof (eds),
The Marshall Plan and Germany, pp. 46–70, or Forrest Pogue, *George
C. Marshall: Statesman 1945–59* (Viking Press: New York, 1987); Dean
Acheson, *Present at the Creation: My Years in the State Department*
(Norton: New York, 1969); Gregory A. Fossedal, *Our Finest Hour: Will*

Clayton, the Marshall Plan and the Triumph of Democracy (Hoover Institution Press: Stanford, 1993); Rudy Abramson, *Spanning the Century: The Life of W. Averell Harriman, 1891–1986* (Morrow: New York, 1992); Wilson D. Miscamble, CSC, *George F. Kennan and the Making of American Foreign Policy, 1947–1950* (Princeton University Press: Princeton, 1992); Alan R. Raucher, *Paul G. Hoffmann: Architect of Foreign Aid* (University Press of Kentucky: Lexington, 1985); Thomas A. Schwartz, *America's Germany: John J. McCloy and the Federal Republic of Germany* (Harvard University Press: Cambridge, Mass., 1991).

Priscilla Roberts, '"All the Right People": the historiography of the American foreign policy establishment', *Journal of American Studies* 26 (1992), pp. 409–34, analyses the group of eastern US businessmen and intellectuals who, in effect, made US foreign policy at this time, and their connections with their European opposite numbers. On the British, see Roy F. Harrod, *The Life of John Maynard Keynes* (Macmillan: London, 1951); Alan Bullock, *Ernest Bevin: Foreign Secretary, 1945–1951* (Oxford University Press: Oxford, 1985); and Alex Danchev, *Oliver Franks: Founding Father* (Clarendon Press: Oxford, 1993). On the French, see Duchêne, *Jean Monnet*, and Robert O. Paxton and Nicholas Wahl (eds), *De Gaulle and the United States: A Centennial Reappraisal* (Berg: Oxford, 1994).

The United States government printed many useful reports, some of which are available in larger libraries. The massive United States, Department of State, *The Foreign Relations of the United States*, is organised by year, region and country, and reprints the most important of the State Department studies and ambassadors' letters. Marshall's offer to help Europe, the CEEC response, the crisis in Europe in late 1947, and the passage of the legislation through Congress all generated many lengthy reports, which were published separately. The most important are the Harriman, Krug, Nourse, and Herter Reports. They are too detailed to describe here, but are outlined in Price, *The Marshall Plan and its Meaning*, pp. 39–70. The Marshall Plan, although a four-year programme, had to be accounted for and renewed annually. The ECA therefore reported regularly to Congress. The ECA was replaced by the Mutual Security Administration on 30 December 1951. Its reports to Congress clearly document the shift from economic to military aid and from Europe to the Third World.

The United Nations study by Ingvar Svennilson, *Growth and Stagnation in the European Economy* (United Nations: Economic Commission for Europe, Geneva, 1954), is a useful study of the interwar period, overlapping into the postwar years. The United Nations, *Economic Report: Salient Features of the World Economic Situation, 1945–47* (Department of Economic Affairs: New York, 1948), records postwar problems clearly. George Woodbridge, *UNRRA: The History of the United Nations Relief and Rehabilitation Administration*, 3 vols (Columbia University Press: New York, 1950) is the official history. The UNRRA, *Operational Analysis Papers*, especially number 49, *UNRRA in Europe, 1945–1947* (UNRRA European Regional Office: London, 1947), is an earlier overview. The United Nations Economic Commission for Europe (Director, Nicholas Kaldor; Assistant Director, Hal Lary; Executive Secretary, Gunnar Myrdal), produced useful annual *Economic Surveys of Europe* (ECE: Geneva, 1948–). The OEEC produced regular reports, from 1948, for the ECA. These were all concerned to make out a good case for the continuation of Marshall Plan support. The ECA Special Mission to the UK, *The Sterling Area* (ECA: London, 1951), is a large, well-illustrated special study. The Economic Commission for Europe, *Economic Survey of Europe since the War* (Geneva, 1953), is a good survey of the progress made to 1953. The IMF, *Balance of Payments Yearbooks* (IMF: Washington, DC, 1949–), provide short, useful 3–25pp. annual balance of payments statements, from 1946 on, for all the UN countries.

The changing balance of transatlantic trade and payments and the increasing problems of the dollar are surveyed in Block, *United States Monetary Policy*, and Andrew Shonfield (ed.), *International Economic Relations of the Western World, 1959–1971*, 2 vols (Oxford University Press: London, 1976), amongst many other works. American investment in Europe is covered by Mira Wilkins, *The Maturing of Multinational Enterprise: American Business Abroad from 1914–1970* (Harvard University Press: Cambridge, Mass., 1974). Raymond Vernon, *Sovereignty at Bay: The Multinational Spread of US Enterprises* (Longman: London, 1971), and Jean-Jacques Servan-Schreiber, *The American Challenge* (Hamish Hamilton: London, 1968), survey some of the results. Robert Gilpin, *US Power and the Multinational Corporation: The Political Economy of Foreign Direct Investment* (Macmillan: London, 1975), links the dollar outflow, the spread of US multinationals and the US foreign economic policy.

The classic article on the convergence thesis is Moses Abramowitz, 'Catching up, forging ahead and falling behind', *Journal of Economic*

History 46 (1986), pp. 385–406. Recent contributions include Richard R. Nelson and Gavin Wright, 'The rise and fall of American technological leadership: the postwar era in historical perspective', *Journal of Economic Literature* 30 (1992), pp. 1931–64, and N. F. R. Crafts, 'The golden age of economic growth in Western Europe, 1950–1973', *Economic History Review* 48 (1995), pp. 429–47. There is a growing literature on the relative United States decline, much of which, in some way or another, blames the costs of the *pax americana* – although not always the economic policy costs. Examples are: Block, *United States Monetary Policy*; David P. Calleo, *The Imperious Economy* (Harvard University Press: Cambridge, Mass., 1982); Paul Kennedy, *The Rise and Fall of the Great Powers: Economic Change and Military Conflict from 1500 to 2000* (Fontana: London, 1989); and Michael A. Bernstein and David E. Adler (eds), *Understanding American Economic Decline* (Cambridge University Press: Cambridge, 1994).

Index

Numbers in italics refer to Figures; those in bold refer to Tables.

The British Association
for American Studies (BAAS)

The British Association for American Studies was founded in 1955 to promote the study of the United States of America. It welcomes applications for membership from anyone interested in the history, society, government and politics, economics, geography, literature, creative arts, culture and thought of the USA.

The Association publishes a newsletter twice yearly, holds an annual national conference, supports regional branches and provides other membership services, including preferential subscription rates to the Journal of American Studies.

Membership enquiries may be addressed to the BAAS Secretary, Philip John Davies, Reader in American Studies, School of Humanities, De Montfort University, Leicester LE1 9BH, UK.